STATES OF BELONGING

STATES OF BELONGING

IMMIGRATION POLICIES, ATTITUDES,
AND INCLUSION

Tomás R. Jiménez, Deborah J. Schildkraut, Yuen J. Huo,
and John F. Dovidio

Russell Sage Foundation   NEW YORK

LIBRARY OF CONGRESS
CATALOGING-IN-PUBLICATION DATA

Names: Jiménez, Tomás R. (Tomás Roberto), 1975- author. | Schildkraut, Deborah J., 1973- author. | Huo, Yuen J., author. | Dovidio, John F., author.

Title: States of belonging : immigration policies, attitudes, and inclusion / by Tomás R. Jiménez, Deborah J. Schildkraut, Yuen J. Huo, John F. Dovidio.

Description: New York, New York : Russell Sage Foundation, 2021. | Includes bibliographical references and index. | Summary: "This book explores interconnections between immigration policy, attitudes about immigrants and immigration, and belonging through an inter-disciplinary political, sociological, and psychological framework. By focusing on immigration policy at the state level, it demonstrates how state and local governments have an active hand in shaping the resources and opportunities immigrants can access and how state and local policy influences immigrants' sense of belonging"— Provided by publisher.

Identifiers: LCCN 2021021437 (print) | LCCN 2021021438 (ebook) | ISBN 9780871544810 (paperback) | ISBN 9781610449083 (ebook)

Subjects: LCSH: United States—Emigration and immigration—Government policy. | United States—Emigration and immigration—Social aspects. | Immigrants—Services for—United States—States.

Classification: LCC JV6483 J56 2021 (print) | LCC JV6483 (ebook) | DDC 325.73—dc23

LC record available at https://lccn.loc.gov/2021021437

LC ebook record available at https://lccn.loc.gov/2021021438

Text design by Matthew T. Avery.

RUSSELL SAGE FOUNDATION
112 East 64th Street, New York, New York 10065
10 9 8 7 6 5 4 3 2 1

CONTENTS

LIST OF ILLUSTRATIONS

ABOUT THE AUTHORS

TOMÁS R. JIMÉNEZ is professor of sociology and comparative studies in race and ethnicity at Stanford University.

DEBORAH J. SCHILDKRAUT is professor of political science at Tufts University.

YUEN J. HUO is professor of psychology at the University of California, Los Angeles.

JOHN F. DOVIDIO is Carl I. Hovland Professor Emeritus of Psychology and Professor Emeritus in the Institute for Social and Policy Studies and of Epidemiology at Yale University.

PREFACE AND ACKNOWLEDGMENTS

Since its very founding, the United States has taken an ambivalent approach to immigration policymaking. Its policies have vacillated over time—sometimes welcoming and encouraging to immigrants, sometimes punitive and expulsive. Attitudes toward immigration have historically divided us politically and socially, as they do today. As this book reveals, however, the divides are not simple: they involve particular combinations of ethnicity and race, political partisanship, and geography. Nor does immigration create fissures simply *between* groups; it also arouses deep personal conflicts *within* groups. As the chapters reveal, many people hold complex, ambivalent attitudes that are a mix of empathy, anger, fear, hope, gratitude, and resentment. This ambivalence reflects our history as a nation. Americans take pride in being a "nation of immigrants," and the vast majority of citizens trace their roots to non-indigenous populations. The poem at the base of the Statue of Liberty, the monument that has greeted hundreds of thousands of immigrants to the United States, extends an embrace: "Give me your tired, your poor, your huddled masses yearning to breathe free." Yet the United States is also a country that, after inviting people from different countries to help build and support the nation (for example, through work on railroads and farms and in factories), rejected these same groups through racially restrictive law and mass deportation campaigns conducted by the federal and state governments. These measures have starkly delineated what kinds of people are seen as belonging in the United States and what kinds are not.

This book explores the interconnections between immigration policy, attitudes about immigrants and immigration, and belonging.

One challenge of writing such a book is the rapid shifting of the social and political landscape relating to immigration. We initiated this project when Barack Obama was president. We wrote much of it during the administration of President Donald Trump. We completed the book after President Joseph Biden took office. However, the dramatic political changes of this historical period in the United States were particularly valuable to our study. The political turmoil at the federal level illuminated aspects of immigrant life in particular states, and the contrasting immigration histories and policies of those states served to anchor the responses from study participants on immigration questions.

We explore how state policies shape belonging through "a tale of two states": Arizona and New Mexico. Our focus on state-level immigration policy may seem counterintuitive, since the federal government bears primary responsibility for immigration law and policy. However, state and local governments have been active in setting their own immigration policies, dictating the resources, institutions, and opportunities that they make available to immigrants. For example, states determine who can get a driver's license and what languages are spoken in schools. Although the two states are geographically adjacent, New Mexico has traditionally welcomed immigrants, while Arizona has enacted the most unwelcoming set of policies. We wanted to understand how these different state policy contexts affect the lives of the people—Latino immigrants, U.S.-born Latinos, and U.S.-born whites—who live under them. We consider a range of outcomes, but a sense of belonging—a basic human need that has a cascading influence on attitudes, actions, and well-being—is our central focus.

Our approach is interdisciplinary, drawing from our training in sociology, political science, and psychology. Although we had a common vision for the book, we came to it from the different professional cultures, professional languages, theoretical perspectives, and methodological tool kits of our different disciplines. Writing the book required us to recognize and respect our differences, grow through misunderstandings, and learn and value what others knew that we did not. That process helped us crystallize our appreciation for difference. It opened our eyes even wider to the challenges faced by immigrants. It also led us to a clearer vision of how policy can maximize the benefits of immigration across a broad swath of the U.S. population.

This book exists because of the vision, dedication, and support of the Russell Sage Foundation. We were part of the Working Group on Cultural Contact and Immigration that the foundation formed in 2010. The goal was to bring together researchers across multiple disciplines to use our disciplinary strengths in complementary ways to analyze the many challenges that face the United States as it experiences immigration-driven diversity, political polarization, and economic uncertainty. Through regular meetings at the Russell Sage Foundation, we learned about each other's work. We came together in smaller research teams to brainstorm about projects we could pursue together, all with the support of the foundation, which served, in effect, as an academic matchmaking service. The process led to a most rewarding and fruitful match for the four of us. We came from different disciplinary backgrounds but shared an interest in understanding how variation in immigration policy across the United States has shaped whether and how individuals feel that they belong. Russell Sage provided us with space and the funding to develop a research project that allowed us to explore our mutual interests.

In the summer of 2012, the foundation sponsored our extended stay in New York so that we could work together to solidify our research plan. Later, the foundation provided the funding to conduct the in-depth interviews in Arizona and New Mexico. Throughout the project, Suzanne Nichols, Aixa Cintrón-Vélez, and all of the other working group members offered intellectual guidance and technical advice. We are grateful to all of them. We are also thankful for an additional benefit we derived from the foundation's matchmaking: our own career trajectories have been reshaped by the work that the four of us did on this project after the foundation brought us together, and by the lessons we learned from one another.

Over the years, we relied on the help of many people, including librarians, research assistants, survey researchers, and staff at our universities. We are ever grateful to Anna Boch, Elliot Brandow, Francine Cafarchia, Felix Danbold, Paula Driscoll, Kim Higuera, Dan Jones, Juan Pedroza, Crystal Redekopp, John Roses, Ariela Schachter, and Zachary Shufro. Chrissy Stimmel at Stanford University adeptly coordinated the grant application across four institutions. Writing a book with four authors across three disciplines is incredibly challenging, and we thank Isabella Furth for helping us communicate with one voice.

And we would have nothing to write about were it not for the people who agreed to be interviewed and surveyed. We know how much time and energy it could take to express their views on the questions we put before them. We are grateful to them for putting their trust in us and allowing us to share their experiences with our readers.

The UPS Endowment Fund at Stanford provided financial support for our survey, and a Presidential Authority Award from the Russell Sage Foundation supported our interviews. The foundation also supported a pilot survey that was crucial for the development of our ideas. In addition, we drew on research support from our respective universities: Stanford University; Tufts University; University of California, Los Angeles; and Yale University.

Audiences at universities and conferences around the world listened to our presentations and provided valuable feedback. Among these opportunities were presentations at the University of California, Irvine; the University of Arizona; Rice University; Princeton University's Population Research Center; Santa Clara University; La Sorbonne (Paris); Casa de Velázquez (University of Madrid Complutense); Harvard University; the annual meeting of the International Society of Political Psychology; Tufts University's Tisch College for Civic Life; the Identity Politics Research Group at New York University; the Centre for the Study of Democratic Citizenship at McGill University; the Society for the Psychological Study of Social Issues and Society for the Australasian Social Psychologists Small Group Conference on Immigration (Ottawa, Canada); the 2017 General Meeting of the European Association for Social Psychology (Granada, Spain); and UCLA's Intergroup Relations Lab. We also want to thank Marie Provine, Monica Varsanyi, Daniel Tichenor, Casandra Salgado, Gabriel Sánchez, Mary Waters, David FitzGerald, and Pham Hoang Van for offering helpful insights along the way. We owe a debt of gratitude to the incredible research assistants who helped us conduct the interviews: Carmela Roybal and Sofia Locklear in New Mexico, and Elizabeth Cantú and Victoria Villalba in Arizona.

Portions of chapters 2 and 3 previously appeared in "A Tale of Two States: How State Immigration Climate Affects Belonging to State and Country among Latinos," *Social Problems* 66(3, 2019): 332–55. Portions of chapter 5 previously appeared in "Local Policy Proposals Can Bridge Latino and (Most) White Americans' Response to

Immigration," *Proceedings of the National Academy of Sciences* 115 (5, 2018): 945–50.

This project is deeply connected to our own experiences as Americans. Each of us has a family story tied to the promise and challenges offered by our country's legacy of immigration. The four of us represent the aspirational mythology and opportunity structure that this "nation of immigrants" inspires. Our own immigrant histories have taught us what it feels like to belong and what it feels like to be marginalized. We are in awe of our family members who started new lives in the United States and deeply grateful for their bravery. We hope our work fosters support for policies to bring about greater inclusion, belonging, and cohesion in this country.

Each of us has a few specific acknowledgments to make as well.

Tomás: My deepest gratitude goes to my collaborators, Debbie, Yuen, and Jack. We began this project when I was an assistant professor. We finished after I became a full professor. In the course of working with my coauthors, they became my role models. Each showed me how to be intellectually rigorous, professionally generous, and an expert and a learner at the same time. It is one of the great joys of my career to have collaborated with these three extraordinary individuals. I had collaborators in other aspects of my life as well. I want to thank my wife, Nova, for her unbending support throughout this project, which came to life just before our second son, Marcel, was born. During a hot summer in New York, I spent large chunks of time working with Debbie, Yuen, and Jack while Nova, seven months pregnant with Marcel, managed our energetic seventeen-month-old son Orlando. It was nothing short of heroic. She also held things down at home while I took trips to Arizona and New Mexico to kick off the interview portion of the project. My two sons, Orlando, now ten years old, and Marcel, now eight, have grown up with this project. They bring me a joy that I could have never anticipated. I dedicate my work on this book to them, *mis hijos*.

Debbie: When the Russell Sage Foundation held its first working group meeting in 2010, I did not go because I was on maternity leave. Shortly afterward, I got a note from Tomás, Yuen, and Jack asking if I would like to join the conversation they had started about projects they might pursue. Though I was familiar with their work, I had never met any of them before. They could have easily pursued a project without me. Not only did they invite me in, but they were also undeterred by the knowledge that I was at home with young and demanding distractions. They offered a true model of welcome, understanding, and inclusivity, a combination that, over the following decade, made this collaboration incredibly rewarding. And speaking of young distractions, my participation on this team would not have been possible without the many kind and dedicated people who helped care for my children in infant care, preschool, and after-school programs, many of whom were themselves immigrants adapting to life in the United States. As I traveled to meetings at the Russell Sage Foundation, RJ was left by himself with the craziness of home. It is hard to put into words how much his support of my work has meant to me. And those two little distractions, Evan and Nate, are not so little anymore. Watching them make sense of the world around them, particularly as they grapple with the types of issues we cover in this book, reminds me of why I do this work.

Yuen: When this project was still in its infancy, the Russell Sage Foundation welcomed me, my husband, and our two young children to New York, where Debbie, Jack, Tomás, and I worked out the outlines of our project and developed the camaraderie and mutual respect that have guided our work in the years since and culminated in this book. Immigration and other such large problems, if they are to be understood, require cross-disciplinary collaboration. I am fortunate to have learned how to engage in this type of project with collaborators who are generous in sharing ideas and supportive in the face of the inevitable challenges. I am thankful for Kay Deaux, who invited me to join the Working Group on Cultural Contact and Immigration that was forming at the Russell Sage Foundation. In the series of meetings of this group, I met and got to know brilliant, dedicated scholars, many of whom I now count among my friends. I came to the United States as a young child with my parents. It has been a joy and a journey to work on a book about the impact of immigrant reception on the lives of the many newcomers to this country. I dedicate this book to my parents, especially my father, Peter Su Huo, who passed away as we finalized the book. In my mind, he represents the indomitable spirit of generations of individuals who had the courage to uproot themselves for the chance to pursue a better tomorrow.

John (Jack): Working on this book reminded me why I love my job so much. I learned so much from so many people. The meetings organized by the Russell Sage Foundation exposed me to new ideas from multiple disciplines and challenged me to think in new ways. I had the opportunity to work closely with people who were outstanding scholars as well as warm and generous individuals on a number of projects over several years. I am indebted to Tomás, Yuen, and Debbie for their patience, support, and inspiration. They continually helped me grow as an interdisciplinary scholar. And I am particularly grateful for their friendship. We developed a special bond that I will value throughout my life. The opportunity to study the topic of immigration with such breadth and depth has also been personally meaningful. All of my grandparents were immigrants to America. I now understand better the challenges they experienced. And this book is one I will pass on to my grandchildren—Dylan, Milo, and Kreider—to remind them that where they come from is as important as where they are going in life.

THE STATE OF IMMIGRATION POLICY

Rafael Ortiz, a forty-two-year-old Latino immigrant from Ecuador who was a naturalized citizen and full-time artist, frequently worked in Arizona.[1] His time there was marked by a constant dull anxiety that occasionally turned sharp at the sight of law enforcement. Rafael was well aware of Arizona's reputation for being hostile toward immigrants and a state where law enforcement officials had been empowered to pull over individuals they suspected of being undocumented. Driving the Arizona roads, Rafael wondered whether his dark skin would arouse the suspicion of police officers or county sheriff deputies. Would he get pulled over? Would his legal status protect him? Or would he end up detained—or worse? Crossing the border to leave Arizona always brought Rafael a palpable sense of relief. As he told us:

> Although I am a citizen, when I come back from Arizona and I cross the [state] border, it's like, phew (*wiping his forehead to signal relief*). I feel like I'm leaving a state . . . where there's pressure. . . . It's just that you never know, you never know what's going to happen. I've heard of cases where citizens were stopped and they put them in detention centers and everything and until they see the papers and . . . "Oh, sorry." . . . That's why, when I'm leaving Arizona, I'm like, (*in English*) Oh yeah phew! (*translated from Spanish*)

The border that Rafael was crossing was not one between two countries. It was a border between two states, Arizona and New Mexico. Rafael's experience during his time in Arizona was such a contrast to life back home in New Mexico because the two states have taken starkly different policy approaches to immigration. While Arizona has made itself distinctly unwelcoming to immigrants,

New Mexico has forged a different path, adopting much more welcoming policies. Rafael highlighted the difference in his comparison of the two states, noting how much New Mexico felt like home:

> It's not like that in New Mexico. . . . I've been here for ten years, and my life is very tranquil. I've never had anything bad happen to me. It's like coming home. I have support from family, from good friends. I think it is still a peaceful state, and I have not had any bad experience because of an immigration situation. And it's relaxed, it's fine. (*translated from Spanish*)

From Lila Ibarra's perspective, Rafael's perceptions of the two states were accurate. A twenty-nine-year-old graduate student and legal permanent resident of Arizona from Mexico, Lila followed politics closely. She characterized Arizona like this:

> We have a bunch of propositions that came about in like [the year] 2000, which prevented undocumented students from receiving in-state tuition, Prop 200 I think it was. . . . I think that was to enforce sanction laws. Then we have politicians . . . state officials who are very proud of their anti-immigrant stance. You have a governor like Jan Brewer, who sucked and introduced SB 1070, which obviously Arizona was known [for] for a long time. . . . So this is a shitty place to be in a lot of ways. If you are a brown person, if you're an immigrant, every turn of the way, you know that in terms of the state, people don't want you here. . . . But in terms of state institutions, it's very clear that the state does not support immigrants, Latinos, brown people.
>
> Actually, you don't even have to be an immigrant because the . . . show me your papers, a lot targeted people who looked like they have the reason . . . suspicion to believe that they were undocumented. So, if you look brown, automatically that . . . maybe meant that you're undocumented. So, no, it's not even immigrants. It's if you're not white.

For Lila, it was not only that Arizona's policies restricted what immigrants could do, but also the fact that they sent powerful signals about who belonged in the state and who did not. The clear indication to Lila was that Latinos—people who "look brown"—did not belong, while white people did.

This book is about the impact of state immigration policies on Latinos, like Rafael and Lila, and on whites, who (as Lila suggested) might be more likely to feel that they belong in a state defined by unwelcoming policies, like Arizona. As Rafael's and Lila's comments suggest, state immigration policies are unwelcoming when they restrict immigrants' access to rights, resources, and institutions, but welcoming when they expand that access to immigrants.

Immigration policies can have a wide range of influences on how people adjust to, cope with, and participate in a new context.[2] We explore how unwelcoming and welcoming policy contexts shape the sense of belonging of the Latinos and whites they affect. The psychologists Gregory Walton and Shannon Brady define "belonging" as a "general inference, drawn from cues, events, experiences, and relationships, about the quality of fit or potential fit between oneself and a setting."[3] A sense of belonging has a profound impact on people personally (for example, on their physical and psychological well-being), socially (on their constructive engagement with others), and politically (such as in how invested and involved they are in the political process). Because of these broad and significant cascading effects, we focus on the sense of belonging and related elements of social identity as core outcomes of interest in this book.

Our focus on state-level immigration policy may seem counterintuitive at first. The federal government remains the primary authority for admitting immigrants, defining their status, and granting citizenship. But state and local governments have been active in setting their own immigration policies, dictating the resources, institutions, and opportunities that immigrants can access. These policies cover everything from who can get a driver's license or attend a state university to what languages are spoken in schools and public offices, how law enforcement interacts with the public, and even what schools teach students about history.

We examine how state policies shape belonging through "a tale of two states": Arizona and New Mexico. These two neighboring states in the U.S. Southwest are historically and demographically similar in many ways. But they differ fundamentally in their approach to immigration policy—the actions taken by the state government or state government officials that are directed at immigrants. As Rafael's and Lila's comments suggest, Arizona is a decidedly unwelcoming policy context for immigrants, while New Mexico is a mostly welcoming context. Using a range of data and behavioral science research methods, we show that living in a welcoming immigration policy context enhances the degree to which Latinos feel that they belong. But the positive effect of welcoming policies is not limited to Latinos. We also find that welcoming policies strengthen the sense of belonging among most whites. Political affiliation, ethno-racial origin, and nativity are important aspects of how both Latinos and whites view their belonging. Despite these axes of difference and a national scene characterized by political divisions, our analysis shows not only that welcoming policies cultivated a greater sense of belonging for the majority of individuals in our study, but also that there are points of consensus among a broad swath of the population about forging a more welcoming way forward in the states and in the nation as a whole.

In his 1932 dissenting opinion in *New State Ice Co. v. Liebmann*, U.S. Supreme Court justice Louis Brandeis referred to states as "policy laboratories" for the rest of the nation. States reveal the consequences—direct and indirect, intended and unintended—of specific policies. Our findings suggest that welcoming policies to help immigrants gain a social, economic, and political foothold can pay a sizable societal dividend.

Constructing Policies and Groups

Rafael's and Lila's portrayals of the two very different states they live in highlight several important characteristics of U.S. immigration policy. The first is that the United States does not have *an* immigration policy that blankets the nation, but rather, a patchwork of immigration policies. This patchwork has grown more varied in the last two decades as subfederal jurisdictions—states, counties, and cities—have become far more active in fashioning their own immigration-related policies. States have been especially active. In 2005, only 25 states passed immigration laws, for a total of 39 laws. In 2010, 43 states passed a total of 207 immigration-related laws. In 2017, 49 states passed a total of 206 laws pertaining to immigration.[4] This burst of state-level immigration lawmaking coincided with a period of the federal government's relative inaction on new major immigration legislation.

Rafael and Lila alluded to a second characteristic of contemporary immigration policies: state and local governments blur the lines between *immigration* policies that spell out the grounds for admission, residency, and citizenship and *immigrant* policies that determine immigrants' access to the rights, resources, and institutions that shape integration. The federal government has been far more active in the former than the latter.[5] States and local governments have been active, however, in creating policies that use federal legal status designations to determine immigrants' access to state and local rights, resources, and institutions. Some state and local governments bestow their own versions of legal membership in the form of driver's licenses, municipal identification cards, and state residency definitions to make these determinations.[6]

The third aspect of today's immigration policy highlighted in Rafael's and Lila's observations relates to the overall climate created by state immigrant policy. Because each state can enact a mix of welcoming and unwelcoming policies, the states can be located on a spectrum of immigration policies from most unwelcoming to most welcoming.[7] On one end of the spectrum are unwelcoming states that restrict the claims that immigrants can make to rights, resources, and institutions. On the other end of the spectrum are welcoming states that seek to protect the rights of immigrants and extend access to resources and institutions. Figure 1.1 is a map displaying where states fall on the welcoming spectrum, according to Huyen Pham and Pham Hoang Van's Immigrant Climate Index (ICI). The ICI tracks city, county, and state immigration laws between 2005 and 2017, classifying them according to how many aspects of life the law affects, whether the law provides a benefit or a restriction, and its geographic reach.[8] The index then assigns a score to the entire state. The map shows a range of state immigration policy climates and brings into relief the immigration policy patchwork across the United States.

Some states have been decidedly unwelcoming in their approach to immigration policymaking. Arizona, where Lila lived, is the most extreme example in the United States. Its score of −103 is the lowest of any state. (California has the highest score, 290.) Through ballot initiatives and the legislative process, Arizona has made itself into the most unwelcoming state in the nation for immigrants in general and unauthorized immigrants in particular in the first decade

Figure 1.1 *Immigration Climate Index, 2018*

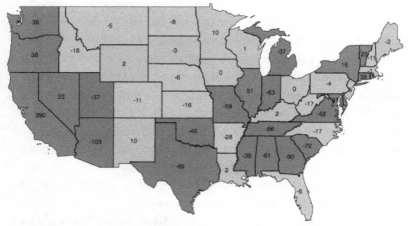

Source: Map constructed by Huyen Pham and Pham Hoang Van. For methodology, see figure 2 (updated August 2018) in "The Immigrant Climate Index (ICI)," Pham Hoang Van (website), https://sites.baylor.edu/van_pham/the-immigrant-climate -index-ici/.

of the new millennium. In a wide-ranging deluge of get-tough-on-immigration state policies, Arizona has instituted laws restricting the rights of unauthorized immigrants related to everything from driver's licenses and in-state tuition to bail and the collection of punitive damages in lawsuits. Of all the state's immigration policies, none is more notorious than SB 1070, which is the most aggressive immigration-related legislation that any state has enacted.[9] Among SB 1070's many provisions is the "show-me-your-papers" component, which requires law enforcement officials, in the course of lawful detention or arrest, to check the immigration status of individuals they suspect of being undocumented.

Other states have followed Arizona's lead. When Arizona passed SB 1070 in 2010, the majority of immigration-related state laws passed around the country aimed to restrict immigrants' rights and the rights of unauthorized immigrants in particular. Georgia, Alabama, Missouri, and North Carolina enacted measures similar to Arizona's.[10] Among the most popular unwelcoming measures are those prohibiting unauthorized immigrants from receiving higher education benefits; requiring local law enforcement to check people's immigration status if they have reason to believe they might be unauthorized; establishing partnerships with federal immigration enforcement agencies; requiring the use of English in public places; limiting bilingual instruction in classrooms; preventing unauthorized immigrants from renting housing; and forbidding access to state professional licenses for the unauthorized. Indeed, states, on the whole, have been following a restrictive, unwelcoming path of immigration policies in the same mold as Arizona's.[11]

But as figure 1.1 shows, not every state has been on this bandwagon. A few, including Rafael's home state of New Mexico, have gone in a more welcoming direction. New Mexico's approach is defined by measures that offer driver's licenses to unauthorized immigrants, allow unauthorized immigrants to pay in-state tuition, and grant unauthorized immigrants access to state aid for colleges and universities. In 2005, New Mexico's then-governor, Bill Richardson, signed an executive order forbidding state law enforcement agencies from cooperating with federal immigration enforcement.

In the 2000s, New Mexico stood out amid the general trend toward unwelcoming policies, but since 2012 the state has gained considerable company in its more welcoming approach. While immigration-related state legislative activity has continued apace after 2012, there has been a sea change in the kinds of laws passed. Rather than instituting overwhelmingly unwelcoming policies, states have begun to pass laws that expand rights for immigrants. California, arguably the most unwelcoming state a generation ago, is now by far the most welcoming state.[12] Illinois, Washington, Oregon, and Connecticut have joined New Mexico and California in passing more welcoming policies that extend rights to immigrants, including granting access to in-state tuition, issuing state driver's licenses regardless of legal status, providing employment protection irrespective of legal status, granting access to state-sponsored medical care, supporting the use of multiple languages in public business, and restricting local law enforcement officials from cooperating with federal immigration enforcement. Since 2012, these more welcoming state policies have outnumbered the unwelcoming policies passed, even though states continue to enact both sorts of measures.[13]

What accounts for these trends in the changing character of subfederal immigration policies? Politics certainly matters. Social scientists have shown that as restrictions on immigration and an emphasis on enforcement have become part and parcel of the positions of the Republican Party and conservatism more generally, Republican elected officials and more conservative voters have instituted state and local policies reflecting that bent.[14]

State-level immigration policies are also increasing in number and variety in response to changing state demography, racial politics, and political organizing. Large and growing immigrant populations, especially those from Latin America, can trigger a sense of threat among established populations, who then pressure their state lawmakers to crack down. The threat may feel particularly acute in bad economic times.[15] Demographic trends, driven mostly by immigration, are also changing the electorate and the ethno-racial makeup of state legislatures. States with greater Latino political power are more likely to limit the ratification of unwelcoming laws.[16] Grassroots organizations matter too. California became one of the most welcoming states in the union in part because local nonprofits pushed for change at the local and state levels.[17] The combination of partisanship, demography, and nonprofit activism that accounts for more welcoming policies in states also plays out in local municipalities. Cities are more likely to establish welcoming policies when the city government is largely liberal, when there is a sizable immigrant voting bloc, and when there is a robust and active network of immigrant-serving organizations that advocate for such policies.[18]

Immigration Policy and Belonging

Understanding immigration policy today requires not only documenting the origins of the policies but also understanding how those policies shape the lives of people who live under them.[19] In 1906, William Graham Sumner, in his classic book, *Folkways*, famously argued, "Legislation cannot change mores," a statement frequently paraphrased as "stateways cannot change folkways."[20] Over one hundred years of behavioral science research demonstrates otherwise. Legislation shapes debate and defines what and who are valued (and what and who are not); it also creates a social structure that influences people's lives in profound ways. Whether such legislation is unwelcoming or welcoming, it affects not only material opportunities for the targets of the policy but also their psychological and physical well-being generally. Policies also have an even broader impact: they *do* change the mores, folkways, values, attitudes, beliefs, and feelings of those who simply become aware of them.

We focus on how immigration policies (and the discourse surrounding those policies) shape whether and how individuals who live in different unwelcoming or welcoming contexts feel that they *belong* where they live. Belonging involves a range of psychological experiences, such as attachment to a particular place or inclusion in a group. It includes an individual's feeling that the place or group is a central component of a sense of self and that others recognize their position in the place or group. Belonging is not merely a state of mind. Feelings of belonging promote physical and mental health, facilitate social cohesion, and encourage cooperation and generosity. Conversely, a lack of a sense of belonging leads to alienation, poor mental and physical well-being, anger, and feelings of resentment that contribute to antisocial and destructive behavior. Belonging is an important outcome to measure because it captures the emotional resonance that drives views about immigration and immigration policy.[21]

Those individual effects of belonging can filter down from policies that offer cues about which groups of people belong. Sociologists and political scientists have documented what federal-level immigration policies indicate about who belongs in the nation. As the political scientist Aristide Zolberg has noted, immigration policies reflect the design of the nation.[22] The national design of the United States and throughout the Americas has historically fashioned immigration policies around race. The U.S. citizenship laws that tightened in the late nineteenth and early twentieth centuries were informed by a belief that a racial hierarchy defined belonging, reflected a preference for fewer immigrants overall, and favored new immigrants to come from northern Europe.[23] No group in the United States today is more targeted in contemporary immigration policy than Latino immigrants. Latin America is the largest source region of today's immigrant population, and the largest share of immigrants in the United States come from Mexico (25 percent).[24] The proliferation of unwelcoming federal and subfederal immigration policies is premised on the notion of Latinos as a cultural and economic threat.[25] Policies, and the rhetoric that promotes them, are part of a "context of reception" in which a combination of laws and societal attitudes shape the immigrant and second-generation experience.[26] If there is a patchwork of immigration policies in the United States, then there is a corresponding variation in how the legal and societal contexts of reception affect the people who live under them.

Lila's observations about Arizona point to the material consequences of a context of reception made unwelcoming through policy. When states like Arizona deny driver's licenses to unauthorized immigrants, routine traffic stops can quickly spiral into arrests, federal detention, and deportation.[27] Those detentions and deportations are extremely detrimental to every aspect of family life, plunging families into poverty, increasing stress, depressing health, and disrupting children's education.[28] Unauthorized immigrants curtail their activities and must go to great lengths to conceal their undocumented status.[29] They become less likely to seek the help of law enforcement and health care providers even when they have a need to do so.[30] When state and local policies turn unwelcoming, Latino immigrants become not only legal outsiders but also part of an ethno-racial "other."[31] Out-of-state tuition costs at state institutions and a lack of access to financial aid can put college out of reach for those denied access to in-state tuition.[32] State laws that go even further than federal policy in restricting hiring and employment can make it especially difficult for unauthorized immigrants to find work.

The material effect of policies is only part of the story. Rafael's and Lila's comments also suggest that the policy context of reception for immigrants has an emotional and psychological impact. Policymakers design measures to have precisely that effect—to express a sense of right and wrong, to demarcate "good" people and "bad" people, and to establish members and nonmembers.[33] Such policies are embedded in a system-justifying ideology that rationalizes the creation and legitimation of policies as fair responses to a problem or issue.[34] Once in place, the policies and the politics surrounding them serve as cues about belonging, reinforcing the message that immigrants are undeserving and unwelcome.[35] Attuned to these cues, Latino immigrants experience a sense of fear that negatively affects their mental health and depresses school performance among their children.[36] This fear even lowers newborn birth weights.[37] An unwelcoming context shapes identity too. In an unwelcoming context, Latinos register a heightened sense of Latino identity and a weakened sense of American identity.[38] A defensive posture can ensue, with Latinos becoming more likely to engage in politics and seek naturalization and to have a heightened sense of identity.[39]

Not all policy contexts of reception are unwelcoming or even hostile. The policies and politics of many states, like New Mexico, construct Latino immigrants as positive—as a population deserving of inclusion, benefits, services, and protections, regardless of legal status. This construction of Latino immigrants informs the more welcoming immigration measures fashioned by these states. What remains unclear is whether welcoming policies informed by positive constructions create a context of reception that leads to beneficial outcomes among Latinos. Existing research only hints at the impact of such a context. Immigrants exhibit better adjustment and more positive intergroup attitudes toward the society in which they settle when their views about integration line up with the dominant ideology.[40] In addition, minorities regard their ethno-racial and national identities as more compatible when they perceive that the society in which they settle values their group.[41] And welcoming policies can create legal categories around which previously excluded immigrant groups form positive social identities.[42] But the context may not even need to be actively welcoming for immigrants to experience a benefit. Even a neutral societal and policy context of reception can facilitate harmonious intergroup relations.[43]

The material and social-psychological effects of different immigration policy contexts do not affect everyone equally. Nativity and ethno-racial background play key roles. As we noted previously, Latino immigrants in the United States bear the material and social-psychological brunt of unwelcoming policy contexts of reception; how welcoming policy contexts affect Latinos is a black box. It can be said, then, that Latino immigrants are *target populations*; the political scientists Anne Schneider and Helen Ingram describe them as "cultural characterizations or popular images of the persons or groups whose behavior and well-being are affected by public policy. These characterizations are normative and evaluative, portraying groups in positive or negative terms for symbolic language, metaphors, and stories."[44] We would add that target populations are the object of the administrative function of a policy that deals with what the law permits, and we highlight the symbolic role that policy plays in signaling the worth and belonging of groups.

Policy contexts of reception, in all of their variation, may shape belonging for non-immigrants too. Lila's observation that Arizona's immigration policies negatively affect people who are "not white" suggests that state-level immigration policies may not affect whites all that much, but that they may affect U.S.-born minorities, especially Latinos. U.S.-born Latinos may not be the target population according to the explicit language of immigration policy. But the enforcement of these policies and their politics make the U.S.-born a *collaterally affected group* that shares aspects of the social categories, like ethno-racial background, that are the basis for the construction of the policy target population. The enforcement and politics of a policy serve as cues that affect the social-psychological well-being of a collaterally affected group that shares these social categories. Policies can also shape the lived experiences of collaterally affected groups through their social ties to target populations. Unwelcoming immigration policies are unambiguously based on notions that some immigrant groups, like Latinos, are a foreign ethno-racial threat.[45]

Sharing an ethno-racial origin with the Latino-immigrant target, U.S.-born Latinos can experience the collateral effects of unwelcoming policies. For example, Mexican Americans whose families have been in the United States for generations internalize the nativism directed against Mexican immigrants, reinforcing their sense of belonging to an outsider group.[46] Second-generation children of immigrants perceive more racial discrimination than do their immigrant parents.[47] These perceptions can move the U.S.-born generations to engage in political protest and even formal politics on behalf of their immigrant parents and grandparents.[48] What remains unclear is how U.S.-born Latinos, as a collaterally affected group, respond to *welcoming* policies.

What also remains unclear is how different immigration policy contexts shape the sense of belonging of groups that do not share ethno-racial or nativity status with the target populations, like whites. In focusing almost exclusively on the impact of immigration policies on immigrants and the subsequent generations since immigration, researchers have tacitly assumed that policies affect only their targeted population and perhaps, collaterally, the U.S.-born generations of the targeted groups. But immigration policies that target groups like Latinos have the potential to affect the sense of belonging of other groups as well.

The sociologist John Torpey's imagery of the "embrace" in his account of the invention of the passport is useful for considering the effect that immigration policies can have on individuals from a range of groups.[49] Torpey argues that to facilitate a sense of national belonging, governments must document membership through censuses, licenses, and passports. This governmental effort is not just a move to exclude nonmembers who are undocumented and uncounted, but also an effort to embrace its citizen members. Applying the embrace metaphor to immigration policies opens the possibility that even individuals who may not share a social category membership with the target or collaterally affected groups can glean a sense of belonging from such policies. Deriving a sense of belonging without sharing a category with a target or collaterally affected group is associated with membership as a *symbolically affected group*.

Generally speaking, lawmakers do not craft immigration policies to target a symbolically affected group. The effect of policy on this group's experiences comes exclusively from the cues they receive from policies about who belongs. History and contemporary research show how immigration policies based on ethno-racial origin have symbolically affected whites. Federal and local policies based on notions of ethno-racial inferiority have had profound effects on the place of other groups in the U.S. ethno-racial landscape.[50] A "relational" construction of ethno-racial groups embedded in policy is evident in federal laws in the late nineteenth and early twentieth centuries that banned immigration from Asia and severely restricted immigration from southern and eastern Europe.[51]

While the policies were unequivocally based on the construction of Asian, southern European, and eastern European immigrant groups as ethno-racial, religious, and political threats, the laws were also cues that belonging in the American nation was reserved for whites with northern European ancestry.[52] By banning immigration from Asia altogether, the laws also opened the possibility for southern and eastern European immigrant groups to eventually claim full membership in the white ethno-racial category.[53] Contemporary research on reactions to immigration-driven changes in U.S. demography offers a similar lesson. It appears that whites view these changes as "zero-sum." Constructions of minority groups as positive and the accompanying policies that embrace them may be seen by whites as a threat to their own group status.[54] Indeed, when whites learn that they will soon become a numerical minority, they express feelings of threat to their group's status, which in turn increases their support for exclusionary policies.[55]

Based on past research, it would be reasonable to expect a straight-forward effect of immigration policies on Latino immigrants, a target population; U.S.-born Latinos, a collaterally affected group; and whites, a symbolically affected group. Latino immigrants would be likely to experience the greatest material and social-psychological hit from unwelcoming policies, as well as the greatest benefit from welcoming policies. U.S.-born Latinos might display a similar, though less intense response. Whites would experience little, if any, material consequences from immigration policies and instead show a response opposite to that of Latinos.

But that is a limited view of the potential effects of immigration policies. Complicating these expectations is ample diversity within these groups, and an important aspect of that internal diversity is political affiliation. Partisan identities are today an important source of social identity.[56] Thus, the impact of immigration policies may have deep resonance with Latinos and whites depending on how the welcoming or unwelcoming nature of the policies aligns with their political identity. While Latinos tend to lean toward the Democratic Party, there is and always has been a significant share who identify as Republican, even among the Mexican and Central American Latinos in the West and Southwest.[57] Latinos with more family generations in the United States are even more likely to identify as Republican.[58]

Whites are also diverse. White identity has always exhibited internal variation, especially along class lines.[59] But today political party identity animates distinctions among whites, especially when it comes to views about immigration and race.[60] Republican whites have views about immigration and race that are likely to conform to a zero-sum view of the world. Views among independent and Democratic whites are going in the other direction. Recent survey findings show that whites who identify as Democrats and liberals have out-looks that rival or even exceed the pro-immigrant, pro–racial justice views of nonwhites.[61] Welcoming policies that embrace immigrants may feel like an embrace to liberal and even independent Latinos and whites because the policies are consistent with their political world-views, and thus their social identity. Conversely, welcoming policies may depress the sense of belonging among Republicans, both white and Latino, who feel as though such policies violate their political worldview and social identity.[62]

Variation in the effect that immigration policies can have on belonging may also come from how individuals view the role of immigration in American civic identity. Many Americans subscribe to what Deborah Schildkraut calls "incorporationism," or a belief that immigration is central to the nation's civic identity, which is charac-terized by a balance between celebrating immigration-driven diver-sity and blending into an American core not explicitly defined by ethno-racial origins.[63] It may be that Latinos and whites who believe in incorporationism see welcoming policies as an embrace of not just immigrants but also of anyone who shares a belief in the central role that immigration plays in the national character. In contrast, Latinos and whites who subscribe to versions of American national identity rooted in the centrality of white identity (ethno-nationalism) or the suppression of individual identities in favor of identification with the civic nation (civic republicanism) could feel excluded from the embracing arms of welcoming immigration policies and thus expe-rience a diminished sense of belonging. In sum, the effect of wel-coming and unwelcoming policies on the sense of belonging among Latino immigrants, U.S.-born Latinos, and whites may cut through rather than circumscribe these groups.

Our book examines the effects of immigration policy on belonging in ways that the existing body of knowledge suggests are important but that remain uninvestigated. Given the patchwork of immigration policies across the United States, we aimed to understand not just the impact of unwelcoming policies but also the effect of welcoming policies on the sense of belonging of people who live under them. We also wanted to know whether and how different kinds of immigra-tion policy contexts shape the sense of belonging among the most targeted population (Latino immigrants) as well as among a collaterally affected group (U.S.-born Latinos) that shares an ethno-racial category with the target population.

We also sought to capture the potential effects of unwelcoming and welcoming immigration measures on whites, a symbolically affected group that does not share an obvious social category with the target group and that has defined legal, social, economic, and political belonging in the United States. The views of other groups are an important part of the national scene when it comes to understanding the effects of immigration policy. However, we focus on whites for theoretical reasons. Whites are unequivocally the most advantaged group in the United States. If immigration policies have a far-reaching effect on belonging, the extent of that reach would be evident among whites.[64]

Because political orientation is such a salient social identity and source of division in the United States, we paid close attention to how political party identification affects feelings of belonging within and between Latino immigrants, U.S.-born Latinos, and whites. Our aim was to answer several related questions: Do immigration policies have a zero-sum effect? Which actions that enhance the sense of belonging of one group diminish the sense of belonging of other groups? Is there an immigration policy approach that benefits the target population *and* pays dividends for U.S. society as a whole?

Drawing insights from existing research, we show how different state-level immigration policy approaches—*both welcoming and unwelcoming*—affect individuals' sense of belonging and the different ways in which that sense of belonging registers for different intersections of ethno-racial categorization (Latinos and whites) and political orientation (Republican, independent, and Democrat). We used survey, experiment, and interview data from Arizona and New Mexico to form a comprehensive picture of the effects on the sense of belonging among those states' Latino and white residents of policies that vary in whether or not they are welcoming. We learned that Arizonans and New Mexicans generally display a greater sense of belonging in their state when policies are more welcoming. The people we studied were also aware, however, of where their state fell on the welcoming spectrum: New Mexico residents saw their state as more welcoming, and Arizona residents—especially Latinos—saw their state as less so. Respondents' awareness came not only from a familiarity with their state's politics and history but also from direct experience with the implemented policies. Foreign-born Latinos in Arizona described exclusion from opportunities and resources in the state, as well as the psychological and emotional sting of that rejection. Their New Mexico counterparts, by contrast, described a generalized sense of welcome that they associated more with New Mexico's history and culture than with policy, which operated mostly in the background. We show that those policies were not just associated with but also were a *cause* of the degree to which Latinos and most whites felt a sense of belonging.

Respondents' sense of belonging was refracted through their political orientation and ethno-racial background. Latinos, both U.S.- and foreign-born, reported a significant sense of belonging in response to welcoming policies and a depressed sense of belonging in response to unwelcoming policies. Foreign-born Latinos were particularly apt to respond this way. We even found similar patterns among U.S.-born whites who identified as Democrats and, to a lesser degree, independents. But welcoming policies are not costless: Republican whites reported a depressed sense of belonging in response to welcoming policies and a greater sense of belonging in response to policies that are more unwelcoming. Republican Latinos, like Republican whites, were generally opposed to more welcoming policies and were concerned about border security and limits on access to a welfare state that they said should be set aside for U.S. citizens. The partisan and ethno-racial differences we discovered hardly marked clearcut divides. When Latinos and whites of all political stripes talked about their views of immigration, significant points of agreement emerged on legalizing unauthorized immigrants and immigration enforcement. These views defied stereotypical notions of where various ethno-racial and ideological groups would stand on the issue. Additionally, for Latinos in particular, merely adopting a partisan identity (regardless of which party) was sometimes associated with a sense of belonging.

Our findings reveal that welcoming immigration policies are not a zero-sum proposition: a greater sense of belonging for immigrants does not amount to a diminished sense of belonging for everyone else. Instead, welcoming policies have a clear benefit for the groups that they target most: foreign-born Latinos. They also benefit the sense of belonging of the majority of individuals (including U.S.-born Latinos and U.S.-born whites) not specifically targeted by these policies.

Disentangling Policy, Culture, and History in Multiple Jurisdictions

Analytically, we focus on the role of state policy as one among the many factors that can cultivate an individual's sense of belonging. As we show, policy, history, culture, economic conditions, and prevailing attitudes combine to form individuals' sense of belonging. These factors implicate each other in giving rise to particular kinds of policies and in how individuals perceive their feelings of belonging in their state. Our analysis takes seriously this swirl of factors, while empirically demonstrating that policy plays a central, independent role in whites' and Latinos' sense of belonging.

The multilevel, jurisdictional patchwork of immigration policy means that individuals' sense of belonging may respond to immigration policies at the federal, state, and local levels, positioned in different places on a welcomeness spectrum. We could not capture the effect of these fine-grained jurisdictional differences, which are important. We focus on states because they have been especially active in immigration policymaking in recent years. As a legal matter, states have historically played—and continue to play—an important role in immigration policy. The U.S. Constitution spells out a role for states in setting their own policies but assigns no such legal role to local jurisdictions. States' legal supremacy over local governments also gives them special power when it comes to setting and enforcing policy, including measures related to immigration.[65]

Although we focus on states, local jurisdictions still matter. Even within a largely welcoming state, differences in city and county approaches to immigration policy can affect immigrants' sense of belonging.[66] The metropolitan areas where we collected our interview data—Phoenix, Albuquerque, and Santa Fe—have county- and city-level policies that are either consistent with the welcoming or unwelcoming bent of state policies or largely neutral. But jurisdictional distinctions do not necessarily register with respondents. As we show in the pages that follow, the people we studied tended to collapse the jurisdictional differences in immigration policies when describing their experiences and outlooks. For example, respondents in Arizona cited the Maricopa County sheriff as a central player in making Arizona an unwelcoming state. Rather than distinguishing immigration enforcement at the county level from enforcement at the state level, they treated unwelcoming policies in Maricopa County as part of the package of unwelcoming policies that prevailed in that county and in the rest of the state. Similarly, respondents in Albuquerque and Santa Fe, cities that have established largely welcoming policies, treated the local-level policy as part of the larger welcoming scene in New Mexico. Where there are differences between local jurisdictions, our research suggests, individuals are more aware of unwelcoming policies than of welcoming policies. Thus, even modest efforts by a city government, like Phoenix, to institute welcoming policies drew less attention from our respondents than the overwhelmingly unwelcoming policies established by the county and state.

Of course, people may identify with their nation, their country of origin, or their city more than they identify with their state. Since, as we have noted, prior research shows that perceptions of reception can affect identity and belonging at the national level, we also examine national identity and belonging. Examinations of the impact of such perceptions on identity and belonging at the state level, however, are lacking. As the past two decades have illustrated, states have had the bureaucratic will and capacity to expand or contract the rights, resources, and access to institutions afforded to immigrants. Allan Colbern and Karthick Ramakrishnan go so far as to argue that state laws now matter more than federal laws for immigrant rights, by virtue of the variations by state and the sheer breadth of the welcomeness spectrum they present.[67] Just as state variation in the quality and scope of policies like Medicaid can have significant effects on civic life and political incorporation, we demonstrate that variation in state immigration policy can likewise shape immigrants' sense of belonging.[68] States, in this sense, are alternative sites of citizenship that can expand who is included in or excluded from a wide range of rights and opportunities, such as educational benefits, business licensing, and access to health care.[69] We concentrate on how variation in those opportunities and in the discourse about those opportunities affect belonging.

That said, our analysis gives us no reason to believe that welcoming or unwelcoming policies at the county and city levels affect belonging differently than what our research shows. Indeed, our research, combined with other research, suggests that welcoming policies, regardless of jurisdiction, increase the overall sense of belonging among immigrants and even U.S.-born individuals.

The Plan of the Book

We lay out our key arguments and the evidence for them in the six chapters that follow. Chapter 2 offers a historical overview of the two states under study, as well as a more detailed look at the unwelcoming policy approach taken by Arizona and the welcoming approach in New Mexico. We also discuss our data and methods in this chapter. Chapter 3 draws on the survey and in-depth interview data to examine feelings of belonging among Latinos in the two states. We show that both Latino immigrants and U.S.-born Latinos in Arizona were well aware of the unwelcoming politics and policies in their state. Our findings indicate that this perception dampened their sense of belonging in their state, especially for U.S.-born Latinos in Arizona. For Latino immigrants in Arizona, a lack of belonging came from direct experiences with the administrative aspects of the state's exclusionary immigration policies. Latinos in New Mexico, in contrast, viewed their state as quite welcoming to immigrants. They did not cite policy as central to their view; instead, they focused on the state's history and generally welcoming culture as the primary reason for their sense of belonging.

Our survey data further reveal that Latinos in both states were equally likely to say that they felt that they belonged in the United States more generally. In interviews with Latinos collected after the election of Donald Trump, Latino respondents explained that they believed that the views and treatment of Latinos in general, and of Latino immigrants in particular, had soured because of the former president's rhetoric and actions. And yet the interviews also show that Latinos in those states saw themselves as contributors to the American story, even if some state policies and politics seemed to be trying to write Latinos out of that story.

Turning to U.S.-born white residents in Arizona and New Mexico, chapter 4 examines their perceptions of how immigrants are treated and the degree to which living under a generally welcoming or unwelcoming immigration state policy regime shaped their own sense of belonging. Our survey and interview data show that whites in Arizona perceived their state as unwelcoming to immigrants because of its immigration policies, while in New Mexico whites saw their state as welcoming because of its history and culture, much in the same way that Latinos in New Mexico saw the state as welcoming. Whites in both states reported a relatively strong sense of belonging; that feeling was particularly pronounced among New Mexicans of all political stripes and among Republican Arizonans. White Democrats in Arizona, by contrast, reported a depressed sense of belonging because the state's politics and policies did not reflect their political preferences. We also found a slightly depressed sense of belonging among whites in New Mexico, owing to the perception among our interview respondents that the top of the state's historic and present-day ethno-racial hierarchy was occupied by Latino residents from families with long-established roots there. The findings from this chapter suggest that welcoming state-level immigration policies do not impose a social-psychological penalty on U.S.-born whites (especially when contrasted with the penalty on Latinos living in unwelcoming settings), but that unwelcoming policies do penalize white Democrats. The effects of living in a welcoming or unwelcoming policy regime did not spill over into feelings of belonging at the national level.

In chapter 5, we use data from an experiment to see whether different state-level immigration policies have a causal effect on feelings of belonging. We found that exposure to information about welcoming policies enhanced a sense of belonging among foreign-born Latinos, U.S.-born Latinos, and even most U.S.-born whites. We also discovered that reactions to welcoming policies were primarily divided along political, not ethno-racial, lines. It was only self-identified Republicans, both white and Latino, who showed depressed feelings of belonging. How respondents expressed their preferences for state policies was influenced more by their political ideology than their ethno-racial background and nativity. Our interviews indicated that Democrats, and to some degree independents, viewed welcoming policies as a mechanism for integrating immigrants and for realizing the economic benefits of immigration and diversity. The same respondents also noted that welcoming policies ought to come with requirements that immigrants display a commitment to contributing economically and socially to the United States. Republican respondents were concerned that welcoming policies would attract too many immigrants. But in explaining their views, they expressed support for measures that would make it easier for unauthorized immigrants already here to legalize their status.

We also wanted to understand whether and how the views of policy we uncovered at the state level scaled up to views about federal policy, since the federal government's power to define legal belonging affects how states carry out their immigration policies. Both the survey and interview data we drew upon for chapter 6 demonstrate that views about immigration, regardless of ethno-racial background, nativity, state residence, or political ideology, do not seem to support the stereotypical portrayals of the immigration debate in the United States today. Latinos, especially Latino immigrants, and Democratic and independent whites favored more generous immigration policies, but they also voiced support for border security. White Republicans favored more aggressive immigration enforcement while also reasoning that unauthorized immigrants who have been in the United States for a long time and who display the potential to be good citizens ought to have a chance to achieve legal status. These findings indicate that there may be more consensus on immigration policies than current and past immigration debates suggest.

The book concludes with chapter 7, in which we summarize the main findings, prescribe approaches to immigration policy, and offer an alternative view, informed by our findings, of where Arizona, New Mexico, and the United States more generally stand on immigration. Our findings reveal that welcoming immigration policies created a sense of belonging among the directly targeted population—Latino immigrants—as well as among a majority of the individuals in our study, including U.S.-born Latinos and whites. Our findings also show that even in this politically polarized time—when immigration often appears to be a focal point of the polarization—there is consensus, tenuous as it may be, in favor of legalizing unauthorized immigrants. Legalization, perhaps the most welcoming policy of all, is not just good policy; it may also be politically viable.

A TALE OF TWO STATES 2

Arizona and New Mexico share much in common. Their political origins are intimately connected, and they have roughly similar demographic profiles. But these two states have fashioned very different contemporary immigration policies. Whereas Arizona has taken the most unwelcoming approach of any U.S. state, its eastern neighbor, New Mexico, is among the states that have adopted a welcoming approach. Their policies are the culmination of the states' different political and ethno-racial histories, which set the stage for not only the development of contemporary policies but also a contemporary cultural and political context that, as subsequent chapters show, combine with policy to shape a sense of belonging among Latinos and whites. History, culture, and politics mutually affect each other, and an understanding of current immigration policies and their impact requires an appreciation of the interconnections of these influences.

Focusing on Latinos and whites, this chapter traces the ethno-racial and political origins of Arizona and New Mexico and describes the approach each state has followed with its immigration policy. These different policy contexts provide an opportunity to compare how different kinds of immigration policy shape belonging. In addition to recounting the states' histories, this chapter explains the methods we used to conduct that comparison.

Arizona and New Mexico: Separated at Birth

It might be said that Arizona and New Mexico, shown in the map in figure 2.1, were separated at birth, both having been born of a sociopolitical ancestry defined by Native American tribes, Spanish

Figure 2.1 *U.S. States Bordering Mexico: Arizona, New Mexico, California, and Texas*

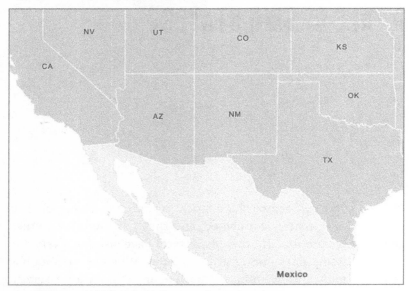

Source: Map compiled by the authors using Social Explorer.

conquest, Mexican rule, and American colonization. Native American peoples—including Hohokam, Mogollon, Ancestral Puebloan, Navajo, Apache, Ute, and Comanche—were the first to live in the territory.[1] There was tremendous diversity among these tribes with respect to language, culture, and territory; the degree to which they were nomadic or sedentary; and the extent to which they engaged in peaceful or hostile intertribal relations. Starting in the early 1500s, Spanish explorers began expeditions to these tribal lands in search of gold, but it was not until 1598 that Spain claimed the territory as part of New Spain. During that time, the colonizing Spaniards imposed strict rule over the Native Americans in the territory, although some tribes met the Spaniards with powerful resistance.

In 1810, Mexico declared its independence from Spain, spurring a decade-long war between Spain and its colony. Mexico emerged victorious and became an independent nation in 1821. Its territory was vast, stretching from its contemporary southern border with Guatemala to a northern border that included what is today the U.S. Southwest. Just two decades after Mexico had established itself as an independent nation, the United States, under the banner of "Manifest

Destiny," was pushing in earnest to have a territory stretching from the Atlantic to the Pacific. White settlers began moving rapidly into Mexico's northern territories, and especially into modern-day Texas, where the settlers' claims of independence ultimately triggered the Mexican-American War in 1846. This war, which raged on for nearly two years, marked the beginning of Arizona's and New Mexico's political incorporation into the United States.

The war ended with the signing of the Treaty of Guadalupe Hidalgo in 1848. Under the treaty's terms, Mexico sold the United States its northern territory, including the contemporary states of California, Arizona, New Mexico, Utah, Colorado, and Nevada, as well as parts of Texas, Oklahoma, Wyoming, and Kansas. The treaty also stipulated that Mexicans living in the new U.S. territories—a population of about seventy-five thousand, concentrated mostly along the newly drawn U.S.-Mexico border—would become U.S. citizens if they remained in the territory; those who did not want to be citizens had to notify the U.S. government within a year of the treaty's signing of their desire not to become U.S. citizens.[2]

In 1850, the United States established the New Mexico Territory, which encompassed the contemporary states of New Mexico and Arizona; this region was home to some sixty thousand former Mexican nationals, who were concentrated in the eastern part of the territory.[3] In 1863, the United States split the New Mexico Territory into two territories: the New Mexico territory (in the eastern part) and the newly established Arizona territory (in the western part).

White settlers flooded into both territories in the ensuing years, and the newcomers quickly moved to seize economic and political power. Even with this influx, the Mexican-origin population of New Mexico continued to be a large share of the territory's inhabitants, and they retained greater power compared to Mexican-origin residents of Arizona and other parts of the Southwest.[4] In more sparsely populated Arizona, meanwhile, federal legislation helped ease the settlement of white people in general and white farmers in particular, and whites quickly overwhelmed the relatively small Mexican-origin population.[5] By the end of the nineteenth century, people of Mexican descent in Arizona, both U.S.- and Mexican-born, made up just 20 percent of the population, down from 40 percent in 1870.[6] While the Mexican-origin population in Arizona shrank as a share of the total population, people of Mexican origin still constituted between 55 and 75 percent of the New Mexico territory by the turn of the twentieth century.[7]

The demographic and cultural milieu of the two territories formed the backdrop for debates about statehood in the territories and in the federal government in Washington, D.C. The ethno-racial character of the territory was a major sticking point. There was some support for making the two territories into a single state. But residents of the largely white Arizona territory rejected that proposal. They feared the large population of Mexican-descent individuals, as well as that of the descendants of Spanish settlers known as "Hispanos." This influential group in the social and political elite in New Mexico also sought to distinguish itself from the indigenous and Mexican-origin populations. White residents of the Arizona territory felt that both individuals of Mexican descent and Hispanos were ethno-racially unfit, and they feared that their large numbers in the New Mexico territory could overwhelm the white-dominated power structure that had taken root in the Arizona territory. The federal government left it to the two territories to offer separate proposals for statehood.

Elected officials in Washington, D.C., were also worried about the large Mexican-descent and Hispano populations in the prospective states. Arizona's white economic and political leaders addressed these concerns through an approach that the historian Linda Noel has called "marginalization": they reassured both territory residents and politicians in Washington that the state's Mexican-origin popula-tion would have no prospect of gaining significant social, political, or economic influence and that they would be temporary workers more than permanent residents.[8] In making their own case for statehood, New Mexico's Hispano ruling class pursued a contrasting "pluralist" approach.[9] New Mexico's Hispanos were largely of Spanish "blood," New Mexico's political elites argued, and thus their European origins made them ethno-racially fit to join the union of states. The pluralist approach not only emphasized the European origins of New Mexico territory residents but also advocated for those residents to maintain their use of Spanish and their pride in Spanish traditions, even as they were encouraged to learn English. Political leaders continually made the case to Washington that even if the territory maintained Spanish language and traditions, its people would consider them-selves Americans first.[10]

In 1912, both territories became states. The newly minted states crafted constitutions that seemed to foreshadow the kinds of state immigration policies each would implement a century later. Arizona's process largely excluded people of Mexican descent and Hispanos. Its constitutional convention included just one Latino among the fifty-two delegates. It established English as the official and only allowable language for public school instruction. The constitution offered no provision for state documents, like ballots, to be translated into Spanish. Not long after statehood, the Arizona state legislature passed legislation further establishing the primacy of English in the state. One bill mandated that anyone holding elected office had to be able to read, write, and speak English. As if to punctuate the English-only school instruction provision in the state's constitution, in 1913 Arizona lawmakers passed another bill requiring that all public school instruction take place in English.[11]

New Mexico's state constitutional process was quite different from that of its neighboring state to the west, as was the outcome. Its convention voted to include language in the constitution explicitly protecting the rights of Hispanos and preserving Spanish-English bilingualism. New Mexico's constitution also declared that the right to vote, to hold office, and to serve on juries would not be curtailed based on "religion, race, language or color, or inability to speak, read or write the English or Spanish languages." It required state-sponsored training so that teachers would be proficient in offering instruction in English and Spanish and mandated that children of Spanish descent never be denied access to public schools or be subjected to school segregation. Although these two states went in opposite directions after statehood, both displayed antipluralist tendencies in the first half of the twentieth century.[12] In New Mexico, antipluralist moves helped state lawmakers bolster the state's claim to racial fitness and American national identity by establishing that Hispanos were in fact white and by vigorously pursuing campaigns against people of German descent during World War I and against Japanese Americans during World War II. Arizona harbored no such insecurities, but it still joined New Mexico in its repression of German Americans and Japanese Americans.

These exceptions notwithstanding, the two states largely continued on the trajectories laid down in their statehood origins. The two world wars further solidified the racial hierarchy in the two states. In New Mexico, whites and Hispanos jointly consolidated political power. In Arizona, on the other hand, power was firmly in the hands of the state's whites. During the first half of the twentieth century, Arizona consistently imported Mexican labor, even lobbying Congress to exclude Mexicans from restrictive provisions, like literacy tests and head taxes, that were imposed on European immigrants. As the state imported Mexican labor, whites consigned these laborers to second-class status. During the Great Depression, for example, the United States is estimated to have "repatriated" (deported) between half a million and one million Mexicans, many of whom were U.S.-born children of Mexican immigrants, and debates raged about whether Mexican immigrants deserved access to New Deal programs.[13] In Arizona, officials debated whether "aliens" there should be removed from welfare rolls. In contrast, New Mexico's officials vigorously defended access to New Deal programs for Mexican immigrants and Hispanos alike.[14]

The differences in the historical origins of the two states and the policy approaches that they pursued thereafter were the forerunners to an explosion of state-level policies enacted in each state near the turn of the millennium.

From the Past to the Present: Contemporary Immigration Policies in Arizona and New Mexico

As with the approaches that Arizona and New Mexico took in crafting their founding documents, the two states have pursued contrasting policy approaches when it comes to immigration. Table 2.1 compares their current demographics and their policies related to immigration.

CONTEMPORARY IMMIGRANT POLICIES IN ARIZONA

No state is more emblematic of an unwelcoming state-level response to immigration than Arizona.[15] Arizona's contemporary embrace of highly restrictive state-level immigration policies dates to the late 1980s. In November 1988, Arizona voters narrowly passed Proposition 106, which would have made English the state's official language had the initiative not been struck down by the courts. Eighteen years

Table 2.1 *Demographics and Immigrant Policies of New Mexico and Arizona*

	New Mexico	Arizona	United States
Demographics			
Total population	2,080,085	6,561,516	318,357,056
Hispanic	47%	30.1%	17.3%
White, non-Hispanic	39.6	56.9	61.9
Foreign-born	9.9	13.5	13.3
Hispanic, U.S.-born	83	72	65.6
Unauthorized immigrants	29	23.5	25.2
Only English spoken in home	63.8	73.2	78.9
English spoken "less than very well"	9.4	9.4	8.6
Immigrant policies			
Driver's licenses for unauthorized residents	Yes	No	
In-state higher education tuition for unauthorized residents	Yes	No	
Higher education financial aid for unauthorized residents	Yes	No	
287(g) agreements (2017)	0	4	
"Show me your papers" provision	No	Yes	
English as official language	No	Yes	
Limits on bilingual education	No	Yes	
E-Verify	No	Yes	

Sources: Varsanyi and Provine 2016; U.S. Census Bureau, 2010–2014; American Community Survey Five-Year and One-Year Estimates; *New Mexico Legislative Council Service Information Bulletin* 18 (July 15, 2011); Pew Research Center 2014, 2015; Migration Policy Institute, "State Immigration Data Profiles" (for 2016 and 2018), https://www.migrationpolicy.org/programs/data-hub/state-immigration-data-profiles.

later, in 2006, Arizona voters once again moved to make English the official language by approving a revised proposal (Proposition 103), with nearly three-quarters casting their ballots in favor.

The English-only measure was only the beginning of a barrage of ballot initiatives and legislative actions unambiguously aimed at making Arizona hostile ground for immigrants in general, and for Latinos in particular. The state moved again against the use of non-English languages in 2000, passing a ballot initiative banning bilingual education (Proposition 203). In 2004, voters approved Proposition 200, which required proof of legal residence to access most forms of state and local social welfare. It also mandated that state and local workers report suspected immigration violators to federal authorities. Two years later, voters passed a deluge of restrictive ballot initiatives: Proposition 100 denied bail to unauthorized immigrants accused of a felony; Proposition 102 forbade unauthorized immigrants from collecting punitive damages in civil lawsuits; and Proposition 300 required verification of immigration status for individuals applying for state-funded services or requesting in-state tuition or financial aid for college, and it also denied subsidies to unauthorized immigrants who wished to access child care or adult education.[16]

Arizona's lawmakers enacted legislation in a similar vein. In 2008, the Arizona state legislature passed HB 2745, a bill establishing a system for reporting workers or employers suspected of being in the United States without legal authorization. The bill also mandated that the state or county attorney report unauthorized immigrants to Immigration and Customs Enforcement (ICE), and it required that all government entities and government contractors use the E-Verify system (a federal database to verify the legal status of employment applicants) for prospective employees. That same year, the state legislature passed SB 1053, a measure mandating that individuals provide proof of naturalization to county recorders when registering to vote. In 2009, state lawmakers approved a budget that included HB 2162, a requirement that anyone applying for any state or local benefit provide proof of citizenship. Also in 2009, the legislature passed and the governor signed a bill (HB 2306) requiring proof of citizenship or authorized "alien status" in order to apply for a driver's license, fortifying a 1996 law that disallowed licenses for individuals who could not prove that their "presence in the United States is authorized under federal law."[17] The following year, Governor Janet Napolitano signed HB 2306, a bill allowing the state to suspend or revoke the business licenses of employers who were found to have hired unauthorized immigrants.

As restrictive as these laws are, no state-level immigration policy in recent history garnered more attention than Arizona's SB 1070. The language in the bill laid out the law's intent as well as, in many ways, the intent behind the collective set of restrictive immigration policies adopted by the state: "The provisions of this act are intended to work together to discourage and deter the unlawful entry and presence of aliens and economic activity by persons unlawfully present in the United States." The law was a comprehensive immigration enforcement measure mandating that immigrants who had lived in the United States for longer than thirty days carry U.S.-government registration documents; state law enforcement officers could demand to see these documents during a detention or arrest or any time they had a reasonable suspicion that an individual was unauthorized. The law also prevented local and state agencies from interfering with the enforcement of federal immigration laws and levied penalties on individuals who hired, sheltered, or transported unregistered immigrants.[18] In 2012, the U.S. Supreme Court struck down some portions of the law: the requirement that immigrants carry documentation proving their legal residency; the provision allowing the state to make arrests without a warrant in certain situations; and the requirement that people applying to work in the state provide federal work authorization. Still, the Supreme Court let many of the law's provisions stand, including the one allowing state police officers to check the immigration status of individuals with whom they came into contact.

Even after enacting this high-profile measure, the state continued to limit the rights of unauthorized immigrants further. For example, in 2011 the state legislature passed HB 2353, a bill that denied bail to any arrested immigrant on whom ICE had placed a hold. That same year, the state strengthened a law that denied punitive damages to any unauthorized immigrant who was the plaintiff in a lawsuit at the state level (HB 2191). Arizona also enacted SB 1046, a law requiring that youth offenders being discharged be turned over to ICE if the enforcement agency had issued a detainer; if the youth was deported and subsequently returned to the United States, their discharge would be vacated and they could be reincarcerated.

Although many of these policies were not ostensibly directed at Latino immigrants, other measures created an unwelcoming climate for Latinos in particular. For example, in 2011 Governor Jan Brewer signed SB 2281, which made it illegal for any school district to include in its programs courses that "promote the overthrow of the United States government; promote resentment toward a race or class of people; are designed primarily for pupils of a particular ethnic group; advocate ethnic solidarity instead of the treatment of pupils as individuals." A year later, the superintendent of Tucson's public schools found the district's Mexican American studies program to be in violation of the law and banned it. In 2017, a federal judge blocked the state from enforcing the law, finding that it violated students' constitutional rights.

Local jurisdictions have also made significant contributions to Arizona's unwelcoming policy bend. While we focus on laws and policies at the state level, local-level policies add to the picture of Arizona as an unwelcoming state up and down jurisdictional levels. Maricopa County, Arizona's largest county and the one in which we conducted our in-depth interviews, was also enforcing policies aimed at expelling unauthorized immigrants and pulsing fear through immigrant and Latino communities. The driving force behind those efforts was former Maricopa County sheriff Joe Arpaio (1993–2017), whose infamous "crime suppression sweeps" targeted Latino immigrant neighborhoods to round up any Latinos whom deputies thought were unauthorized.[19] In 2015, a federal judge ruled that these raids violated the civil rights of Latinos and issued an injunction requiring that they stop; when the raids continued, Arpaio was found to be in contempt of court. (President Trump pardoned him in 2017.) Even after leaving office in 2017, Sheriff Arpaio remained an icon to supporters of restrictionist immigration policies, frequently speaking out on national news programs against unauthorized immigrants. Figures like Arpaio and the policies he enforced, in conjunction with a host of state and local measures, have earned Arizona the distinction of being the least welcoming state to immigrants in the union.[20]

But even outside of Maricopa County, other local jurisdictions largely reflect the state's overwhelmingly unwelcoming policy orientation. The University of Denver's Westminster Law Library maintains a comprehensive list of "sanctuary" policies dating back to the late 1970s.[21] The sanctuary policy designation is broad but generally includes measures that "resist entanglement of state and local law enforcement in federal immigration."[22] The database contains only six sanctuary actions in Arizona in nearly forty years. The dearth of sanctuary jurisdictions continues even today. In 2017, a report published by ICE listed one Arizona jurisdiction, Maricopa County Jails, where Arpaio's successor, Sheriff Paul Penzone, stated that the county would not honor ICE requests to hold individuals.[23]

The consistency between Maricopa County and Arizona's state-level policies can also be seen in the degree of cooperation between county and federal immigration enforcement. Maricopa County was one of the most aggressive enforcers of Secure Communities, a program that required county sheriff departments to conduct immigration background checks on arrestees in county jails and to retain immigrants flagged by an ICE database until ICE could take the immigrant into custody. The program ran from 2008 until 2015; the Trump administration revived it in 2017. During the program's first iteration in 2013, the federal government required all counties to participate, but not all counties participated equally. Some counties made few arrests, especially given the size of their immigrant population, and others refused to participate altogether. Others, like Maricopa County, were enthusiastic participants. According to data provided by the sociologist Juan Pedroza, between January 2009 and May 2013 nearly twenty-two thousand immigrants in Maricopa County were detained and deported.[24] Only slightly more than one-third of these deportees fell into the top-priority category reserved for immigrants who have committed serious crimes, like murder and rape. Perhaps more telling is the share that received relief from deportation. Under Secure Communities, sheriff departments could exercise some discretion in handing off arrestees to federal authorities. Pedroza's calculation of the share of arrestees receiving "deportation relief" indicates that 70 percent of arrestees were ultimately not deported, below the average for all Arizona counties (76 percent) and well below the national average (86 percent).[25]

Civil society groups have certainly stepped in to defend the rights of immigrants in Arizona, but the organizational resources that might dull the sharp edges of Arizona's unwelcoming policies are in short supply. Arizona offers limited support to immigrants in the state, particularly those with low income. In 2020, Arizona was home to 320,024 immigrants considered low-income (150 percent or less of the federal poverty line), but had only 36 immigration legal services providers—a rate of one legal service provider for every 8,890 low-income immigrants.[26]

It is important to note that there may be evidence of retrenchment in Arizona's immigration policies at the local level. Bubbling up is a more pro-immigrant stance in the state's local jurisdictions. For examples, several Arizona local jurisdictions, including Phoenix, Tucson, Tempe, Mesa, Goodyear, and Coconino County, have joined Cities for Action, a coalition of mayors that advocates for pro-immigrant policies at the federal and subfederal levels.[27] In recent years, Phoenix has come to look more like a pro-immigrant big city as well, electing as its mayor Kate Gallego, a longtime advocate of immigrant rights. Still, as we show in later chapters, these changes have hardly put a dent in the view among Arizona's residents that the state is unwelcoming to its immigrant population. Indeed, with an Immigrant Climate Index (ICI) score of −103, Arizona remained at the time of our research the most unwelcoming state in the nation.[28]

CONTEMPORARY IMMIGRANT POLICIES IN NEW MEXICO

If Arizona represents an unwelcoming extreme, New Mexico, Arizona's neighbor to the east, hews toward the welcoming end of the spectrum. According to Pham and Van's ICI, New Mexico has a score of +10, which places it amid a set of states, like Minnesota and New Jersey, that are moderately welcoming, and certainly a far cry from Arizona's score of −103.[29]

The contemporary origins of New Mexico's more welcoming approach can arguably be dated to 1986, when Governor Tony Anaya declared New Mexico a "sanctuary state" for asylum seekers fleeing the civil wars in Central America. Just a year after Arizona first voted to make English the state's official language, in 1989 New Mexico issued an "English-plus" declaration: "The people of New Mexico promote the spirit-of-diversity-with-harmony represented by the various cultures that make up the fabric of our state and nation."[30] In 2005, Governor Bill Richardson issued an executive order forbidding state law enforcement officers from asking about the immigrant status of criminal suspects.

The welcoming state context in New Mexico is further highlighted by a series of policies that make the rights of unauthorized immigrants nearly equivalent to those of its citizen residents. One of the most hotly contested issues in states around the country has been whether unauthorized immigrants should be able to obtain driver's licenses. While states like Arizona have resisted such efforts, New Mexico has allowed its residents, regardless of legal status, to obtain driver's licenses since 2003.[31]

An equally contentious issue is whether unauthorized residents of a state can enroll in state-sponsored colleges and universities. New Mexico was among the first of only nineteen U.S. states to permit unauthorized immigrants to pay in-state tuition at public colleges and universities. In 2005, New Mexico passed a measure allowing any student to pay in-state tuition at the state's public colleges and universities who had graduated from high school in New Mexico after attending for at least one year or had received a general educational development certificate. Even fewer states—just eight—offer unauthorized immigrants state-sponsored financial aid at state colleges and universities. New Mexico has been one of them since 2005, when state lawmakers passed SB 582. This bill also explicitly prohibits colleges and universities from discriminating against students based on their immigration status. Other laws that add to the state's more welcoming policy climate include a bill that recognized medical licenses obtained abroad (SB 171 in 2003) and another bill that expanded unemployment benefits to several categories of noncitizens (HB 261 in 2003).

These measures proactively constitute a welcoming context for immigrants. But New Mexico's welcoming state policy context is also defined by what the state has *not* done in the way of state-level immigration policy. Unlike Arizona, where four local law enforcement agencies and the state department of corrections had "287(g) agreements" with ICE allowing them to carry out immigration enforcement, at the time of our research there were no such agreements active in New Mexico.[32] Although there had been one in 2007—under which ICE provided training for state prison officers to carry out immigration enforcement—the agreement did not result in significant numbers of deportations: between 2006 and 2011, New Mexico's program identified ten candidates for removal. By comparison, the nine Arizona jurisdictions that had 287(g) agreements identified over fifty thousand candidates for removal.[33] New Mexico's 287(g) agreement was terminated in 2013. In 2014, the state declared that none of its county jails would honor ICE detainer requests.

More recently, however, Governor Susana Martinez (2011–2019) moved to blunt some of the state's welcoming policies toward immigrants. She worked out a compromise whereby driver's licenses would be issued to individuals who could not prove they were in the United States legally, but these "driver authorization cards" would bear a mark signifying that the card was not valid for federal purposes, such as boarding a plane. (In 2019, New Mexico renamed these documents "standard driver's licenses" to distinguish them from licenses that complied with the federal Real ID Act.) In 2011, Governor Martinez issued an executive order to compel state law enforcement agencies to inquire about the immigration status of criminal suspects and to share the information with federal immigration enforcement agencies. Martinez also overturned the 2005 order issued by former governor Richardson that prevented law enforcement agencies from cooperating with federal immigration law enforcement. These measures represent the exception rather than the rule in the political history of New Mexico.

Across New Mexico, the policies enacted by counties and cities are largely consistent with the welcoming bent of state policies. According to the University of Denver's Westminster Law Library, New Mexico state and local governments have enacted twenty sanctuary policies since the late 1970s (compared to six in Arizona).[34] The list maintained by ICE recorded six jurisdictions that had some sort of ICE noncooperation policy in 2017, including a state policy mandating that none of the state's county jails were to honor ICE detainer requests.[35] New Mexico's two most populous counties, Bernalillo (which contains Albuquerque) and Santa Fe (which contains the city of Santa Fe), are included on that list. Both Albuquerque and Santa Fe have sanctuary policies. Albuquerque even declared itself a "welcoming city," joining a national network of states and counties that have vowed to create a welcoming context for immigrants. (No Arizona city, county, or nonprofit has made such a declaration.)[36] Local governments, including the two largest in New Mexico, have also been much less aggressive in their cooperation with federal immigration enforcement efforts, even when required to do so.

The contrast in approaches to immigration policy at the state and local levels between Arizona and New Mexico becomes clearer when considering the participation by New Mexico's two largest counties, Bernalillo and Santa Fe, in the federal Secure Communities program. Less than four years after Bernalillo County began participating in the program in the fall of 2009, 655 immigrants had been deported under the program, less than one-quarter was in the top-priority category, and 80 percent of arrestees were not deported. Santa Fe County activated its Secure Communities program later than Bernalillo County (February 2011); it had reported just 94 deportations by mid-2013, and nearly 90 percent of arrestees received deportation relief, equaling the average for all counties in the state. (Recall that Arizona's average was 76 percent.) On top of having more welcoming state and local policies, New Mexico possesses a more robust legal services infrastructure for low-income immigrants. In 2020, New Mexico had 26 immigration legal services providers and 79,145 low-income immigrants, or one legal services provider for every 3,044 low-income immigrants—nearly three times greater than the rate in Arizona.[37]

Generally speaking, New Mexico has laid out a welcome mat for immigrants.[38] As we show later in this book, these more local welcoming policies, combined with the state's welcoming approach, add up to a life for immigrants in New Mexico that is largely unencumbered by the fear of detention, deportation, and harassment so prevalent in Arizona.

Studying Arizona and New Mexico

Arizona and New Mexico offer an opportunity to investigate whether and how immigration policy shapes people's sense of belonging and intergroup experiences. We bring together multiple methods and disciplinary insights to craft a deeper understanding of how sub-federal immigration policies are playing out in different parts of the United States, like Arizona and New Mexico. We draw upon disciplines that study interpersonal, intergroup, institutional, and political influences on behavior, and we unite methods commonly used in sociology, psychology, and political science. Our data include a telephone survey of a representative sample of 1,903 Latino and white residents in Arizona and New Mexico in which an experiment is embedded; we replicated the survey experiment with a national sample of 904 U.S.-born Latinos and whites. For information about the methodology and key sample characteristics for both studies, see our online appendix.[39] The survey instrument and experiment stimuli are also available in the appendix. We then conducted in-depth interviews with 123 residents of both states. The appendix contains a detailed description of the interview-gathering process. Each of these different kinds of data enabled us to answer the different but interrelated central research questions of this book.

One of our questions was simply whether individuals' ethno-racial background, political orientation, and the policy context in which they lived—in this case Arizona or New Mexico—led to differences among them in feelings of belonging. To answer that question, we fielded the Survey of Immigration and Belonging with U.S.-born whites, U.S.-born Latinos, and foreign-born Latinos in Arizona and New Mexico. Our main outcome measures focus on multiple elements of belonging. We present our analysis of those measures in chapters 3 and 4. While a survey can describe group and state differences, we wanted to identify whether these group and state differences in how much people felt they belonged could be *caused* by differences in policy. To answer that question, we used an experiment embedded in our survey that allowed us to see whether randomly exposing individuals to different stimuli while holding other factors constant changed the outcome. We were interested in whether exposure to different policy proposals would have a causal effect on the extent to which respondents felt welcomed and on their emotional state. For obvious reasons, we could not carry out a field experiment, such as randomly distributing whites and Latinos between the two states, exposing them to the policy context in those two states, and then testing whether that exposure shaped their feelings of belonging. Instead, we told respondents that lawmakers in their state were considering adopting policies that were either more welcoming or less welcoming toward immigrants and then assessed the impact of that information on their feelings and sense of belonging in the state. This experiment does not re-create an actual welcoming or unwelcoming environment. But *discussions* about policies, even if those policies are never enacted, can signal a psychologically impactful message of inclusion or exclusion. It is that feeling that we sought to emulate when we raised the possibility that welcoming or unwelcoming approaches were soon to be on the political agenda in respondents' states. We explain the experiment in more detail in chapter 5, along with related findings.

We were sensitive to the possibility that the differences we found between residents of Arizona and New Mexico, including how they responded to our experimental manipulation, could be unique to those states. We therefore replicated our entire survey with a national convenience sample recruited through Amazon's Mechanical Turk (MTurk) platform. In that survey, we replaced all references to New Mexico or Arizona with a more generic reference to "your state." Throughout the following chapters, we show consistent similarities between what we find in the two states and what we find in the national sample.

We took a data-driven approach to interpreting our survey and experimental findings and to gaining insight into how individuals make sense of immigration and policy. To obtain that perspective, we turned to in-depth interviews with individuals from each of our groups of interest in each state—U.S.-born whites (thirty-five in Arizona and thirty in New Mexico); foreign-born Latinos (twenty in Arizona and twelve in New Mexico); and U.S.-born Latinos (nine in Arizona and seventeen in New Mexico). The interviews allowed respondents to explain how they came to a particular perspective and offered a more textured picture of how they grappled with one of the most contentious issues of our time. Throughout the following chapters, we quote extensively from our interviews. When we do, we use pseudonyms to protect the identities of our respondents. We also conducted several of the interviews in Spanish. We use English translations when we quote from these interviews, noting when we have translated the text.

Conclusion

States present natural laboratories for testing the consequences of policies—in this case, immigration policies and laws—in ways that can inform politicians, policymakers, behavioral scientists, and the general public of the far-reaching and often unintended social consequences of legislation. We bring a range of behavioral science tools—representative surveys, experiments, and in-depth interviews—to decipher whether and how the different immigration policy contexts in Arizona and New Mexico affect the sense of belonging among the Latino immigrants, U.S.-born Latinos, and whites who live in those states. Comparing and contrasting the impact of immigration policies on the sense of belonging among residents of Arizona and New Mexico—policies intertwined with the diverging histories, cultures, and political legacies of these two states—can offer new insights of practical importance to the current immigration debate.

THE IMMIGRATION POLICY CLIMATE AND LATINOS' SENSE OF BELONGING

There can be little doubt that the states of Arizona and New Mexico, despite being founded in the same year (1912) and having similar present-day demographics, reflect different political histories and have adopted divergent approaches to state-level immigration policies. Arizona has constructed an unwelcoming, seemingly hostile, policy context of reception for a Latino-immigrant target population. New Mexico offers a welcoming context. How do those policies shape the sense of belonging of the people who live under them? What general inferences do they draw from these policies about the quality of fit or potential fit between themselves and their state? This chapter begins to address that question, focusing on the experiences of Latino immigrants, who are the targets of these policies, and U.S.-born Latinos, who are a collaterally affected group by virtue of the ethno-racial origin they share with Latino immigrants.

Belonging represents the experience of "fit" within a group or a particular setting. Recall that Walton and Brady define "belonging" as a "general inference, drawn from cues, events, experiences, and relationships about the quality of fit or potential fit between oneself and a setting. It is experienced as being accepted, included, respected in, and contributing to a setting, or anticipating the likelihood of developing this feeling."[1] We draw upon original survey data collected in 2016 (before Trump's election) in Arizona and New Mexico and in-depth interview data collected in 2018–2019 (during the Trump presidency) to show how Latinos perceived the climate for immigrants and Latinos in their state; how much Latinos felt that they belonged in their state and the nation; how much they felt that others in their state and in the United States welcomed them; the level of pride they felt in their state and in the United States; and the importance they placed on their ethnic, national, and state identities.

Latinos in Arizona and New Mexico largely reflected the portrait painted in the previous chapter when it came to how welcoming they thought their state was: Latinos in Arizona were far less likely than Latinos in New Mexico to say that their state was welcoming to immigrants. In speaking about whether their state was welcoming to immigrants, respondents, collectively, drew cues about their belonging from a swirl of history, culture, and state and local policies. But the ingredients in that swirl differed between the two states. Latinos in Arizona pointed to the state's policies and politics—and to some degree local policies and politics—as the primary reasons why Arizona was unwelcoming to immigrants. Respondents were so familiar with the policies that many could cite by name the specific laws, the politicians behind the laws, and the individuals who enforced the laws. In New Mexico, by contrast, Latinos seldom cited policies as the source of their feeling that their state was welcoming to immigrants. Instead, they focused on the state's history and culture to explain why immigrants in New Mexico generally feel that they belong. It is not that policy is irrelevant in New Mexico. Rather, welcoming immigration policies in New Mexico are a "dog that does not bark" in that they simply contribute to an absence of the kind of fear among Latinos that is pervasive in Arizona.

Our survey results also reveal that Latinos in the two states had dramatically different views about the level of discrimination against Latinos in their state. Latino Arizonans were far more likely than their New Mexican counterparts to see discrimination against Latinos in their state, and the U.S.-born Latinos in Arizona were especially likely to have that view. Despite differences in perceptions about how welcoming their state was to immigrants and about discrimination against them, Latinos in the two states were equally likely to say they were proud to live in their state and that their state identity was important to them. However, the sources of the pride were different. Arizona Latinos said that their pride stemmed from the sense of home they felt in their neighborhood and in their community, but not necessarily in the state as a whole. Latinos in New Mexico cited the state's cultural uniqueness and general openness to all comers as the source of their pride. At the same time, during in-depth interviews U.S.- and foreign-born Latinos in both states explained how the different levels of belonging revealed in our survey were tied to state-level policies, which they often collapsed onto local policies that reflected a general state-wide climate.

And yet Latinos in both states, regardless of their nativity or how welcome they felt in their state, maintained similar perspectives on their sense of belonging in the United States more generally. The interviews added texture to the survey findings on this count, showing that both immigrant and U.S.-born Latinos found ways to write their biography onto a larger American national identity. However, they also recognized that their belonging might be contested: the in-depth interviews, gathered after Trump's election, show that Latinos were attuned to the souring views toward immigrants and Latinos characteristic of the policies and politics of the Trump administration.

If there is a jurisdictional patchwork of immigration policies, there is an equally complex social-psychological response to these policies. Even as Latinos and immigrants make strong claims to membership in the U.S. polity, they are well aware that the places where they live—in the country and in subfederal jurisdictions—may or may not hold out a welcoming hand. When unwelcoming immigration policies shun them, Latinos are keenly aware of it, even as they assert that they belong.

A Welcoming Hand or a Closed Fist? Perceptions of the State Policy Context

Before evaluating what immigration policies signal about belonging, we wanted to explore whether Latinos recognized the differing policy contexts in the two states we studied. We therefore posed the following question to survey respondents: "In general, do you think that [your state] tries to make immigrants feel: very welcome, somewhat welcome, somewhat unwelcome, or very unwelcome?" Overall, 40.8 percent of Latinos felt that their state tried to make immigrants feel somewhat or very unwelcome. There were clear differences by state. Latinos in New Mexico were much more likely to see their state as welcoming than Arizona Latinos were to say the same about their state: 51.3 percent in New Mexico versus 21.3 percent in Arizona.

In our statistical analysis, we attempted to determine whether living in either Arizona or New Mexico played an independent role in Latinos' outlooks. To do so, we included other potentially relevant variables aside from state of residence that might affect respondents' sense of belonging. It is reasonable to expect that nativity and English-language ability would play a role in shaping the attitudes examined here—specifically, that Latinos who were U.S.-born and English-dominant would exhibit a greater sense of belonging.[2] As such, all of our models included measures for nativity (66 percent of our Latino respondents were born in the United States) and language used at home (57 percent primarily spoke English at home).[3] We also included a variable capturing the interaction between being U.S.-born and state of residence. We used this variable to test whether the U.S.-born in Arizona were more aware of their state's climate than the foreign-born.[4] We also accounted for educational attainment and income, both of which provide security and stability that could enhance an individual's sense of belonging.[5]

Finally, we accounted for partisanship by assessing whether the respondent either identified as a Democrat, Republican, or independent or declined to pick one of these three options.[6] The fact that Latino are often uncomfortable placing themselves in traditional partisan categories indicates that adopting any kind of partisanship is itself a form of acculturation.[7] It may therefore be the case that partisans, regardless of which party they choose, feel a greater sense of belonging than people who lack a party affiliation. It is also likely that Democrats and Republicans feel differently about several of the measures examined here. Since the two political parties increasingly diverge on issues pertaining to immigration, Democrats would be expected to be more likely than Republicans to perceive discrimination.[8] In our sample, 53 percent of Latino respondents identified as Democrats (strong, weak, or leaning), and 18 percent identified as Republicans. Only 6 percent identified as independent, while 22 percent either skipped the question or said that they did not think of themselves in partisan terms.

The effect of partisanship may differ across states if the character of each party differs by state (such as if Democrats in one state tend

Figure 3.1 *How Welcoming Is My State? Predicted Probabilities among Latino Respondents, by State and Birthplace*

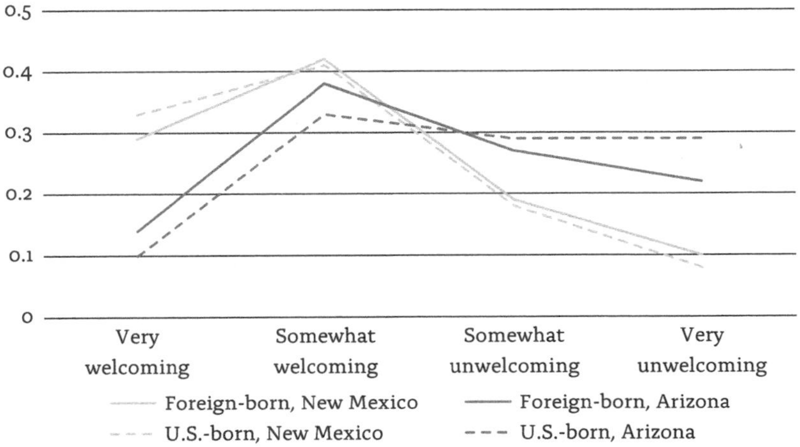

Foreign-born, New Mexico   Foreign-born, Arizona
U.S.-born, New Mexico   U.S.-born, Arizona

Source: Survey of Immigration and Belonging (Dovidio et al. 2016).

to be more moderate than Democrats in another). Our survey did not include policy questions that would allow us to capture this possibility directly, but we did ask respondents whether they considered themselves liberal, conservative, or moderate. Latino Democrats in the two states were equally likely to identify as liberal (28 percent in Arizona and 31 percent in New Mexico), while Latino Republicans were more likely to identify as conservative in Arizona (65 percent in Arizona and 54 percent in New Mexico). That Democrats were so similar and that over a majority of Republicans in both states were conservative suggests to us that, at least ideologically, the two parties are more similar than different for Latino respondents in these states.

All these political factors might reasonably be expected to affect respondents' view of whether their state was welcoming or not. But our analysis revealed that the respondent's state of residence still mattered after taking these other factors into account.[9] We present our results in terms of predicted probabilities, showing the likelihood of giving a particular response to a survey question once we have accounted for all of the variables described here. We pay attention both to statistical significance and to substantive significance.[10]

The results, depicted in figure 3.1, are striking in how differently Latinos in the two states perceived their state: Latinos in Arizona were far more likely to say that their state was unwelcoming to immigrants, and this perception was especially strong among the U.S.-born.[11]

The responses to this question in the interviews were just as striking. Latino respondents from Arizona were unequivocal that their state was unwelcoming to immigrants, and especially to Latino immigrants. As noted in the previous chapter, Arizona passed a torrent of unwelcoming legislation during the 2000s. For most Latino Arizonans, these measures were tantamount to a series of storms that made for a long and dark winter. Rather than seizing on any one policy or measure, they characterized the entire period as a demonstration of the state's unwelcoming character. When we asked Latinos how immigrants were treated in their state, they rarely had to think long; the answer seemed obvious to them. Take, for example, Lara Aguiano,[12] a thirty-three-year-old Mexican immigrant, naturalized U.S. citizen, social worker, and liberal Democrat. When asked how immigrants are treated in Arizona, she responded:

> Very badly. I feel there's a lot of racism here. I think you feel it right away. I think you feel the tension. Once you come to Arizona, 'cause I have family in California and the atmosphere and everything's so different from here. Here, I feel that it's nothing but racism and fear. I don't know, I don't think that Arizona is welcoming to immigrants. (*translated from Spanish*)

Nelia Torres was a twenty-nine-year-old construction manager, immigrant from Mexico, and Arizona resident who identified with the Democratic Party. She had been in the United States since she was ten months old. She also was a "Dreamer," a Deferred Action for Childhood Arrivals (DACA) recipient; this program created by the Obama administration in 2012 allowed undocumented immigrants who were brought to the United States as children and who met certain conditions to apply for a two-year, renewable work authorization permit. Here is her description of how immigrants were treated in Arizona:

> You know, definitely not the place to come if you're an immigrant. . . . You need to go somewhere else, to definitely a more liberal state or a more welcoming state. New York is nice to people, but Arizona is

not. There's a lot of opportunities, of course, there's a lot of work here—landscaping is year-round because of the weather that we have, and a lot of immigrants go into that, but it's definitely not an immigrant-friendly state, no.

Latino Arizonans' sense of belonging as immigrants in their state was not just based on intuition. They cited specific aspects of the policy and political landscape that targeted them. If there was one policy that figured more prominently than others, it was Arizona's SB 1070, the 2010 "show me your papers" law that made it illegal to reside or work in Arizona as an undocumented immigrant; required law enforcement to check the immigration status of anyone detained or arrested; and, most controversially, required law enforcement to check the immigration status of anyone they perceived as likely to be undocumented. In addition to these policies, respondents mentioned individuals who symbolized just how unwelcoming the state was, including former governor Jan Brewer (2009–2015), who signed a number of unwelcoming measures, including SB 1070. But it was former Maricopa County sheriff Joe Arpaio who was *the* focal character of the state's unwelcoming bent toward immigrants. Take the recollections of Mario Mendoza, a fifty-two-year-old construction worker in Arizona who said his views aligned with Democrats. Mario was originally from Mexico and now resided in the United States without legal authorization. Mario compared the situation at the time of the interview, when Arpaio was out of office, to a time not so long before when Arpaio's enforcement was a local version of the state's overall approach to punishing Latino immigrants:

Arpaio was like Trump, only he was more direct. They apply the law of injury, not federal law or state law; they just want to cause damage. . . . When Arpaio was in office it was pretty stressful, because if I ever got home later than expected, they would get scared and they would start asking me why I hadn't arrived sooner. That used to happen all the time, back when Arpaio was enforcing all of those laws. Same with the kids, if they went out at night and didn't come home until the next day, you'd think migration caught them. It used to be very stressful, but it's all better now, thankfully. (*translated from Spanish*)

Arpaio figured prominently in other respondents' accounts as well. In both our survey and in-depth interviews, we asked respondents specifically about the state. But Mario and other interviewees collapsed state and local policies as they articulated their experiences and perceptions of belonging in Arizona more generally. Although Sheriff Arpaio was a county official, his reputation was national, and he became a figurehead not just for an unwelcoming county, but also for the state's overall unwelcoming context.

Comments like Mario's underscored the symbolic as well as administrative impact of unwelcoming policies. Some respondents mentioned the potential effect of these policies on their undocumented parents. Others who were undocumented themselves told us about how their lives had been directly touched by the state's unwelcoming policies. We describe how the administrative aspects of policies factored into Latinos' feelings of belonging later in the chapter. Suffice it to say here that in Arizona unwelcoming policies informed the view among Latinos that their state was firmly unwelcoming to immigrants.

Latinos in New Mexico discussed their state's treatment of immigrants and Latinos quite differently. Whereas Latinos in Arizona pointed directly to policies in articulating their perceptions, Latinos in New Mexico had various explanations for why Latinos were treated the way they were in the state. The latter were also vague in laying out the role of immigration policy in making their state welcoming. Latinos in New Mexico cited a host of factors, including history and culture, and only occasionally referred to policy. But welcoming immigration policies were a dog that did not bark. Because the policies were largely welcoming, immigrants in New Mexico went about their daily lives free from the kind of fear prevalent among immigrants in Arizona. New Mexico respondents took that sense of freedom for granted and thus did not readily mention it. Some interviewees, especially the immigrants, simply expressed a general sense that state laws were more welcoming. María Araya, a thirty-seven-year-old retail clerk and immigrant from El Salvador living in the United States under temporary protected status, put it this way:

If it were like in other states, which has a lot to do with immigrants, maybe it is [unwelcoming]. But here in New Mexico I don't feel that way. I feel more protected, that the laws are more flexible with us, because there are many organizations that support us and other people who kick us out, like the governor. But otherwise, I feel good. I feel safe. (*translated from Spanish*)

The factors that facilitate a sense of belonging include, but are not exclusive to, policy. Local organizations that serve immigrants, for instance, cultivate a sense of belonging. Even though New Mexico's Latino respondents believed that the state was largely welcoming in its policies, to the extent that they mentioned policies at all they described the less friendly measures taken by former governor Susana Martinez as an exception. As we noted in the previous chapter, Martinez led a push to stop giving driver's licenses to unauthorized immigrants in New Mexico. But the Democratic state legislature pushed back. So, too, did local immigrant advocacy organizations, which, as we discussed in chapter 2, abound in New Mexico compared to Arizona. These organizations form a larger welcoming context that includes welcoming immigration policies. Everyday contact between members of different national-origin and ethno-racial groups also determined the degree to which immigrants reported a sense of belonging. Research conducted by Michael Jones-Correa, Linda Tropp, Helen Marrow, and Dina Okamoto on Mexicans, South Asian Indians, whites, and African Americans in Atlanta and Philadelphia demonstrates that more positive intergroup interactions cultivate a sense of belonging among immigrants, as does intermittent cordial contact.[13] This contact is an interpersonal version of the policies in place in New Mexico. Both contribute to a normalcy in everyday life that signals belonging precisely because immigrants are not preoccupied with the threat of conflict and exclusion.

With the welcoming policies largely operating in the background, Latino respondents offered New Mexico's culture as an important and pervasive cue that provided immigrants with a soft landing and integration process. New Mexico's political origins, its large and long-residing Hispano population supplemented by later-generation Mexicans, and its subsequent waves of Latino immigrants have all sustained a culture that was recognizable and welcoming to the state's Latino immigrants. Respondents homed in on the pervasiveness of the Spanish language as well as a larger cultural sensibility that created a sense of everyday ease for Latinos. In both its tangible and intangible elements, New Mexico's welcoming context emerged clearly in the comments of Amy Garza, a thirty-six-year-old college counselor, daughter of Mexican immigrants, and registered independent. She grew up in New Mexico and had moved to Arizona just three years before we interviewed her. Frequent conversations with her best friend, an Arizonan, made her particularly aware of the climate in Arizona, and just how different it was from New Mexico. She told us:

> I was aware of policies by Jan . . . Jan Brewer, the former governor. I knew about Sheriff Joe Arpaio. I knew about SB 1060. Is it 1060? (*She was referring to SB 1070.*) I knew about, you know, just how a lot of crime was kind of scapegoated against Latinos. . . . And so part of my hesitation in moving here, was because I knew the political climate. . . . New Mexico is its own little unique area in . . . the whole union. And a lot of it goes back to the history. There was a lot of resources there that really attracted other settlers. So the communities are Native American and Spaniards, and then Mexicans. The whole identity is completely different compared to Arizona. And so I feel that there's a lot more politicians who reflect the constituents, as far as them being not necessarily Caucasian; they're usually more Latino. But there's also that strong identity of Spanish among them too, even though they could be mixed with Mexican. It's completely different.

As Amy's comments suggest, the question of whether their state was welcoming to immigrants gained sharper clarity when respondents drew comparisons between New Mexico and Arizona. New Mexico's Latinos often did just that without our prompting. Those comparisons led respondents to move New Mexico's relatively welcoming policies to the foreground in their accounts of how the state treated immigrants. When we asked Luis Ramirez, a thirty-nine-year-old construction worker, naturalized U.S. citizen from Mexico, and registered Democrat, about how welcoming New Mexico is to immigrants, he too offered up Arizona as a foil:

> Here I only know of the governor, Susana Martinez, who wants to take away people's licenses, and I completely disagree with that. . . . People want to screw with the immigrants' lives in Arizona, that's why people moved to New Mexico, here is not how it is there, the sheriff [Joe Arpaio] kicked many people out of Arizona. I put myself in their place and told my wife to imagine that we were

living in Arizona and that we had to go to run an errand in our car—what would we do if we got stopped by the police and we're undocumented? A lot of people couldn't go out because of this. I have relatives in Arizona who were afraid and had to move from there. (*translated from Spanish*)

As Luis's comments make clear, former Arizona sheriff Arpaio's stature as a figurehead for unwelcoming policies resonated in New Mexico. Even though he was a local law enforcement official, his actions and rhetoric appeared to our respondents as emblematic of the entire state's approach. New Mexico's Latinos could not always quite put their finger on what made New Mexico welcoming, but they knew that their state was nothing like Arizona. As we show later in this chapter and the next, comparisons between New Mexico and Arizona were a leitmotif of the interviews as respondents evaluated the degree to which they identified with, belonged in, and experienced discrimination in their state.

The Immigration Policy Context and *Latinos'* Belonging and Identification

It is not just that Arizona and New Mexico Latinos differed in their perception of how warm the welcome was to immigrants in their state; they also had distinct feelings of belonging emanating from the different state policy and cultural contexts they navigated. These differences emerged from our survey, which asked whether they felt that they belonged in their state, whether they felt like an outsider, and whether they perceived discrimination against Latinos in their state; our survey also asked how much pride they had in their state and how important their state identity was to them. The differences also came through in the interviews: respondents explained how their lived experiences and outlooks had been shaped by the unwelcoming policies in Arizona for that state's Latinos and by their state's general culture of welcome for New Mexico's Latino residents.

STATE BELONGING AND DISCRIMINATION

Clearer differences between Latinos in the two states emerged from responses to survey questions that tapped into Latinos' perceptions

Figure 3.2 *Do I Feel That I Belong in My State? Predicted Probabilities among Latino Respondents, by State and Birthplace*

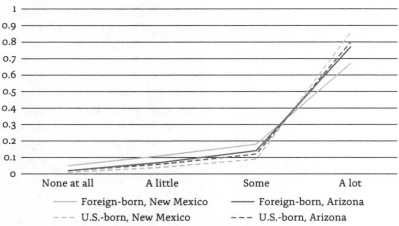

Source: Survey of Immigration and Belonging (Dovidio et al. 2016).

of their own belonging and the level of discrimination against Latinos in their state. We asked survey respondents whether they felt that they belonged in their state, whether they thought *other* people felt that they (the respondents) belonged, and whether they felt like outsiders. We also asked about the degree to which they felt that Latinos were discriminated against in their state. Over 75 percent (76.8 percent) of Latinos felt that they belonged "a lot" in their state, and differences across the two states were minimal: 74 percent in Arizona and 79 percent in New Mexico.[14] Nonetheless, there were a few notable differences. Once again, state of residence and nativity combined in unique ways: U.S.-born Latinos in Arizona were less likely than U.S.-born Latinos in New Mexico to say that they felt that they belonged in their state. As figure 3.2 shows, although U.S. nativity enhanced the sense of belonging, the U.S.-born in Arizona were six percentage points less likely to feel a sense of belonging than the U.S.-born in New Mexico. This effect is not particularly large, but it is both statistically significant and indicative of a pattern that appears with some of our other measures as well. It's noteworthy that foreign-born Latinos in New Mexico are less likely to report belonging in their state than their Arizona counterparts. Given the differences in immigration policy approaches between the two states, this survey finding seems vexing. However, the interview findings we present later in the chapter offer clarity. Interviews show that foreign-born Latinos in Arizona find belonging in a close-knit Latino community in response to the level of perceived discrimination; their New Mexico counterparts referenced the intra-Latino hierarchy alongside the state's relative overall cultural openness. As we show later in this section, levels of perceived discrimination diverge dramatically by state of residence. It is also noteworthy that, on this measure, both Democrats and Republicans were more likely than nonpartisans to say that they belonged, indicating that the mere adoption of a political party can be a measure of integration.

When considering Latinos' perception of whether *other* people in their state felt that they belonged, we found that although respondents were likely to report feeling themselves that they belonged "a lot," they were much less likely to believe that other people shared that view. Overall, 57.4 percent of Latino respondents said that they thought others felt that they belonged "a lot" in the state (versus 76.8 percent who personally felt that they belonged a lot). However, respondents in New Mexico were more likely to report feeling this way than respondents in Arizona (65 percent in New Mexico versus 50 percent in Arizona). The state difference remains statistically significant in our multivariate analysis when we account for other factors, while also showing that it is the U.S.-born who were most affected by where they lived. As figure 3.3 illustrates, the views of U.S.-born Latinos in Arizona resemble those of foreign-born Latinos in both states more than they resemble those of U.S.-born Latinos in New Mexico. Indeed, there was a 67 percent chance that U.S.-born Latinos in New Mexico would say that others felt that they belonged "a lot," but only a 55 percent chance that U.S.-born Latinos in Arizona would say the same.[15] As with our findings on self-reported belonging, foreign-born Latinos in New Mexico are slightly less likely than foreign-born Latinos in Arizona to report feeling that others think they belong in their state. Interview findings we report later in the chapter help explain this survey finding and the findings on self-reported belonging.

Another way to assess belonging is to consider whether people feel that they are excluded—the opposite of a sense of belonging. When we asked respondents whether they felt like an outsider in their state, 17 percent agreed ("somewhat" or "strongly"). Latinos in Arizona were

Figure 3.3 *Do Other People Feel That I Belong in My State? Predicted Probabilities among Latino Respondents, by State and Birthplace*

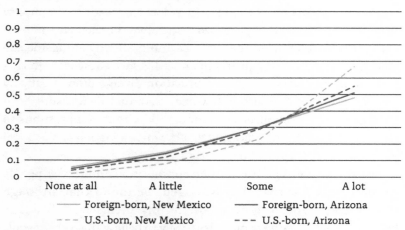

Source: Survey of Immigration and Belonging (Dovidio et al. 2016).

more likely to feel this way than Latinos in New Mexico (22 percent in Arizona versus 13 percent in New Mexico), but this difference was not statistically significant once we took into account other factors that could shape these perceptions. On this question, both nativity and language were strong predictors of feeling like an outsider: in both New Mexico and Arizona, U.S.-born respondents and respondents who primarily spoke English at home were less likely than others to say that they felt like an outsider in their state.

An additional measure of belonging among Latinos is whether they felt that there was discrimination against Latinos in their state of residence. It was on this count that we found the most disparate perceptions between Latinos in the two states. To perceive discrimination is to think that group members are being treated as less than full members of the community and given less access to the range of rights and opportunities that full members enjoy. Perceptions of discrimination therefore suggest awareness of exclusion. When asked about state-level discrimination against Latinos overall, 34.5 percent felt that there was "a lot" or "a great deal" of discrimination in their state. Arizona Latinos were far more likely to feel this way than their New Mexico counterparts (49 percent in Arizona versus 20 percent in New Mexico).[16] This finding held true for both the U.S.-born and the

Figure 3.4 *Are Latinos Discriminated against in My State? Predicted Probabilities among Latino Respondents, by State and Birthplace*

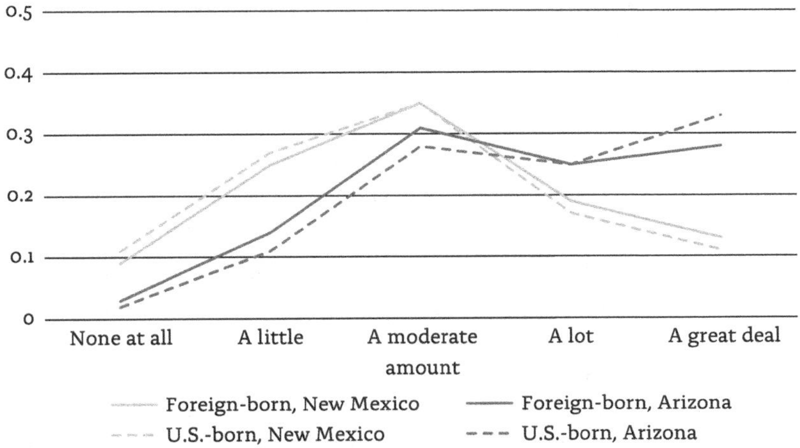

Foreign-born, New Mexico — Foreign-born, Arizona
U.S.-born, New Mexico — U.S.-born, Arizona

Source: Survey of Immigration and Belonging (Dovidio et al. 2016).

foreign-born in Arizona, even after accounting for other variables. Figure 3.4 displays the extent to which Latinos perceived discrimination against Latinos in their state. Respondents in Arizona were much more likely to perceive a "great deal" of discrimination compared to respondents in New Mexico.[17] This was also one of the only instances where we found a partisan divide: Latino Democrats were more likely than nonpartisans to say there is discrimination in their state while Latino Republicans were less likely (see online appendix).

A STATE FOR US?

Another way of assessing the sense of connection that Latinos felt in the state where they lived is to measure how strongly they identified with that state—a key form of social identity in their daily lives. Social identity, which can involve state as well as ethno-racial identity, relates to the way individuals perceive their connection to a group and what the group represents.[18] According to Henri Tajfel, "social identity is that part of an individual's self-concept which derives from his [sic] knowledge of his membership of a social group (or groups) together with the emotional significance attached to that membership."[19] Two key dimensions of social identity relate to the esteem that an individual has for the group and the importance this individual assigns to being a member of a group.[20] Social identity and belonging are likely to be positively related because people who take pride in their group membership and view that membership as important are motivated to belong to the group.[21] Another reason is that people who belong to a group aspire to promote the status and interests of the group.[22] Typically, people are not proud of a group unless they see themselves as belonging to it in a substantial way.[23] Among Latino survey respondents, feelings of greater pride in their state and of the greater importance of their state identity were positively associated with a feeling of belonging in their state.

Our survey delved into the degree to which Latinos identified with their state by asking them how strongly they agreed that "I am proud to tell people I am from [my state]." Seventy percent of Latinos across the two states agreed strongly with that statement. Those living in New Mexico exhibited more pride than those living in Arizona (77 percent in New Mexico versus 64 percent in Arizona). This difference, however, was not statistically significant once we accounted for other variables. We also found that nativity was not statistically significant, nor was partisanship (see results in the appendix). And so it appears that Latinos in New Mexico and Arizona, regardless of whether they were U.S.- or foreign-born, were equally proud to tell people they were from their state of residence.

Our survey also asked respondents how important being from Arizona or New Mexico was to them. Greater importance indicates stronger social identification with the state. Across the two states, we found that 58 percent of Latinos said that being from their state was very important. Latinos in Arizona were less likely than Latinos in New Mexico to feel this way (56 percent in Arizona and 62 percent in New Mexico). Differences between the two states remained even when we accounted for other relevant variables. We also found that the effect of state residence was influenced by nativity. The results, shown in figure 3.5, reveal that U.S.-born Latinos in Arizona were by far the least likely to say that their state identity was very important to them. Even after accounting for income, education, partisanship, and language use, U.S.-born Latinos in Arizona were fourteen percentage points less likely than the U.S.-born in New Mexico to say

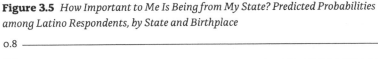

Figure 3.5 *How Important to Me Is Being from My State? Predicted Probabilities among Latino Respondents, by State and Birthplace*

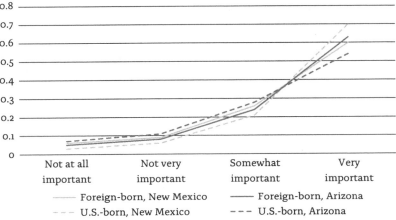

Source: Survey of Immigration and Belonging (Dovidio et al. 2016).

that being from their state was very important (54 percent versus 68 percent). Differences between U.S.- and foreign-born Latinos in New Mexico and foreign-born Latinos in Arizona were not statistically different.

Latinos in the two states had mostly similar levels of pride in and identification with their home state (the U.S.-born in Arizona being an exception), with the foreign-born slightly more likely to report they belonged and that others saw them as belonging. But across the two states, the sources of that pride and identification differed.

Although no clear explanation emerged from our in-depth interviews for these patterns of belonging and identification with their state, the data suggest that Arizona Latinos worked to define their belonging by carving out a narrow geographic context, such as their neighborhood or home, within which they found a coethnic community that cultivated a sense of belonging. The closeness of these (usually predominantly Latino) communities stemmed from the kind of factors that bring minority communities together in general: a shared national origin, a shared ethnic background, economic opportunities, a common language, and a sense of protection from discrimination.[24] As we show in the next section, Latinos across the board agreed unequivocally that whites felt most at home in Arizona.

But when respondents reflected on their notion of what it *meant* to feel at home, they often spoke, not of the state in general, but of the specific neighborhood where they grew up or where they were currently living. Indeed, the feeling of exclusion in one area can promote a sense of belonging in another.

Take, for example, Pancho Vigil, a twenty-nine-year-old Mexican national, self-described political liberal, and professional translator, whom we interviewed over the phone from his new home in Mexico City. He had lived in Arizona for most of his life, but he was deported not long before we interviewed him. When we asked him what group of people felt most at home in Arizona, he replied that "it would have to be the middle white class and up, because everyone else stresses. But when it comes to feeling at home, I can close my eyes and think that I'm driving and feel right at home. That's what the issue is, that there's a lot of people that see Arizona as home because they've been there for so long, they don't know another home." Asked to describe "home" for himself, Pancho first gave his address, Sixty-Fifth and Montgomery. We asked him to elaborate:

> Momma's house, the places you can go to . . . I mean yes, I had my apartment, but that was home base, we still had Christmas parties, go visit after work and end up falling asleep on our couch. . . . Those things, Mexican mom stuff, you wake up and she has this caldo [Mexican soup] waiting for you. (*translated from Spanish*)

As Pancho suggested, the very conditions that created an unwelcoming environment in Arizona, and thus made the coethnic community indispensable, helped instill a sense of home rooted not so much in living in a political and cultural territory known as the state of Arizona, but in being part of a local coethnic community that provided respite in state and local policy contexts and societal contexts of reception that were decisively unwelcoming.

Latinos in New Mexico emphasized what they perceived as their state's cultural openness and diversity as their source of pride. That diversity derives from the presence of the longtime Hispano population, people of Mexican descent, and the Native American population. Among these groups there is a clear ethno-racial hierarchy rooted in a history of colonization that prioritized closeness to European ancestry—thus Hispanos are at the top of that hierarchy.[25] And yet there remained a sense of pride in the state's multiethnic makeup. The Latinos we interviewed perceived New Mexico's embrace of this diversity as a factor that seemed to make it easy for them to find their own place in the state. Take, for example, the comments of Miguel Ocampo, a nineteen-year-old Mexican immigrant and DACA recipient who identified with the Democratic Party. Miguel worked as a substance abuse prevention specialist. His description of his home state captured the same sources of pride mentioned by many others, regardless of their birthplace:

> I would describe it as diverse and beautiful, because that's what makes it beautiful, you know? It's just different, there's so many people, the cultures, the views. . . . I think that New Mexico is amicable, it's amicable, and, and I guess it's just welcoming because, like I said, its different cultures, different peoples. . . . New Mexico itself doesn't discriminate, it does not, you know? That's what I feel; how I would describe New Mexico.

Felipe Gastelum, a thirty-four-year-old marketing specialist and Republican from a well-established New Mexico family, echoed Miguel's comments when he characterized what made New Mexico welcoming:

> Because you have space to breathe. You have places to go. There's spots that you could frequent, and you could build a little bit of a community. I would say there's enough diversity, but there's not that many black people here, which is really weird. But, there's enough diversity for people to get a range of people, just like the different fields. You know, shared upon a common theme, it's like work, or maybe it's sports, of course.

For these respondents, diversity was a lived experience that gave New Mexico an allure not only for people who had spent their whole lives there but also for newcomers, whether from abroad or from other U.S. regions. One respondent described the state as a "land of entrapment," a play on New Mexico's popular motto, "land of enchantment." Because of the beauty of the landscape and the welcoming people, this respondent said, anyone who has ever spent time in the state becomes emotionally attached and has a hard time leaving.

Across the measures of belonging the survey captures, a clear picture begins to emerge. Latinos in Arizona and New Mexico alike appeared to identify with their state, but those in Arizona were more likely to perceive that others rejected them as full members of the community. What accounts for these divergent perceptions? The Arizona Latinos we interviewed offered a portrait of belonging in their state that adds texture to our survey data. Some of that texture arises from their answers to a question about which group of people they thought felt most at home in their state. Among Latinos in Arizona, the answer seemed obvious: whites, and especially white Republicans. Across the interviews, a clear consensus emerged that an ethno-racial hierarchy prevailed in the state that had whites planted firmly at the top. Lara Aguiano, the thirty-three-year-old naturalized U.S. citizen we quoted earlier, summed up that consensus. When asked who felt most at home in Arizona, she replied: "Republicans.... Definitely white, white people, and old people, very conservative people."

INTERVIEWER: And how do you compare yourself to them—to white, conservative, old people?

LARA: I'm not, I'm nothing like them.... I'm not conservative, I'm not. I'm not white to begin with. I'm brown. I'm Mexican. I'm more about justice and fairness and equal opportunity and equal rights and I'm just different from them. I don't see it like Arizona, like the U.S. belongs to me and you guys are just immigrants, you guys don't belong here. I see it more like this is Arizona, this is the home for everyone, and we all deserve to be treated equally.

INTERVIEWER: And how would you describe the people that feel least at home in Arizona?

LARA: Like me, people like me: immigrants, minorities, African Americans, those their social, economic status being low. . . . That's something that I struggle with every day because I don't understand why I'm still living here—with all this racism. But I feel that I don't like it, yet I have

> my family here, and it's not fair for me to just run
> away from it, you know? Because I also live here
> and I deserve to be here. (*translated from Spanish*)

Note that Lara asserted a principle that everyone, regardless of background, ought to belong in Arizona. And yet she, like other respondents, distinguished this aspiration from the reality she perceived: that racism made not just Latinos but other minorities, including African Americans, feel like they did not belong in the state. Lara's comments echo the observations made by Lila Ibarra in the opening pages of the book in identifying whites as the group that most belongs in the state. But Lara went even further, questioning why she still lived in a state "with all this racism." Lara foreshadowed our analysis of experimental data in chapter 5, where we show that welcoming policies cause Latino immigrants like her to feel a greater sense of belonging, which includes being less likely to want to move away from a welcoming state. Her comments also illustrate that decisions about where to live are multifaceted, with family and work ties counterbalancing the repulsion of unwelcoming policies.

When Arizona's Latinos linked their sense of not belonging to the series of unwelcoming immigration policies that proliferated in the first decade of the new millennium, the role of policy in responses to the state like Lara's was even more explicit. For these respondents, those policies animated the state's capacity to make daily life miserable for Latinos in general, and for Latino immigrants in particular. Virtually all of the Latinos we interviewed in Arizona referenced unwelcoming policies as a source of discrimination against their ethno-racial group. Taken together, their comments portrayed a pall of anti-Latino sentiment in the state that hung over daily life in both symbolic and material ways. Cristina Suarez was a twenty-six-year-old paralegal and daughter of Mexican immigrants. She was also a registered Democrat and someone who took pride in being from Arizona. But that pride hit a limit when she described the situation of most Latinos since 2010, the year SB 1070 passed:

> In 2010, I was eighteen [years old], so I feel like that's a very transformative age too, but after, I just felt like there was this feeling, this very dark veil kind of feeling, like [in the] back of your throat.

Everything that I did, I just started carrying and carrying this burden for all of my friends and family members that I knew that were undocumented. I kind of acquired this worry for them. And it hasn't gone away. . . . It wasn't like where you could just point at something or someone and say that's the bad thing. . . . It was just everywhere, like a veil. . . . [I felt] just very worried and almost hopeless. And it's like you're yelling, trying to get your point across, but the person you're yelling to has headphones on. That's how I describe it. You know, or they are like not even looking at you. They are like ignoring you, and you're like yelling and fighting for your life.

Cristina's use of the veil as an image echoes W.E.B. Du Bois's use of the same metaphor to describe physical, emotional, and psychological distinctions between African Americans and whites.[26] For Du Bois, the veil is the filter through which African Americans view and interpret their place in the world, as well as make sense of the views that others have of them. Cristina's veil is colored by the ethnoracial and legal status distinctions through which she interpreted virtually every situation after 2010, the year SB 1070 went into effect. The veil gave her view of the world bleak hues. But it was not just the symbolism and political rhetoric that cast a shadow over the Latino experience in Arizona. A concern that unwelcoming policies would have a material effect on the lives of Latinos, both immigrant and U.S.-born, shaped their perceptions of belonging. As Cristina indicated, this concern emerged in physical, visceral ways, especially among children of Latino immigrants. Cristina, like other children of immigrants, feared for her friends and family members who lacked legal documentation. But more than that, she and others worried that all Latinos could become targets of the policies. In explaining why she protested SB 1070 when it passed, Cristina articulated the sort of concern we heard from other U.S.-born Latinos:

Because I knew my parents were immigrants and also family friends that were immigrants and undocumented. Even though I knew my whole life they were undocumented and immigrants, the fear they had to go through every day, I feel I didn't know until that point. I probably don't know it because I don't live it, but I felt I was able to just understand them more. . . . I remember thinking back then, my kids are going to be born here, but they're Mexican. What kind of racism are they going to go through as they grow up? I don't know. I don't want them to go through this. Who am I going to marry and have kids with? I don't know. If they have to go through this shit, I want them to be able to stand up for themselves or to know what to stand up for.

The comments from our U.S.-born respondents provide insight into our survey results showing that U.S.-born Latinos in Arizona were particularly likely to see discrimination against Latinos in their state. It may seem paradoxical that U.S.-born Latinos, who were a collaterally affected group not directly subject to the administrative aspect of immigration policies, were more likely to perceive discrimination than Latino immigrants, who were the target of those policies, both administratively and symbolically. Many Latinos living in Arizona and New Mexico are what the anthropologist John Ogbu calls "involuntary minorities," either because they trace their roots in the region back to a time before it was part of the United States or because they are the U.S.-born descendants of immigrants.[27] U.S.-born Latinos have a catalog of cues, events, experiences, and relationships tinged with racism often going back generations in their family.

Whereas Latino immigrants can compare their experience in the United States to their experience in a home country where they probably had a higher status than they do in the United States, U.S.-born Latinos have no other country to serve as a comparison point for their experiences of discrimination in the United States; they have always been ethno-racial minorities. U.S.-born Latinos may thus have greater expectations that they enjoy the rights that come with citizenship and their established presence in Arizona and New Mexico. When unwelcoming policies, like SB 1070, puncture that expectation, they become more likely to see discrimination than foreign-born Latinos.[28] Moreover, their experiences growing up in the United States have socialized them to be more aware of and attuned to the racism visited upon Latinos.[29]

It is one thing to live in an unwelcoming policy context as a collaterally affected group. It is another to experience the dual impact of the cues and the sharp administrative teeth of those policies. The undocumented Latino immigrants in our interview sample were the ones who most clearly articulated feeling the sharp edges of those teeth in their lives. Federal, state, and local policies all contributed to an enforcement bite that often had ruinous effects on the lives of the people we interviewed. In places like Arizona, federal, state, and local immigration enforcement work in concert. Federal definitions of legal status inform policies at the state and local levels that exclude unauthorized immigrants from accessing state institutions and resources. State and local law enforcement also collaborate with federal immigration enforcement, as they do in Arizona. For example, in a state like Arizona that does not allow unauthorized immigrants to get driver's licenses, an unauthorized immigrant who gets pulled over for a traffic infraction and is detained by state or local law enforcement for driving without a license can wind up in deportation proceedings.[30] Federal and subfederal policies could also work independently of one another, and at different times, in the lives of Latino immigrants. Perhaps none of our interview respondents articulated this dynamic more clearly than Pancho Vigil, the deportee living in Mexico City whom we quoted earlier. As he explained, Arizona's SB 1070 compelled him and other immigrants to move to New Mexico to find a more welcoming context. When he moved back to Arizona some years later, federal policy reared its head when ICE detained him in a workplace raid at the Taco Bell that employed him. In moving to New Mexico, he had joined a kind of intra-United States stream of refugees looking for sanctuary in a more welcoming state:

> When they passed SB 1070, they started asking people for all this other information. I put all my stuff in my Jeep and drove over to New Mexico, and I moved to Albuquerque. The reason why I bring this up is because I remember that people said that in Phoenix, at the time, they used to brag about how clear the streets were; they weren't getting as congested as before. But on the other side, people didn't realize that there was all these Arizona license plates now in New Mexico. . . . For a second, Albuquerque—New Mexico— was a sanctuary for all these people who were running away from SB 1070. It was really a migration, a flock of people that kind of got lost in history, and people don't realize it, but I used to work with them. I remember the tire shops they built up, all these new restaurants started coming up from all these people who were migrating from Arizona to New Mexico. (*translated from Spanish*)

The administrative impact of subfederal immigration policies could directly target Latino immigrants, as Pancho's experience suggests. Laws like SB 1070 and former Sheriff Joe Arpaio's infamous crime suppression sweeps were enforced with a heavy and aggressive police presence in Latino immigrant neighborhoods. The sweeps were ostensibly about suppressing crime but, in reality, used ethno-racial profiling to detain unauthorized immigrants.[31] The undocumented were also targeted for exclusion from resources and institutions in the state's control: they were denied driver's licenses and deemed ineligible for in-state tuition at public colleges and universities and for state-supported funding to attend those colleges and universities. These exclusionary laws could be just as painful in their impact.

Among our interviewees in Arizona were several Dreamers.[32] Their cases highlight the powerful role of subfederal immigration policies in systematically excluding a population. Because these Latinos were protected from deportation by their DACA status, the exclusion they experienced because of their legal status stemmed largely from state policies. Some of those subfederal policies blurred the line between immigration and immigrant policies and used federal immigration status designations to enforce exclusionary state policies. Nelia Torres, the construction manager and DACA recipient in Arizona we quoted earlier, began attending college in the early 2000s with the help of state grants. But in 2006, Proposition 300 went into effect, prohibiting undocumented immigrants from receiving in-state tuition. The change made college unaffordable for Nelia. She explained her situation and the fallout from it:

> Straight out of high school, I did go to the university. I went up to [Northern Arizona University]. But shortly, I think that first year I was there, my scholarship got pulled due to a proposition that was put in place here in the state of Arizona. So they pulled my scholarship. I came back and kind of found work to do until I was able to go to the company where I'm at now. . . . I was pretty devastated. I really didn't know what I was gonna do, what was gonna [become] of me. My whole childhood, all I had planned for was going to a university, and, you know, getting educated, and I knew that it would be a struggle afterwards, to work because of my status. I wasn't ready to face it just yet. My focus was, get educated. If you get educated, good things will come, and when that got pulled from me, I remember being at home for the first few

months, and after a while, I just felt like I was starting to lose my mind. I didn't know what to do. I was not just bored out of my mind, but I was lost. I was completely lost.

The active targeting of immigrants in Arizona and their exclusion from rights, institutions, and resources, combined with policies not directly related to immigration, created an atmosphere of palpable ethno-racial discrimination against Latinos in the state. Nevertheless, our respondents could only infer that Arizona's bevy of unwelcoming laws targeted Latinos. After all, the laws did not name Latino immigrants specifically; as written, they applied to immigrants in general. But the politics surrounding these laws suggest that Latino immigrants are indeed the targets. That the spate of policies passed in the last two decades target Latinos specifically appears evident alongside other, non-immigration policies that likewise appear to target Latinos. Recall from the previous chapter that Arizona's HB 2281 banned courses and programs in K-12 schools, including a popular Mexican American studies program in Tucson, on the grounds that "public school pupils should be taught to treat and value each other as individuals and not be taught to resent or hate other races or classes of people." (A federal district court found the ban unconstitutional.) The state also passed an initiative mandating English-only instruction (Proposition 203) in 2000. The Arizona Latinos we interviewed included these policies in their evaluation of discrimination against Latinos in the state. Catarina Cortez, a twenty-nine-year-old naturalized citizen from Mexico, school administrator in Arizona, and registered independent, noted the impact of bilingual education and changes in the law on her and her family:

Well, I mean, Arizona . . . in the schools, it's English only. And I feel like it only hurts the population here, especially the young ones. . . . When I was in kindergarten, I didn't know any English, right? I was just a monolingual Spanish speaker. At that time, there were bilingual programs in public schools. So, I was in this bilingual program at the same school all my brothers went to, [the high school near my house]. I want to say third grade, all my teachers . . . I was taught both English and Spanish. So I learned to also read and write Spanish at the same time as I was learning English. So I was having the two languages. By the time my brother, who's five years younger than me, entered kindergarten, I think there was a law [banning bilingual education] here in Arizona.

Our survey data and interviews paint a clear picture of Arizona as a state where policies and politics punctuate and even combine with federal policies to dampen the sense of belonging among Latinos, U.S.-born and foreign-born alike, and make them feel like outsiders.

A very different picture emerged from our New Mexico respondents. Recall that our survey data showed that Latinos in New Mexico, regardless of nativity, were less likely to see discrimination against Latinos in their state. Not only did New Mexico Latinos differ on this score from their Arizona counterparts, but the basis for their greater sense of belonging in New Mexico diverged as well. Whereas Arizona's Latinos cited unwelcoming policies as a key reason they felt they did not belong, New Mexico's Latinos' sense of belonging stemmed not so much from welcoming policies as from a larger social, cultural, and political milieu that mostly welcomed immigrants and Latinos; for them, policies were a largely indistinguishable part of this milieu. In contrast to the consternation we heard from immigrants in Arizona, Latinos from New Mexico described their state as a tranquil place where immigrants could live without worry for the most part. Also in contrast to what we heard from Latinos in Arizona, Latinos in New Mexico almost never cited the state's welcoming immigration policies as a basis for their sense of belonging. Instead, they located their sense of belonging in the widespread use of the Spanish language and a general sense of friendliness in the state. New Mexico made space for Hispanic culture from its inception and Latinos have enjoyed more political power in the state compared to Latinos elsewhere, but very few of our respondents referred directly to these historical roots of the state's friendliness. Nor did many mention the contemporary policies (outlined in the previous chapter) that have secured New Mexico's place on the welcoming end of the spectrum. Because those policies combined with the prominent historical and contemporary presence of Latinos in New Mexico to create an environment with lower levels of ethnic tension and an assumption of acceptance, respondents seemed not to notice them.

Of course, Latinos in New Mexico have also experienced discrimination. Historical research has well documented the mistreatment and systematic efforts to marginalize Latinos in New Mexico.[33] But compared to other southwestern states like Texas and Arizona, New Mexico's Latinos have maintained a degree of power and influence. With that comes a sense that being Latino is a less stigmatized identity in New Mexico than it is in other states. When we asked Latinos in New Mexico who they believed felt most at home in the state, they resoundingly said Latinos—in contrast to responses from Arizona Latinos, who almost without fail said that whites felt most at home in their state. Monica Gonzalez was a twenty-three-year-old youth recreation facilitator and self-described independent conservative; her mother was from Mexico, and her father came from an established Hispano family. Her parents moved to the state from El Paso, Texas, in part because they viewed New Mexico as welcoming to Latinos— largely, Monica felt, because of the size of the Latino population there:

> INTERVIEWER: Here in New Mexico, in your opinion, who do you think feels more accepted in New Mexico, more at home?
>
> MONICA: Latinos, Hispanics.
>
> INTERVIEWER: Why? How did you reach that conclusion?
>
> MONICA: I came because there are more of us here, we see ourselves more. If you come to Española (a city in New Mexico), here where we are most of the people, we are mostly Hispanic, Latino. And with that there are people here of indigenous people. Also if you go to other smaller towns to the north there are also many Hispanic people. And when you go further south, again Mexico is when you see more people who are . . . Caucasian or white. Because Texas—Texas is there.

Juan Arellano, a thirty-nine-year-old industrial technician and regis-tered Democrat with deep generational roots in New Mexico as well as a connection to more recent Mexican immigrants, put it more directly:

> Because a lot of people from New Mexico have the background of the Latino, there's a lot of Latinos in New Mexico, I think more so

than in a lot of other places. So if you're a Latino living here, and you see other people that look like you, you're going to feel a little more accepted in a way. I mean, when you go somewhere where all you see is blue eyes and blond hair, you kind of feel like the oddball in a way. And it's not like that here. I mean, like I said, you have a mix of different people, but the vibes here in New Mexico are, for the most part, pretty good, I think.

One of the few Latino respondents to cite policy was Felipe Gastelum, a conservative Republican and native New Mexican whom we quoted earlier. In offering his view of who feels at home in New Mexico, he noted with a mix of dispassionate observation and subtle resentment just how welcoming things are for immigrants and Latinos in general:

> The majority here is Hispanic. It's almost like a minority to everyone else, but whites are . . . people tend to be more respectful of our culture. . . . I think there's a lot of immigration here, and I think that we're a sanctuary state, which I don't necessarily agree with. It's hard to feel at home in a place that you don't really know, your future could change in an instant. So I'm sure that's got to feel uncomfortable [for immigrants]. Anyone that's Mexican, or doesn't speak English, and only speaks Spanish, would feel right at home there.

With the political power that Latinos held on to leading up to and after statehood and the sustained Hispano culture across multiple generations, Latinos in New Mexico felt that they were operating on a cultural home turf. It is important to note that not all Latinos felt equally at home. Respondents largely saw the most generationally established Latinos—those whose families had been in the region since statehood or before and who could claim a distinct Spanish identity—as having the greatest claim to belonging. Some Latinos took from that claim a sense of superiority that led them to look down on Latinos whose family origins in New Mexico were established in more recent immigration waves. Take, for example, the comments of Angelina Cordova, a thirty-nine-year-old salesperson whose family had been in New Mexico for multiple generations. Angelina was aware of the intra-Latino division, and she was working hard to bridge the divide through volunteer work with Mexican immigrants. She described the lines of division among Latinos:

> The weird thing about here is that, people here in New Mexico think they're Spanish. So they have a little bit more of an arrogance, and they think that they're better than other Mexicans that come through, or any other Latino race. They're arrogant, and they're racists. I've had people who have little girls who are, you know, half black, and the little Chicana girls don't like them. And they torment them, because they're black. But they don't realize we're in the same boat. It's kind of weird like that. But it's a lot of arrogance. People here don't want to be identified as having any Mexican heritage, they want to be Spanish, Spanish, Spanish. And they don't even speak Spanish. It's kind of weird like that.

Just as the sociologist Cassandra Salgado found among her respondents in New Mexico, individuals whose families has been in the state for many generations may try to distance themselves from more recently arrived Mexican immigrants by asserting Spanish family ancestry.[34] And yet these assertions are nested within a claim to a larger Mexican American identity that encompasses both the long-established and the newly arrived. Javier Flores was a forty-five-year-old small-business owner and registered Republican in New Mexico who was originally from El Paso. He noted that the big-tent notion of Mexican American identity in the state coexisted with perceptions of status differences:

> In New Mexico, the people who are at home, love it, and wouldn't change a thing, are the ones who can trace their lineage to having been here at least a hundred years. So that plays a huge role in who's comfortable. So when somebody will say, "I'm a Lujan or I'm a Rodriguez or a Montoya or Lucero," they will say, "Because my family has been here for almost 150 years." I think it gives them a sense of privilege and entitlement which is very important because that's what has helped to create the identity that's here. And so those are the people who feel most comfortable here. . . . I am from El Paso. So I've been here for twenty-two years, which makes me an absolute newcomer. As I said, if you haven't been here for more

than 150 years, you're not from here. So it's very difficult to enter into this culture, but it's an amazing culture. And the reason that I say that is because it's mine too. I'm just as much a mix of Spanish and Mexican and Native American and all of those other things. So to me, the culture's the same, I get to be able to see it through the same lens. And if somebody says that it's a little bit more this or I'm missing a little bit more of that, that's all right, I'm cool with that. Because in the end, we're all recognizing the same food, the same traditions, the same song. Even though it's slightly different here or there, we all love to listen to mariachis, we all love to listen to and watch a flamenco dance, and it's a part of our culture.

New Mexico's distinctiveness as a welcoming state for immigrants might not have emerged so clearly were it not for the way that politics and policies in Arizona and nationally served as foils. Several of our Latino New Mexican respondents were familiar with Arizona because they had once lived there, had relatives in the state, had experience working there, or had read the news about it. Their perceptions of Arizona as unwelcoming echoed what we heard from Latinos in Arizona. But for the Latinos in New Mexico, the Arizona comparison informed their sense that New Mexico lacked this kind of animosity. Take, for example, the response of Nora Martínez, a forty-four-year-old food service worker and undocumented Mexican who had lived in New Mexico for twenty-three years and did not identify with a political party, when we asked her how immigrants were treated here in New Mexico:

> Well . . . good. I say that because I know a lot of people and we all have a good living. . . . Every state is different, and there are states that, indisputably and sadly, are really racists. Really, really racists and don't treat the different ethnic groups equally. . . . I just have visited, for example, you know, Arizona . . . which is a really difficult place to live in for an immigrant in the last few years. Even a few years ago, when Arpaio toughened the policies, how many families had to leave Phoenix and came here to New Mexico— entire families. . . . It's one of the things we most heard about in the last few years, which you can see in the people that came from there and that got here to New Mexico. You could see . . . the fear on their faces. A lot of people even went back to Mexico or to

their countries, the same people that lived in Arizona and got there after escaping from the difficult situations a few years ago. Sadly, sadly, there are states that are pretty harsh with us Latinos. Thank God, I say, New Mexico is not a state like that . . . it's not so hard to live in an immigrant community, for a Latina like me, a Hispanic. (*translated from Spanish*)

For Rafael Ortiz, the naturalized citizen from Ecuador and successful artist, who was also a registered Democrat, the sense of belonging in New Mexico registered emotionally:

Yes, yes, I feel that I belong here. I've liked it since I came. I liked the Sandia Mountains. I feel at home. Everything I have done has opened the doors for me, and I am advancing, moving forward, and I feel happy. I feel happy here with the people. . . . I think people from different cultures here have grown together— Natives, gringos, then there's no reason for racism here. No, no. They know how to survive together. They have all grown together. (*translated from Spanish*)

It is worth offering again the quote at the beginning of chapter 1, in which Rafael described the threat that weighed on him when he made one of his frequent trips to Arizona to show his work, and how he always felt when returning to New Mexico:

Although I am a citizen, when I come back from Arizona and I cross the [state] border, it's like, phew (*wiping his forehead to signal relief*). I feel like I'm leaving a state . . . where there's pressure. . . . It's just that you never know, you never know what's going to happen. I've heard of cases where citizens were stopped and they put them in detention centers and everything and until they see the papers and . . . "Oh, sorry." . . . That's why, when I'm leaving Arizona, I'm like, (*in English*) Oh yeah phew! . . . It's not like that in New Mexico. . . . I've been here ten years, and my life is very tranquil. I've never had anything bad happen to me. It's like getting home. I have support from family, from good friends. I think it is still a peaceful state, and I haven't had any bad experience because of an immigration situation. And it's still calm, it's fine. (*translated from Spanish*)

Why did discussion of actual policies register so strongly in Arizona but not in New Mexico? Although our data do not offer a definitive answer, some evidence points to differences in the content and volume of information available about immigration policies in the two states. We explored whether the states differ in the volume of news coverage devoted to immigration by searching the full text archives of the *Arizona Republic* and the *Albuquerque Journal*, the two largest newspapers in each state, from January 1, 2005, to December 31, 2016.[35] We found that while the *Arizona Republic* had 19,332 articles that mentioned immigration or immigrants, the *Albuquerque Journal* had only 2,644. Additionally, 14.5 percent of the articles in New Mexico that mentioned immigration or immigrants referred to Arizona or one of its major cities.

In addition to the different amount of attention paid to immigration in the two states, the differences in perception among Latinos in Arizona and New Mexico may have to do with the tendency for individuals to assign greater importance to negative than to positive information.[36] Coverage that casts Arizona negatively may resonate more than any coverage of New Mexico's more welcoming policies simply because negative information tends to have more cognitive staying power. Welcoming policies in New Mexico thus become part of a quiet background that combines with the history and prevailing culture in the state to create a greater sense of belonging. Our data do not give us purchase on the validity of these explanations for our respondents. But as others have shown, when a context is free of conflict, the resulting sense of belonging becomes an unstated norm that only becomes obvious when an incident, politics, or policy puncture that norm.[37] The closest thing to such a puncturing force that New Mexico respondents could identify was the policy environment of its western neighbor. Indeed, the public discourse in both states was marked by the broad and negative attention that Arizona received for its unwelcoming immigration policies.

This Land Is Your Land, This Land Is My Land: Latinos' National Belonging

The layered nature of immigration policy—with federal, state, and local governments simultaneously creating and enforcing their own, often competing, immigrant policies—may send an overarching message about whether Latinos belong in the American nation: a group of people united by political claims and a culture emblematic of political belonging.[38] It is well established that people who feel discriminated against in the United States are less likely to consider being American an important part of their identity.[39] Given our findings thus far—that the unwelcoming climate in Arizona is associated with lower levels of belonging compared to the more welcoming climate next door in New Mexico—we might expect that Latinos in Arizona would be less likely to feel that they belong in the United States compared to Latinos in New Mexico. Does the contrasting climate for Latinos in Arizona and New Mexico affect their sense of national belonging?

To answer that question, we turned first to our survey. For each of the measures of belonging targeted at the state level described earlier, we matched questions that tapped into respondents' sense of belonging at the national level. We asked survey respondents if they were proud to be American; if being American was important to them; if they felt like they belonged in the United States; if they thought that *other* people felt that they (the respondents) belonged in the United States; if they felt like an outsider in the United States; and how much discrimination there was against Latinos in the United States.[40] We also asked people how important being Latino was to them.

The results indicate that state of residence does *not* play a significant role in Latinos' sense of national attachment. And much as is the case at the state level, it appears that while Latinos assert a sense of belonging, they also perceive others as taking an unwelcoming stance toward them. We found that Latinos were likely to say that they were proud to be American and that being American was very important to them. Eighty-two percent of Latinos agreed strongly that they were proud to be American, with those in New Mexico especially likely to feel this way (78 percent in Arizona versus 86 percent in New Mexico). A similarly large share of Latinos—86 percent—said that being American was very important to them (85 percent in Arizona versus 87 percent in New Mexico). Additionally, 82 percent of Latinos said that they felt like they belonged in the United States "a lot" (78 percent in Arizona versus 87 percent in New Mexico), and only 17 percent agreed "somewhat" or "strongly" that they felt like an outsider in the United States (20 percent in Arizona versus 15 percent in New Mexico).[41]

Even though our survey results show that state of residence largely did not affect feelings of belonging in the United States, Latinos in Arizona and New Mexico had much to say about what it means to be American and about their own place in American society. Some of what they told us in the interviews, which took place after the 2016 election, related to sea changes in immigration politics and policy during the Trump presidency. Although the in-depth interviews do not offer a broad view of how Latinos' views might have changed since we fielded our survey, they do provide insight into what it was like being Latino in this country after Trump was elected. Even during the Trump presidency, what we heard from respondents—U.S.- and foreign-born alike—reflected the survey results from before the 2016 election: Latinos asserted themselves as members of the American nation even as they felt that discrimination against Latinos and perceptions of their social exclusion were on the rise. Latino interviewees across the sample consistently wrote themselves into the American national narrative, playing up legal, cultural, and ancestral aspects of their own histories that fit with some notions of what it means to be American, and downplaying some elements of their histories that were not such an easy fit.

Claims of ancestral belonging were especially available to multigenerational Hispanos in New Mexico, some of whom claimed roots in present-day New Mexico going back centuries. Take, for example, Dennis Amaya, a sixty-year-old small-business owner, self-described conservative, and someone with deep family roots in New Mexico:

> And even though I have ancestors that go back to the territory of New Mexico and even into the Mexican occupation and probably into Spanish and Native Americans, I think that an American is somebody that resides within the boundaries of the United States. And I'm a true believer that I was born in the United States, my parents were born in the United States, their parents were born in the United States, my great-grandparents probably were part of Mexico at one time. But we have to consider ourselves something. . . . We have a country and in this case [it's] the United States, so I'm proud to be an American. I'm not so proud of some of the past things that happened, and policies and stuff. But I'm proud to be an American today. And there's been a lot of

things that have forged this country that we are not so proud of maybe. . . . And this country was forged by a lot of different nationalities and a lot of different ideas, all based on liberty and freedom for all.

Other later-generation Latinos, and especially those in New Mexico, noted that their families had been in the present-day United States far longer than most Americans. They premised their claims to American identity on ancestry, but not on ancestry alone.[42] The Latinos we interviewed also drew on a notion of incorporationism: the belief that immigration and the contributions of immigrants are elemental to American identity.[43] They also asserted claims to a civic republican model of American identity rooted in participation in American institutions. Some offered a family history of military service and civic engagement as evidence that Latinos have not merely existed in the United States for generations, but have also contributed to its formation.

For most Latinos, however, those sorts of claims were not readily accessible. Latino immigrants stood out from U.S.-born Latinos in the degree to which they wrestled with legal status and culture as they asserted their own belonging. For immigrants who were either legal permanent residents or naturalized citizens, legal status was a premise for belonging. Recognizing the association between Latinos and illegality, they cited their own legal status as part of the foundation for their belonging and a shield against the pernicious effects of the Trump administration's more muscular enforcement of immigration policies.[44] Consider the comments of Cindy Rubio, a twenty-five-year-old health care representative in Arizona who was also a Mexican immigrant and DACA recipient and who identified with the Democratic Party:

> I consider [the United States] a home because this is where I grew up. . . . Of course, I don't remember Mexico—when I [left I was] about three years old, but this is pretty much where I grew up, where I learned a different language, where I met people, where I attended school, where my parents, you know, where, where we met the people we know now. So like, pretty much like, this is all I know. Mexico—I hardly have any memories because I wasn't there. . . . I understand when people talk about illegal immigrants,

like "this is not your home." But I feel like they don't know what other people go through, so it's easier for them to judge in a way because they were born here.

When legal status claims were not available, undocumented Latino immigrants rested their assertions of belonging on culture and economic contributions. Even if the United States did not recognize them as legal members, they said that they behaved like members of the American nation in cultural displays and in their work ethic. For Nelia Torres, the construction manager and DACA recipient, assertions of cultural belonging played out in interpersonal interactions at work, where some of her coworkers were openly supportive of stricter immigration policies:

I would avoid the question [of legal status]. I would talk around it. I know my U.S. history. I worked really hard to make sure I learned English very well. So I just carried myself in a way where people couldn't question me. There was nothing to question. . . . I avoided it. Until this day, there's people that, you know, that have known me for fifteen years and still don't know what my status was or currently is. . . . And so, no matter how much I opened up, that was always a piece that I kept to myself. And that would be from boyfriends to friends, to colleagues, to anyone. I just, you know, no matter how much I trusted, I never really trusted anybody with that.

Possessing the cultural elements of American identity gave non-citizen respondents a sense of "legal passing"—the ability to conceal their legal status under a cloak of cultural know-how that included facility in speaking English and knowledge of American history and culture.[45] But respondents saw their possession of this know-how as more than a cover for their legal status. They viewed it as proof of their de facto, if not legal, belonging in the American nation. Pancho Vigil, for instance, continued to stake a cultural claim to the United States even after his deportation:

Waking up every day and singing the Pledge of Allegiance before school and reciting and memorizing this made one believe that there truly was equality for everybody. We recited it so often that nobody questioned it. The true American I would describe as somebody who doesn't give up and makes the best out of the resources he has available. Being just a human being and helping one another.

We asked Pancho whether he identified as an American:

> PANCHO: Yeah, everywhere I go.
>
> INTERVIEWER: Can you tell me about that?
>
> PANCHO: I know Spanish, but it's a different culture, it's a different Spanish, I can talk a little chilango (in the style of Mexico City) to blend in and bargain and what not and you have to do it. It's a very strict survival skill, but it's just different. You can tell right away if you're walking on the street and you hear someone speaking English with your accent. People from the U.S. come here all the time, and you end up bonding and meeting up and hanging out, it's crazy. (*translated from Spanish*)

There is no firmer assertion of the state's rejection of an individual's claim to membership than deportation. And yet for Pancho, the experience of living in Mexico after having spent most of his life in the United States underscored just how culturally American he had become.

The self-declared sense of belonging that we found in abundance in our survey and in-depth interview data bumped up against respondents' views about whether they thought other people agreed that they belonged. More than half of our Latino respondents, 51 percent, felt that there was "a lot" or "a great deal" of discrimination against their group in the United States, with those in Arizona more likely to feel this way than those in New Mexico (54 percent in Arizona versus 47 percent in New Mexico). Only 57 percent of Latino respondents said that other people agreed that Latinos belong in the United States (54 percent in Arizona versus 61 percent in New Mexico). Even though the bivariate comparisons across these measures suggest that Latinos in New Mexico may feel a greater sense of belonging in the United States than Latinos in Arizona, when we accounted for other factors that might affect feelings of belonging, the state-level differences were statistically insignificant in all cases but one: pride in the United States. We found that acculturation—speaking English and being a U.S. citizen—boosted pride, but that this boost was lower for the U.S.-born if they lived in Arizona.[46]

The in-depth interviews lay bare how this delineation plays out, and how the Trump presidency gave it greater weight. For all the respondents' assertions of their American national identity, the Trump administration's policies and rhetoric suggested to many of them that they did not, in fact, belong in the country. Take Marco Meza, a twenty-nine-year-old teacher in Arizona and registered independent. Marco came to the United States when he was eight, was undocumented for a period, and later became a U.S. citizen. His wife was still undocumented, however, at the time of the interview. Trump's stance on immigration made Marco concerned mostly for his wife, but also for his own ability to stay in the United States:

> I don't wanna lose my wife. I don't want one day to get a note from immigration telling her when she's gonna be deported. I don't want something like that. When I tell people that, especially at work, I . . . I talk about it. But, you know, it scares me. . . . This is when [Trump] was first running. . . . Trump said he's gonna go after the illegals and he said he was gonna go after what they call anchor babies. Basically, he said on live television that he's gonna not only go after illegals, he's gonna go after American citizens; Mexican Americans that were born in America. He's talking about me. . . . Bill O'Reilly of all people told him, "You can't do that." And you know what? With a straight face, Trump said, "I have some people that are working on it." You were just told on national television you can't do that. And you have the balls to say that you're gonna still try to get that done? That scares me. Something's wrong with this son-of-a-bitch. . . . I'm now scared that shit can happen to me, and it's disheartening. A lot of people that are privileged like me— you don't think about it until it happens to you.

When we asked Latino respondents their opinion on who felt most at home in the United States, the most common answer was "white people," as many had said about the state in which they resided. If anything, they felt that the current national leadership made that even more the case. The observation made by Evan Chávez, a twenty-seven-year-old hairdresser and undocumented immigrant from Mexico living in Arizona who identified as a political independent, captured the distinction between Latinos' assertions about their own sense of belonging and the growing awareness that many others did not agree with them that they belonged:

> This is practically where I've built a whole life, built up everything, and I feel like I'm at home. I feel like if I was to go back to Mexico or anything like that, I would be completely lost. . . . Unfortunately, I think it's white people [who feel the most comfortable in the United States]. And I don't like to label people or categorize, but I honestly feel like they do. . . . It's sad how white people feel like they own . . . like this is their land. . . . But the first group of people that pop in my head [when you asked who feels most at home in the United States], it's the white . . . ever since the new president came along, I would say. I feel like there is a lot of racism, a lot of marches, a lot of . . . even the whole KKK that's been so public now that they've been doing things like attacking other people just because they feel like this is their land and should just be them living here. (*translated from Spanish*)

Trump's politics and policies seemed to have replicated at the national level what Arizona's Latinos had known for the better part of two decades. But even in New Mexico, where Latinos described a more welcoming environment, Latinos' perceptions of the impact of the Trump presidency on their sense of belonging in the nation as a whole looked similar to what we heard in Arizona. Camila Cardoza, a seventy-one-year-old social worker, registered Democrat, and New Mexico resident of Puerto Rican and Dominican ancestry, told us:

> [It's] very difficult to be where we are right now, knowing that we're not seen the same way that we were seen before, that I feel like people look at us and question what the hell are we doing here, where we should be back in our country, or if we speak Spanish that we shouldn't be speaking Spanish because this is America. "Let's make America great again." And to me, it translates [to] "let's make . . . let's make America white again."

Likewise, Elena-Delia Guerrero, a fifty-four-year-old elder care provider, New Mexico resident, and legal permanent resident originally from Mexico who described herself as politically moderate, prefaced her objections to a list of Trump's immigration policies with the following remark:

> Now, with this new president we can see there is racism. . . . A lot of the people who are living here, sometimes we have felt discriminated against. We have felt like you are not very accepted in this country, but I can see that there is a lot of discrimination against Mexicans . . . and [what] I can now see with this new president is that there is a struggle. It's like a fight that he does not accept Mexicans, and it's something that is very obvious right now in the United States. (*translated from Spanish*)

Over and over, we heard that President Trump's policies and rhetoric were stoking discrimination against Latinos and deepening our respondents' feeling that however much they felt that they belonged in the nation, that feeling was not reciprocated by an American society that increasingly saw them as outsiders. In reality, anti-Latino prejudice went down during Trump's political rise and presidency. Using a host of measures, the political scientists Daniel Hopkins and Samantha Washington show that Trump's rhetoric did not heighten anti-Latino prejudice and may have even dampened it during that time.[47] Still, the drumbeat of his anti-immigrant rhetoric weighed heavily on the perceptions of our respondents. Whether they lived in the more welcoming context of New Mexico or the more unwelcoming context of Arizona, the Trump administration was a shadow hanging over the heads of all Latinos, and especially foreign-born Latinos.

Our findings are in line with the examination of attitudes of Latino immigrants across the country conducted by the political scientists James McCann and Michael Jones-Correa.[48] These scholars classified respondents as living in a state that was restrictive, accommodating, or neutral with respect to its immigrant policy. They examined a range of attitudes about the United States, including whether the country was on the right or wrong track, the degree to which respondents loved the United States, and how good they felt when they saw the American flag. McCann and Jones-Correa find that the state policy climate is unrelated to all of these measures. They also find that state policies are unrelated to feelings about President Trump. These results reinforce our own in establishing that people differentiate between the federal government, on the one hand, and state and local government, on the other.

Conclusion

The findings from this chapter give credence to the notion that policies signal which populations belong socially, politically, and economically.[49] They also illustrate that those policies can shape experiences that influence a sense of belonging.[50] Our survey showed the broad strokes of Latinos' sense of belonging in Arizona, New Mexico, and the nation. That sense of belonging began with perceptions of whether the state in which they lived was welcoming or unwelcoming to immigrants. Survey data revealed that Latinos living in Arizona perceived their state as very unwelcoming to immigrants, while their New Mexico counterparts saw their state as welcoming. The interviews showed that respondents conflated state and local policy in forming a view about whether their state was welcoming. They also conflated history, culture, and policy. But there were differences in how respondents saw the relative role of each of these ingredients in creating their sense of belonging. In Arizona, unwelcoming policies at both the state and local levels were central to Latinos' perceptions of belonging in that state. New Mexico's Latinos, in contrast, relied on history and culture to explain why they thought their state was more welcoming; policy operated in the background as they formed their perceptions.

It was not just that Latinos perceived differences in how welcome they were in their home state; they also experienced these differences. Latinos in both states staked a claim to belonging, saying that they identified with their state and that their state was important to them. However, they had different views about whether others in their state agreed with their claims of belonging. Our survey data show that Arizona's Latinos were far more likely than New Mexico's Latinos to see discrimination against Latinos in their state. In in-depth interviews, Latino immigrants in Arizona said that they saw themselves as the targets of the state's unwelcoming policies, and they described how both the symbolism of unwelcoming policies and their administrative teeth played into their perception of discrimination. U.S.-born Latinos' comments about their state suggested that, although they were not subject to the letter of these unwelcoming laws but only symbolically affected by them, these laws nonetheless had a negative impact on their sense of belonging. The state's far-ranging unwelcoming policies and the people who pushed for them and enforced them were central reasons why both immigrant and U.S.-born Latinos saw their state as unwelcoming to immigrants. In New Mexico, state immigration policy took a back seat to what Latinos saw as the state's overwhelmingly welcoming history and culture. If New Mexico's immigration policies came to the fore at all, it was largely through comparisons with Arizona: Latino New Mexicans saw Arizona's immigration policies as a foil illustrating just how welcoming New Mexico was. This raises the question of whether our conclusion that welcoming policies foster a sense of belonging while unwelcoming policies undermine it is transferable to other states. We believe that it is, and we discuss why in later chapters.

State-level policies did not seem to have an impact on Latinos' perceptions of belonging in the nation. Our survey, conducted before the Trump presidency, shows that Latinos across the two states, both U.S.- and foreign-born, were similarly likely to assert a sense of belonging in the United States. However, in our interviews, which were conducted during the Trump presidency, the federal picture eclipsed state-level policies. Latinos in both states staked a claim to belonging in the American nation, much as they asserted a claim to belong in their state, drawing on elements of their own personal history—their legal status, ancestry, culture, economic productivity—that they could link to available notions of American identity. Yet they were unequivocal in their perception that a political move, led by Trump, was under way to write Latinos out of the national narrative.

These findings begin to show whether and how national and subfederal immigration policies construct a sense of belonging. In the picture that begins to emerge, unwelcoming policies targeted at a particular population—in this case Latinos—send a clear message that this population does not belong. But that is only part of the picture. The findings from this chapter also illustrate the surprising resilience of Latinos' claims to belonging, even when the state and national policy and political contexts are decidedly hostile.

Clearly, Latinos are not the only ones living in these policy and political contexts. Do welcoming and unwelcoming contexts affect the sense of belonging of groups that do not appear to be directly targeted or collaterally affected by the laws? It is to that question that we turn next.

THE IMMIGRATION POLICY CLIMATE AND WHITES' SENSE OF BELONGING

4

It is perhaps not altogether surprising that state-level immigration policy has a significant effect on the Latinos residing in that state. After all, Latinos, and especially the foreign-born among them, are the targets of state-level immigration policy, regardless of where those policies fall on the welcoming spectrum. The previous chapter showed that policies affect not only the target population but also a collaterally affected group: U.S.-born Latinos are swept up in the web of measures explicitly targeting immigrant members of the same ethno-racial group.

Does the effect of unwelcoming or welcoming state-level immigration policies extend beyond the Latino immigrant targets and the U.S.-born Latinos who are collaterally affected? This chapter explores the far-reaching influence of the immigration policy context of reception on the sense of belonging of a symbolically affected group that is not materially affected by immigration policies but for whom they provide cues about who belongs: U.S.-born whites.

We follow the same line of analysis as in the previous chapter, drawing on survey and in-depth interview data to examine white residents' views of whether their state welcomed immigrants and whether white residents felt that they belonged in their state and in the nation as a whole, as well as how they felt about their ethno-racial identity.

As we noted in chapter 1, feelings of belonging have significant effects on people's well-being and on how they think and feel about others. White people can feel threatened by policies that support multiculturalism when they perceive that they are being excluded by these initiatives. From this perspective, welcoming immigration policies could diminish whites' sense of belonging. However, white people also commonly react negatively when they perceive that their group has treated others unjustly. They may question their "fit" with their own ethno-racial group and weaken their identification with their group, and their esteem for their group may be diminished.[1] This view suggests that unwelcoming immigration policies could adversely affect whites' ethno-racial identity.

In this chapter, we answer the question about how welcoming and unwelcoming immigration policies affect whites' sense of belonging and social identity: both depend on where they live (Arizona or New Mexico) and their party identification (Republican or Democrat). Taking a full view of our findings among whites at the state level, our analysis shows that, on balance, whites' sense of belonging is not diminished by living in a state that offers a welcoming climate for immigrants. Additionally, their state's welcoming or unwelcoming climate has no effect on whether whites feel that they belong in the United States in general, nor does the state's level of welcoming affect white respondents' views about white racial identity in general. Instead, white Republicans in New Mexico cited examples of what they perceived as discrimination against whites in hiring, social policy, and college admissions, while white Democrats, by contrast, wrapped their view of white identity in critical analysis of white privilege, often explicitly noting that they themselves had benefited from it.

The findings from this chapter, combined with those from the previous chapter, indicate that when policies contribute to a welcoming context of reception for immigrants, those policies do not appear to impose a social-psychological penalty on U.S.-born whites. At the same time, unwelcoming policies alienate not only U.S.- and foreign-born Latinos but also white Democrats. Together, these populations make up a plurality of individuals in the two states. If policy ought to be designed to do the greatest good for the greatest number of people while protecting rights and liberties and minimizing harm, then what emerges from our analyses thus far is that welcoming immigration policies offer a large payoff.

How Do White Residents Perceive the Immigration Policy Climate?

Our analysis of historical and contemporary immigration politics and policy places Arizona and New Mexico at opposite ends of a welcoming spectrum. Before we examine how whites understand their own identity and sense of belonging in the context of these two states, we look at their assessments of how welcoming their state is for immigrants.

In our survey, we asked whites in Arizona and New Mexico how welcoming they thought their state was to immigrants.[2] Across the two states, 38.8 percent of white respondents felt that their state tried to make immigrants feel very or somewhat *unwelcome*. Breaking down the white sample by state reveals that whites, like Latinos, were cognizant of differences in the level of welcome extended to immigrants in their state. Whites in Arizona were far more likely than whites in New Mexico to see their state as unwelcoming: 46.8 percent in Arizona versus only 17.0 percent in New Mexico.

Our survey data allow us to look at whether those patterns hold when accounting for other factors that might influence respondents' views. These analyses, and others that follow, focus on whether respondents reside in Arizona or New Mexico as the primary factor of interest. A secondary factor is partisanship (Democrat, Republican, independent), which for whites has become an intense dividing line on many issues, including immigration.[3] We tested whether state of residence (Arizona versus New Mexico) and partisanship independently or jointly related to how whites viewed the immigration policy climate in their state.[4] With respect to partisanship, we were mainly interested in the comparison between Democrats and Republicans. Among white survey respondents, 31.6 percent identified as Democrats and 42.6 percent as Republicans. This split was roughly the same in both states (Democrats: 30 percent in Arizona and 33 percent in New Mexico; Republicans: 45 percent in Arizona and 41 percent in New Mexico). We examined the effects of state of residence and partisanship over and above any influence of respondents' levels of income and education.[5] (Full model results are available in the online appendix.) Figure 4.1 presents how welcoming white

Figure 4.1 *How Welcoming Is My State? Predicted Probabilities among White Respondents, by State and Political Party*

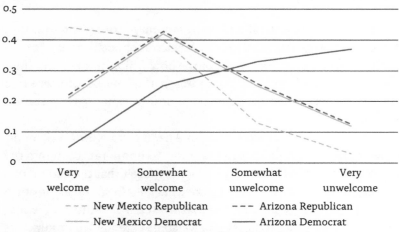

Source: Survey of Immigration and Belonging (Dovidio et al. 2016).

respondents believed their state was toward immigrants, broken down by respondents' state of residence and partisan affiliation.

As in the previous chapter, we looked at whether the ideological identification of partisans differed by state. Our survey indicates that Republicans in the two states were equally likely to call themselves conservative (69 percent in Arizona versus 66 percent in New Mexico), while Democrats in New Mexico were far more likely to call themselves liberal than Democrats in Arizona (62 percent in New Mexico versus 40 percent in Arizona). As our results later in this chapter show, it was Democrats in Arizona who appeared most sensitive to their state's immigration policy context, suggesting that the immigration climate in Arizona is all the more noteworthy in its impact. White Democrats there displayed alienation, even though they mostly considered themselves to be politically moderate.

Figure 4.1 illustrates that white respondents in New Mexico were more likely than Arizona whites to see their state as welcoming to immigrants. It also shows that partisanship played a role. While white Arizona Democrats were far more likely than any other group to view their state as unwelcoming, white New Mexico Republicans were more likely than any other group to perceive their state as welcoming.

Our survey data show that even though whites were not the targets of immigration policies, they were nonetheless aware of the climate in their state.

How did whites in Arizona and New Mexico explain what made their states welcoming or not? In-depth interviews revealed that, although they recognized a number of different contributing influences, respondents saw their state's approach to immigration policy as central to defining its immigration climate. The role of policy was more salient to whites in Arizona—the state perceived to have an unwelcoming immigration climate—compared to whites in New Mexico. White Arizonans' strong view that their state was unwelcoming for immigrants was rooted, in part, in observations that this topic had dominated state politics for the better part of a decade. Emily Scott was a twenty-nine-year-old education adviser and registered Democrat whose husband was Latino. For her and other Democrats, Arizona was clearly unwelcoming to immigrants because of the effect of its policies on her husband's family and because of the prevalence of the immigration issue in the state's politics:

> There's people crossing the border from Mexico into Arizona in the desert. It's just genuinely happening. But I think people lose sight of—and there's this horrible rhetoric that happens around these people: [that they] are criminals, [that] these people are smuggling drugs, that they're doing all sorts of horrible things. When the reality is that they're fleeing from horrible things in their country. And I think that is what the rhetoric is lacking. What is it that they would be running from, to risk their children's lives for however long, and then risk them being separated at the border? They're so much that they're risking, to get away from what? And I don't think that that is discussed very often. In effect, these people are refugees and a lot of times Arizona treats them as if . . . and the narrative behind it treats them as if they're criminals and trying to infiltrate this country with drugs and other crazy things.

Whether Republican or Democrat, white residents of Arizona perceived their state as unwelcoming to immigrants partly because they were aware of Arizona's national reputation for unwelcoming immigration policies. The comments of Peter Evans, a thirty-eight-year-old nonprofit director and registered Republican, were typical in connecting the effect of unwelcoming policies to Arizona's economy and reputation:

> I think with SB 1070, hopefully we learned a huge lesson, that that type of legislation is not in the best interests of our state. I think we took a pretty significant hit, not only economically, which was pretty significant, but culturally and reputationally as a state. I think there's a good deal of motivation not to repeat that.

Not only were white residents of Arizona aware of the state's unwelcoming stance toward immigrants, but they were also attuned to its effect on the state's national reputation.

Whites in New Mexico echoed what we heard from Latinos in New Mexico: they saw their state as welcoming but also offered history and culture—not policy—as the primary drivers. When we asked white New Mexicans how they thought immigrants were treated in New Mexico, they resoundingly replied that the state was welcoming. Even if they were not fully aware of the details of New Mexico's history, white New Mexicans noted that the social and political prominence of Hispanics in the state, extending back generations, made it a more welcoming place for immigrants culturally. Their views reflected the historical record: Hispanos in New Mexico have traditionally wielded political and economic power, and they continue to do so. White respondents felt that New Mexico's history of Hispanic cultural and political prominence and the "live and let live" attitude that they saw as pervasive in the state offered immigrants a softer landing and easier settlement.[6] John Horn, a seventy-six-year-old retired engineer and registered Republican who had lived in New Mexico for a quarter-century, saw the state as welcoming to immigrants. When asked why, he echoed the views of other whites across the political spectrum, noting that Latino immigrants in New Mexico felt like they belonged there partly because they could blend into the state's Latino milieu, which allowed the unauthorized among them to live with less fear than unauthorized residents elsewhere. We asked for his sense of how New Mexico handled undocumented immigrants. "I think we look the other way," he said. "Let's say we have a large Spanish population, a lot of the undocumented immigrants are Hispanic background, so they kind of just meld into the group."

New Mexico does not necessarily "look the other way," but it has instead instituted policies that grant unauthorized immigrants access to state-sponsored resources and institutions. White New Mexicans' assessment of the role these policies play in welcoming immigrants was similar to the assessment Latinos provided. As we reported in the last chapter, New Mexico's Latinos treated these access-providing policies as working in the background of a larger welcoming milieu in which they foregrounded the state's history and culture. Of course, as the previous chapter showed, Latinos do not necessarily see themselves as melting into one group, as John suggested. Indeed, they recognize significant differences among Latinos based on national origin and generation in the United States, among other factors.[7] Whites, however, tended to downplay these differences in favor of a view that there were enough commonalities among Latinos to offer the newcomers among them a sense of cultural and even civic home.

When New Mexico's respondents spoke of policy, they cited the current policy context rather than the legacy of welcoming policies that the state had enacted in the previous three decades. New Mexico first declared itself a sanctuary for Central American immigrants in 1986, and its largest county, Bernalillo, is also a sanctuary jurisdiction. Yet for many of our respondents, those policies only seemed relevant because of the political moment in which we conducted the interviews, when the Trump administration was ramping up detentions while also waging battle against jurisdictions that had declared themselves "sanctuaries" for immigrants and were limiting their cooperation with federal efforts to enforce immigration law. These recent events, not the decades of welcoming policies, were what our New Mexico respondents raised when they mentioned state policy. This finding, which highlights the importance of state-level policies in how people think about immigration and immigrants, presents a stark contrast to findings from the Arizona interviews: in that state, respondents routinely invoked the state's actions regarding immigration over the past few decades.

If white New Mexicans did not point to their state's specific policies as reference points for explaining its welcoming context, they frequently invoked the state's western neighbor, Arizona, to clarify where New Mexico stood in relative terms. Respondents often made this comparison without our prompting, a pattern that emerged in our interviews with New Mexico's Latinos as well. Jack O'Grady, a fifty-five-year-old Albuquerque resident and moderate Democrat who worked in the state's burgeoning film industry, cited the historical roots of the two states' differing levels of welcomingness when we asked him about his sense of how immigrants were treated in New Mexico:

> I think [it's] probably better in New Mexico than other places. My brother lives in Arizona. [Both states] came into the union at the same time—1912—and they went a different route. That state is a lot more Anglicized and has a lot more money than New Mexico. We somehow held on to a lot more of our traditional cultural. . . . Manifest destiny somehow kinda went around New Mexico. We still have nineteen Pueblos and our Native American population, for the most part, at least we held on to their cultures. I mean, they wiped out everybody in Arizona. . . . I think in the old New Mexico, it's a nicer place for immigrants. We have agriculture, we have jobs where these people, immigrants, have a better chance, and we welcome that.

Jack's comments echo our account of the history of the two states in chapter 2, where we briefly chronicled the demographic, political, ethno-racial, and policy histories of the two states. That history figured in respondents' sense of just how different Arizona and New Mexico were when it came to their treatment of immigrants specifically, and of Latinos in general. Jack's use of the word "we" reveals an inclusive view of his state in which supporting the sense of belonging of other groups, such as Latinos and Native Americans, enhances his own feelings of belonging.

Even those less well versed than Jack in the Southwest's history knew about Arizona's reputation as an unwelcoming place for immigrants and thought of New Mexico as a place that did things differently. Arizona's policies and politics grounded what was otherwise a vague sense of New Mexico as a welcoming place. As Doug Johnson, a twenty-five-year-old writer and Democrat originally from rural New Mexico, put it: "I feel like Arizona has just had such a negative image regarding immigration that New Mexico has been able to look great by comparison." Clearly the fear expressed by some Arizonans that their home state had a reputation for being unwelcoming to immigrants had merit. As we noted in the previous chapter, immigration-related news coverage in the two states differed considerably: immigration policy loomed far larger in Arizona news, and many of the immigration news stories covered in New Mexico focused on Arizona. We believe that this difference in coverage, along with the tendency for people to seek out and remember negative information more than positive information, helps explain why Arizonans referenced policy more often in our interviews than New Mexicans did.[8]

The Immigration Climate, White Identity, Belonging, and (Reverse) Discrimination in Arizona and New Mexico

Laws such as Arizona's SB 1070, one of the strictest anti-immigration measures in the nation, were ostensibly aimed at all unauthorized immigrants regardless of national origin. Nearly 30 percent of the state's population was foreign-born at the time of the law's passage, and Latino immigrants made up the vast majority of that total. With the U.S.-Mexico border as Arizona's southern boundary, the law unambiguously targeted Latino immigrants, and immigrants from Mexico in particular.[9] As we have discussed, however, even if policies target one group, they may affect other populations that are not the intended targets. In this case, whites were a symbolically affected group, as state-level immigration policy informed their sense of their own belonging.

How does a welcoming or unwelcoming immigration context affect whites? Do whites' perceptions of Arizona's and New Mexico's immigration climates shape how closely they feel connected to their state of residence and whether they perceive their home state as a place where people like them belong? The answer is not straightforward. It depends on where a person lives and their political orientation. This social context determines whether white individuals are likely to see an exclusionary state policy as fair or unfair, whether they view an increase in immigrants as threatening or mutually beneficial, how connected they feel to their state of residence, and whether they perceive their home state as a place where people like them belong.

Political affiliation is important here. In an era of hyperpartisan-ship, policies, the messages they send, and the messengers who deliver them are viewed through red and blue (Republican and Dem-ocratic) partisan lenses.[10] The Pew Research Center has found that both Republicans and Democrats have become more supportive of legal immigration in recent years: in 2006, 15 percent of Republicans and 20 percent of Democrats said that they wanted legal immigra-tion to be increased; in 2018, the shares were, respectively, 22 percent and 40 percent. Still overall levels of support remain dramatically different between Republicans and Democrats.[11] There are also dif-ferences in how white Democrats and Republicans respond to information about immigration, with Republicans more affected by threatening information.[12]

DO WHITE RESIDENTS FEEL CONNECTED TO THEIR STATE? PRIDE AND IMPORTANCE OF HOME STATE IDENTITY

In our survey, we asked white residents of Arizona and New Mexico how much pride they felt in being a part of their state and how important being from their state was to them. These are two of the most influential elements of social identity, esteem and centrality.[13] Although, as we explained earlier, social identification with a state (feelings of pride and importance) is conceptually distinct from a sense of belonging in the state, they are related. In our survey, whites who felt greater pride in their state and who believed that their state was important to them also felt a greater sense of belonging.

We first consider whether whites said that they were proud to be from their state. In the aggregate, 64 percent agreed strongly that they were proud to tell people they were from Arizona or New Mexico. How-ever, a smaller share of white Arizonans than white New Mexicans expressed pride in being from their state (60 percent in Arizona versus 68 percent in New Mexico). Figure 4.2 shows that these patterns persist when we account for party identification alongside other vari-ables that might affect pride.

The lower degree of pride in Arizona is largely driven by the state's Democrats, who were nearly twenty-five points less likely to agree strongly that they were proud to be from their state. In Arizona—

Figure 4.2 *Am I Proud of Being from My State? Predicted Probabilities among White Respondents, by State and Party*

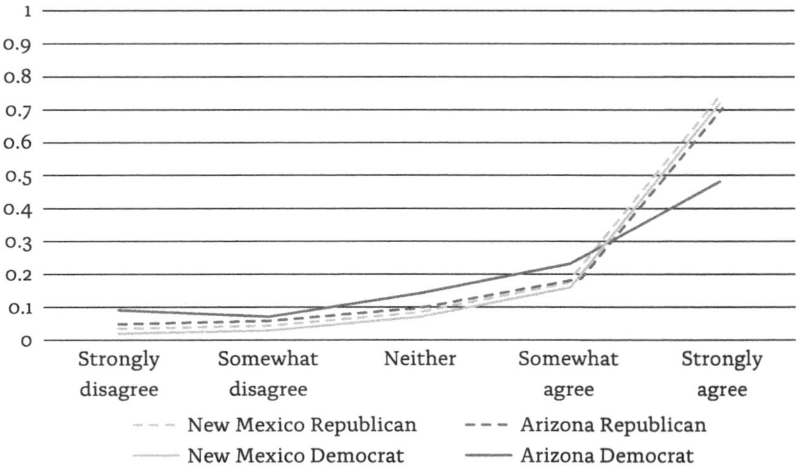

Source: Survey of Immigration and Belonging (Dovidio et al. 2016).

a state with unwelcoming immigration policies—white Republicans expressed pride in their state and were likely to say that being from Arizona was important to them; by contrast, white Democrats felt much less pride in their state and said that being from Arizona was much less important to them. White residents of New Mexico, however, whether they were Republican or Democrat, took substantial pride in their state, which had welcoming immigration policies. In sum, our survey analysis finds no evidence that living in a welcoming state decreases state pride among whites. In fact, the opposite is true: living in a state with unwelcoming policies seems to decrease state pride, at least among white Democrats.

With respect to importance, overall 27 percent of white survey respondents said that being from their state was very important to them. White New Mexicans expressed that sentiment more often (30 percent) than white Arizonans (24 percent), and these descriptive findings hold when other variables are taken into consideration.[14] As figure 4.3 shows, respondents in Arizona were less likely than respondents in New Mexico to say that their state identity was important to them. Paralleling the results for pride, white Republicans in Arizona were more likely to say that being from Arizona was important to

Figure 4.3 *How Important to Me Is Being from My State? Predicted Probabilities among White Respondents, by State and Party*

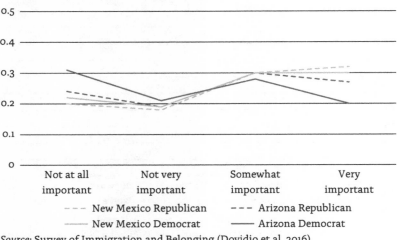

Source: Survey of Immigration and Belonging (Dovidio et al. 2016).

them than were white Democrats. In New Mexico, whether they were Republican or Democrat, white residents felt that being from there was important to them. In sum, our survey analysis finds no evidence that living in a welcoming state decreases the degree to which whites identify with their state in terms of pride or importance. In fact, living in a state with unwelcoming policies seems to decrease state identification, at least among white Democrats.

Our in-depth interviews add texture to these findings, illuminating ways in which the state immigration policy climate may factor into respondents' personal sense of connection to their state. In New Mexico, white respondents mentioned repeatedly that their state's unique culture—one formed by a prominent Hispano population, Native Americans, and Latino immigrants—distinguished the state from others in a way that inspired a sense of pride. White New Mexicans described their state as open to differences, which on its own was a point of pride. But more than that, the state's cultural admixture required a degree of adaptation among whites that, once achieved, allowed them to feel like carriers of the state's culture. Consider what we heard from John Horn, the retired engineer and registered Republican we quoted earlier. Well aware of the influence of Hispanos and Latino immigrants in New Mexico, John and his wife took steps to fit in upon moving there, and they found that the adjustment was easier than they anticipated:

> We kind of had an impression that we were going to have to assimilate to New Mexico. So we had a Spanish tutor. We'd go over to her house and have a Spanish lesson once a week. . . . It was our thinking that we needed to adapt to the community that we were moving to. . . . One of the things I recall when we were coming to New Mexico, we were traveling here in a 1960 Ford fastback. . . . We were looking for some help with the radiator. . . . They were very friendly, warm, and helpful and didn't charge us a lot of money to try to get us on our way for the day. Then we got into Albuquerque, and we stopped and asked for directions. It was at a gas station, and we weren't buying gas, we were just stopping. And the guy was real friendly, and he told us what we were looking for. So it was that experience and how warmly people treated a newcomer. And we found that to be very typical of most of the Hispanic population. They're very warm and open. That's been my experience. . . . The people who feel most at home is anybody that wants to come here! If you want to come here and be part of the community, you should be comfortable.

The strong presence of a Hispanic population and culture in New Mexico requires some degree of adjustment among whites. Whites are the numeric majority and at the top of the social hierarchy in the United States, but New Mexico may not reflect white status nationally. The size and status of the state's Hispanic population yields a more symmetrically "relational" form of assimilation.[15] That is, whites, the state's established Hispanics, Native Americans, and more newly arrived Latinos mutually influence each other's ways of life and outlooks.[16] New Mexico may not be unique in this respect. Historical examinations and ethnographic research in U.S. metropolitan areas with large immigrant populations show that immigrants and subsequent generations can have a profound influence on the mainstream and the established populations thought to be its standard-bearers.[17]

The Horns' level of intentional assimilation into New Mexico's version of mainstream culture was hardly universal among whites in the state. But it illustrates the kind of cultural belonging that whites

discussed as the anchor for a state identity. The whites we interviewed depicted belonging in the state as multiplicative: the sense
of belonging of any one group only expanded the belonging of others.
In describing New Mexico's openness to immigrants, some respondents drew on their own experiences moving there from out of state.
Diane Aikman, a fifty-seven-year-old florist and registered Democrat
in Albuquerque, compared what it was like growing up in her native
rural Midwest to living in New Mexico, where her reception as a gay
woman highlighted the general sense of welcome:

> There are so many different types of people that are living out here.
> It's much more welcoming. I'll give you a quick little story. Kansas
> is one of the states that can refuse to serve gays. And we knew
> that going in, when we were going back there. We actually went
> to a Jimmy John's right down the street from where my mom's
> house was. And we walked in and they're like, "Oh . . ." You could see
> them whispering back there. And they never really made an effort
> to come up to wait on us. . . . I think when I moved out here—
> for example, when I started playing softball. I was playing with
> Hispanics, with Mexicans, with blacks, whites. And we were a
> team, we were a group, we were all friends. It wasn't like this team
> was Hispanic and that team was black. It was all integrated, and
> it was the first time really that I had ever participated in anything
> like that. I'm like, "They really are just like me! They're just dif-
> ferent outside." . . . I became involved with a white married woman,
> a Hispanic woman, another Hispanic woman, white woman. . . .
> But the Hispanic women that I was with, two of them I was with
> for almost six years each. I was welcomed into their family. There
> was no racial bias, nothing. Couldn't understand what they were
> saying half the time, but you know? . . . I've always felt at home
> here I guess because of being different. . . . So I came out here and
> I was accepted, no matter what, by no matter who. It made it nice,
> comfortable.

If New Mexicans felt that their state was welcoming to everyone
in general, they believed that it was particularly open to immigrants.
They based their views not so much on specific policies, but rather
on an overarching openness to diversity and a Hispanic cultural
salience that included widespread and unremarkable use of the
Spanish language.

While Arizona resembles New Mexico in some respects—Arizona also has a large Hispanic population and a large Native American population—white respondents in Arizona had a sense that their state was rapidly changing. Arizona has experienced rapid population growth, especially in the Phoenix metropolitan area, where we did most of the interviews, and that growth is driven overwhelmingly by new domestic and foreign arrivals. More people moved to Maricopa County, the state's largest, than to any other U.S. county between 2012 and 2017.[18] Arizona is also a popular winter home for "snowbirds"—retirees from cold-weather states who come to Arizona to spend the winter in a warmer climate. As a result, white Arizonans felt less of a sense of attachment to their state than whites in New Mexico, both because many of them were themselves migrants to the state and because the influx of people from so many other U.S. regions and parts of the world was diminishing the state's sense of collective rootedness. As Elaine Hatley, a thirty-five-year-old registered Republican and director of a nonprofit, reported, "It's kind of a melting pot of people. There's not a lot of Arizona natives that have grown up in Phoenix, and so there's a lot of diverse people. Demographic-wise, the snowbirds that come down here, it's really diverse." Immigration-driven diversity can dampen the sense of connection that residents have to a place. Some research has shown that diversity drives down trust and is negatively associated with a host of collective behaviors, ranging from views about the welfare state to census response rates.[19] In the case of Arizona, and Phoenix in particular, it is not just immigration from abroad but also from other U.S. states that contributes to residents' slightly weaker sense of identity with their state.

And yet the partisan differences within Arizona were clearly major drivers of respondents' sense of identification and pride. The survey data suggest that white Arizona Democrats had the weakest identification with and pride in their state and the lowest sense of belonging among the whites we surveyed. In-depth interviews reflected their sense of political outsiderness. It was not so much that they explicitly cited their party identification, but rather that they noted that the state's prevailing conservative political and social views misaligned with their own more liberal views. Consider the response of Nolan Taylor, a white, thirty-eight-year-old insurance sales representative and registered Democrat from Arizona, when we asked him what would make him more comfortable living in Arizona: "I don't know. Probably if the political climate was . . . I think we're fairly Republican here. If the political climate was more in line with what I felt, I think would be one of the things that would help."

Feelings of Belonging among Whites

Our central research question is how state-level immigration policy regimes relate to, and potentially affect, people's sense of belonging. As we noted earlier, social identity is built on aspects of the psychological connection between an individual and a group (for example, the pride an individual has for a group and the importance of being a member of the group). Belonging reflects the fit that individuals experience within a group, which involves not only their personal comfort and security within the group but also perceptions of their acceptance by other members of the group.

To assess whites' sense of belonging we draw on three questions from our survey: (1) feelings of belonging, (2) feelings of being an outsider, and (3) perceptions of discrimination against whites. Overall, a large majority of whites expressed a strong sense that they belonged in their state (65 percent). Differences between white Arizonans and white New Mexicans were minimal (67 percent in Arizona versus 64 percent in New Mexico). Figure 4.4 presents results from our multivariate analysis, in which party identification and state of residence are the main explanatory variables. Our statistical analysis seems to bear out the descriptive finding that whites have considerable pride in their state: Arizona Republicans were the most likely to say that they belonged "a lot," Arizona Democrats were the least likely to provide that response, and white New Mexican Republicans and Democrats were equally likely to say that they belonged in their state. Importantly, although white Arizona Republicans showed a belonging boost and white Arizona Democrats a belonging penalty, majorities of all groups of white respondents expressed high levels of belonging in their state.

Another way of getting at belonging is to examine its social-psychological opposite: exclusion. Our survey asked people how strongly they agreed with the statement "I feel like an outsider in my state." The responses affirm the picture emerging from the belonging

Figure 4.4 *I Belong in My State "a Lot": Predicted Probabilities among White Respondents, by State and Party*

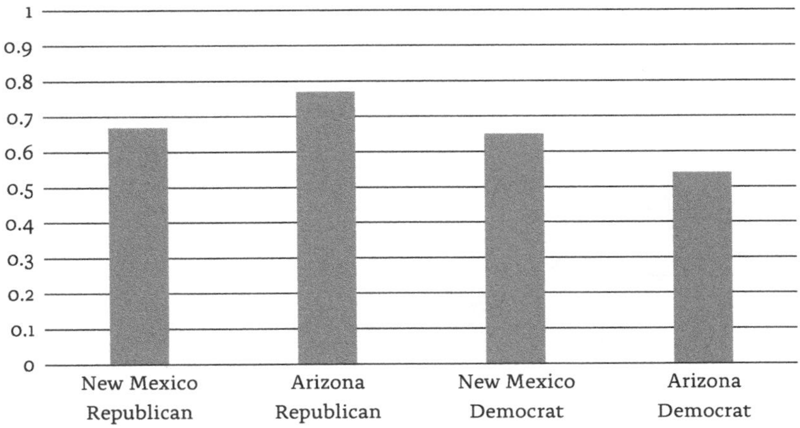

Source: Survey of Immigration and Belonging (Dovidio et al. 2016).

question. Only 16 percent of white respondents agreed strongly that they felt like outsiders (16 percent in Arizona; 17 percent in New Mexico). Arizona Democrats were the most likely to feel this way, and Arizona Republicans were the least likely; New Mexicans from both political parties fell in between these two extremes (see figure 4.5).

We also sought to understand whether white respondents saw discrimination against whites in their state. In general, the overall level of anti-white discrimination perceived by whites was considerably lower than the level of anti-Latino discrimination perceived by Latinos. More than 50 percent of the Latinos in our survey perceived "a lot" or "a great deal" of anti-Latino discrimination in their state; among all white groups analyzed in this chapter, only 5 to 21 percent saw similar levels of anti-white discrimination.[20] Only 13.4 percent of white respondents felt that there was a lot of discrimination against their racial group in their state; this perception was slightly higher among whites in New Mexico (11 percent in Arizona versus 16 percent in New Mexico). We found that whites in Arizona were more likely than whites in New Mexico to say that there was no discrimination at all against whites in their state. Partisanship also made a difference on this question: white Republicans were more likely than white Democrats to perceive discrimination against white Americans. As

Figure 4.5 *Do I Feel Like an Outsider in My State? Predicted Probabilities among White Respondents, by State and Party*

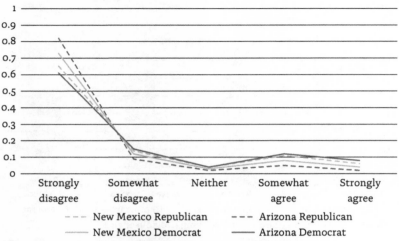

Source: Survey of Immigration and Belonging (Dovidio et al. 2016).

shown in figure 4.6, our statistical model predicts that 57 percent of New Mexico Republicans would say that there was at least a moderate amount of discrimination against whites in their state, compared to only 25 percent of Arizona Democrats. This measure demonstrates that while living in a welcoming state does not tend to decrease white residents' pride in their state, it may diminish their sense of belonging. We explore that proposition in our in-depth interviews in the next section.

In summary, our survey results regarding feelings of belonging—whether people felt that they belonged in their state, whether they were proud to be from their state, whether they felt like an outsider in their state, and whether they perceived discrimination against whites—show that whites overall felt like they belonged in their state. However, state and party differences emerged prominently: white Republicans in Arizona displayed the greatest sense of belonging across our analyses in this section, and white Democrats in Arizona displayed the lowest. New Mexico Democrats and Republicans displayed little difference in their sense of attachment to their state. There is one notable exception, however: whites in New Mexico were slightly more likely to say that they perceived discrimination

Figure 4.6 *Are Whites Discriminated against in My State? Predicted Probabilities among White Respondents, by State and Party*

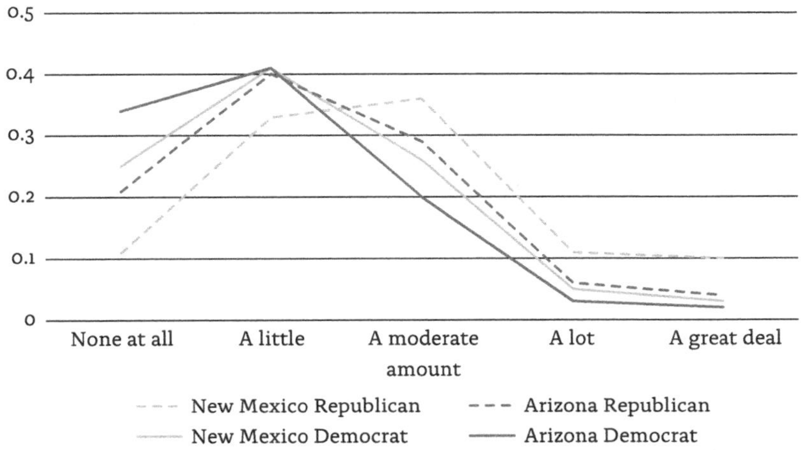

Source: Survey of Immigration and Belonging (Dovidio et al. 2016).

in their state. Overall, it appears that if there is a belonging penalty that accrues to whites living in a state with a welcoming immigration policy regime, white New Mexicans may experience it to a slight degree. And if living in an unwelcoming state exacts a belonging penalty for whites, it is the white Democrats in Arizona who are paying that price.

WHITENESS AND RACIAL HIERARCHY IN NEW MEXICO

There is a paradox in our quantitative finding: compared to whites in Arizona, whites in New Mexico more strongly identified with their state, but they were also more likely to see discrimination against whites in their state and to say that they did not feel like they belonged. Our interviews offer an explanation for this apparently paradoxical finding.

Recall that white New Mexicans tended to strongly identify with their state because of its unique cultural milieu and because they perceived the state to be culturally open to all. And yet a distinguishing feature of the state is the economic and political prominence of a Hispanic population with roots in the region dating back centuries. In the in-depth interviews, we asked respondents a broad set of questions meant to tap some of these themes: Who did they think felt most at home in the state? And how did their own situation compare to the situation of those who, in their opinion, felt most at home?

The responses revealed what whites perceived to be a downside of the state's cultural uniqueness: even if it was easy to fit in, whites did not quite feel like the high-status group in the state. For whites in New Mexico, there was a near-consensus that the state's long-residing Hispano population, more than others, felt the most at home. They cited this population's historic and contemporary political dominance as well as the continued visibility of Hispanic culture, including food and language. For our respondents, the status position of Hispanos presented a contrast to the prevailing ethno-racial status hierarchy in the United States. For example, when asked about the kinds of people who felt most at home in New Mexico, Ann Myers, a thirty-two-year-old graphic designer and registered Democrat, observed:

> It's definitely not the same kinds of people that you would think are most at home in America at large. New Mexico is so different. I think of people who have Spanish descent, whose families have been here since forever. And have this really deep connection with the land and with the culture and the traditions that are here. I feel kind of envious, honestly, of having such a deep-rooted connection to a place. I imagine that would be pretty cool to have ten generations to point to and say, "We came here in 1508," or whatever. If that doesn't make you feel at home, I don't know what would.

Similarly, Aaron Donnelly, a white twenty-nine-year-old customer service representative and registered Democrat from Albuquerque, observed:

> The people who probably feel the most comfortable here would be people of Spanish descent, Mexican descent. Just because it's really honored and valued here. I wonder. If somebody grew up with an idea . . . homogenous community is good, if they thought that one type of community is good, then they might feel uncomfortable here where it's not that way. It's diverse. So my white aunts from New York . . . [were] kind of uncomfortable here.

Aaron's observation hinted at why white New Mexicans may have perceived more discrimination against whites in their state compared to their Arizona counterparts. Note that Aaron described people of Spanish descent as having an honored and valued position, suggesting a hierarchy in which whites might not necessarily feel on top. At the same time he made this observation, however, Aaron also commented on the state's diversity, saying that it could pose a challenge for whites unaccustomed to ethno-racial difference. His implication was that the state's diversity was a net positive, even if it challenged a sense of white dominance.

This view of hierarchy emerged even more clearly when respondents discussed Hispanic power in state politics. They observed what historians and contemporary observers of New Mexico have noted: unlike Hispanos in other southwestern states, Hispanos in New Mexico retained a fair amount of political and economic power after the Mexican-American War and the annexation of the contemporary Southwest by the United States.[21] With that history in mind, white respondents occasionally reflected on instances in which they did not feel entirely like insiders in the state because they lacked Hispanic heritage. Doug Johnson, whom we quoted earlier arguing that the immigration climate in Arizona was so unwelcoming that New Mexico looked good by comparison, said that when he was a child he had been bullied for being white. As welcoming as New Mexico might be, he still had a lingering sense that the state's true insiders were those residents whose Spanish heritage was deeply rooted in the region:

> I feel like there have been good and bad encounters that I've had with Hispanic people. There have been some really awesome times, say when I was at a small restaurant in a rural part of New Mexico and found out a little too late that they can't run cards there. And I would say, "Do you mind if I come back in thirty minutes after I hit an ATM?" And they're like, "Yeah, no problem." And that felt like a level of trust that I don't think that I would be afforded by a lot of people, let alone people that have different identities than myself. I feel like the in-group, out-group mentality can exist. In high school it wasn't always easy interacting with some of the Hispanic students. I feel like because I was white, I was targeted

for some bullying. One of my old elementary school classmates that I consider to have been a good friend, by the time we got to high school, he didn't like me anymore. And I don't think it was my personality because we weren't close or anything. It was just that some years down the road I would see him and I would say hello and he would make fun of me for my appearance. Maybe if he was making fun of me for something else it wouldn't have hurt as much as it did. But yeah, those are two contrasting examples that come to mind. . . . It was just some impermeable barrier that kind of obstructed us from being friends the way that I saw it. . . . I tried not to generalize and that's something that in general I try not to generalize. I feel like that has been good so far in life. When that happened, it hurt my feelings, but I tried not to internalize it and I didn't extrapolate from that one incident, I guess. Or even from many incidents. Because I know that that's not the entirety of it. That's not the scope of it, and that's not necessarily the reality of the situation.

Any perceived exclusion that Doug and others noted was counterbalanced in their view by a long list of harmonious interactions and friendships and a larger belief about New Mexico as welcoming of different groups of people.

Respondents also mentioned Native Americans as a population that felt at home culturally in the state. However, no respondent attributed political and economic power to this population. If anything, they were quick to assert that there was a notable lack of power among the state's large Native American population, and they attributed this to a history of racism that continues today.

What white New Mexicans did *not* mention about what made them feel like they belonged in their state was also revealing: no respondents cited the state's welcoming immigration policy as a reason they felt they did not belong, and the modest partisan divide that appears in our quantitative models was not very noticeable in the interviews. The absence of such mentions provides further evidence that policies that are welcoming to immigrants do not drive down whites' sense of belonging. Welcoming policies, once in place, are not seen by whites as a zero-sum proposition in which a gain for

Latino is a loss for themselves. The findings we present in the next chapter lend support to the suggestion that welcoming immigration policies were not responsible for the modest differences in feelings of belonging between New Mexican whites and Arizona whites. We test that proposition experimentally, showing that welcoming policies can heighten a sense of belonging for some whites in either state, particularly those who are liberal.

WHITENESS AND RACIAL HIERARCHY IN ARIZONA

In Arizona, whites felt no sense of being outsiders because of their racial background. But, like all Americans, they were operating in a hyperpartisan climate: political parties have increasingly come to represent not only a political but also a social identity that shapes where Americans live, with whom they socialize or form romantic partnerships, and their cultural tastes.[22] As the Republican Party has become increasingly white in its makeup and known for looking out for white interests, partisanship has divided whites.[23] Party identification and views about immigration are also more correlated than ever. It used to be that immigration was a bipartisan issue. Driven by the changing outlooks of its white members, the Democratic Party has become far more accommodating in its views about immigration and race in recent years; among Republicans, views have either become less accommodating or remained unchanged.[24]

This is the backdrop for white Arizona Democrats seeing their party affiliation as an outgroup marker, and themselves as symbolically affected by unwelcoming immigration policies. Democrats grounded their sense of outsiderness in a host of state-level policies and politics that cut sharply against the grain of Democratic political beliefs: lack of support for the poor, paltry funding for schools and teachers, and aggressive policing. But it was also clear that Arizona's unwelcoming immigration policies and aggressive enforcement strategies were cues contributing to Democrats' feeling that they were not on political home turf—that they were a symbolically affected group. Take Daniel Colbert, a seventy-year-old registered Democrat and retired military officer who was doing advocacy work for veterans. His reflections about returning from Afghanistan to settle permanently in the state echoed the views of other Arizona Democrats:

> It was still the lovely, conservative state—and I say that . . . kind of sarcastically—that it always was. . . . From a legislative stand- point, I saw that the government got far more conservative than it had ever been before. That to me was a red flag, progressive that I am. (*chuckling*). . . . One of the things I found was that the state government is not representative of its constituency, of the citizens here. That to me is painful. . . . I think that if you go through the major issues of the day, whether it's immigration, the economy, education, those are top. Defunding education at every level started a decade ago, in 2008. Admittedly, the economy was tanking and a lot of things going on. But they did absolutely nothing. In fact, there were a lot of things I thought they did that exacerbated the economic downturn. And then just from a policy standpoint, the tax policy was continually advantaged to those who were in the upper income levels.

Daniel's remarks were echoed by other white Arizona Democrats, many of whom felt that they were part of an out-group in a state where politics has been dominated by Republicans. Although white Arizonans did not say that they felt like outsiders because of their racial identity, race played a prominent role in how they described belonging in their state. Whites in Arizona described a state racial hierarchy quite different from New Mexico's: in Arizona, whites were clearly on top. That picture of the hierarchy emerged implic- itly. We asked every respondent to describe the people who felt most at home in their respective states and those who felt least at home. The Republicans we interviewed mostly avoided explicit references to race in their replies. The racial subtext was clear, however, and often took the form of suggestions that people who were already comfort- able in Arizona would feel most at home. Elsa Lowen, a forty-five- year-old financial analyst and registered Republican, chuckled when we posed the question:

> It's funny. Old, white people? People that are retiring? Phoenix, Arizona, we have the snowbirds. People like to come here for the weather. People don't want to deal with the winters. That would

be a stereotypical citizen. But most at home in Arizona? I would say I don't know.

David Kahn, a seventy-five-year-old retired government worker and independent who said he leaned "more toward the liberal side," captured the dynamic succinctly. When asked who felt comfortable in Arizona, he replied, "The people who could say, 'This is the way we did things fifty years ago and there's no need for any kind of change. As long as we keep on feeling that way, I feel comfortable.'"

The rather circular reasoning reveals that these Arizonans believed that the people who feel most comfortable in their state are those who are comfortable with the state's status quo. In that status quo, whiteness rests incontrovertibly at the top of the state's social and economic hierarchy. As sociologists have noted, a characteristic of white racial identity is a taken-for-granted sense of whiteness as the norm: an unstated category imbued with the power to define what it means to belong and against which all others are judged.[25] The fact that white Republicans did not mention race in their rendering of what it means to belong is a reflection of just how widely accepted whites are in the state and the degree to which their sense of belonging is a given.

If white Republicans were reluctant to say outright that race was a factor in who feels welcomed in Arizona, white Democrats were quicker to call it out. Even in Arizona, however, white Democrats tended to speak not in terms of whites feeling most at home, but in terms of Latinos feeling *least* so. Their views were informed by a combination of recent high-profile unwelcoming state policies, the notoriety of former sheriff Joe Arpaio, and the Trump administration's enforcement efforts. Take Lena Bell Gladstone, a thirty-one-year-old entrepreneur and libertarian from Phoenix whose views on social issues were decidedly left of center.[26] When asked who felt most at home in Arizona, she hesitated, speculating that she might need to take a survey to figure out the answer. But when asked who felt least at home in Arizona, she was quick to answer:

> Honestly, the Hispanic population. I can't imagine they feel safe. I wouldn't, being that close to the border and just the alienation that's happening in so many ways. If I was gonna think through that, but this is an assumption. . . . I would say there's gotta be

some people who have come up from Mexico, especially, who don't feel safe, who don't feel at home. . . . One of my good friends from high school is not a citizen of the U.S. She was born in Mexico, and both her kids were born here. Her husband is also not a citizen, so neither one of them are. They were both born in Mexico and she's afraid every day. She's like, "At any point they could kick me out of this country and I don't know what I would do." Because her whole life is here. Her job is here, everything is here. She's kind of the example I have in terms of being intimately close to people who are dealing with that issue. And it's heartbreaking to even talk about that.

Lena Bell's personal connection to an immigrant from Mexico made Latinos' position at the bottom of the hierarchy in Arizona more vivid to her. Of course, the broad group of Latinos also includes individuals with deep generational roots in the United States. Yet even though white Democrats acknowledged that some Latinos might be less vulnerable because of their U.S.-born status, it did little to change their view of who was least at home in Arizona. Indeed, many saw Latinos as a population under siege.

But they also saw the status quo as likely to change, given Arizona's immigration-driven demographic change. David Kahn, who was quoted earlier describing how many white Arizonans were comfortable with the state's existing racial hierarchy, saw that status quo in flux:

DAVID: It's probably changing to where maybe in five or ten years they're gonna be the ones that feel uncomfortable. I don't know. But I think the ones that feel the least comfortable in Arizona, I would think, probably would be the Hispanics who are here, who have been here for a long time, but still don't have citizenship.

INTERVIEWER: And why do you think they would feel least at home?

DAVID: Because they're not sure where they stand from day to day. They're not sure what's going to happen with them. Even Hispanics that are here as citizens, I would think, a lot of them would feel

> uncomfortable because if somebody looks at them and says, "Oh look at that, they probably aren't legal." So, I would think that would make them feel uncomfortable.

When they did talk directly about their ethno-racial identity, white Democrats used language from popular and academic discourse on race in their descriptions of which groups felt most at home in their state. Many white Democrats asserted that whites feel at home in Arizona because the state's white ethno-racial politics enhances white privilege, which includes the material and psychological dividends enjoyed by individuals identified as white. Critiques of white privilege were particularly prominent among the younger white Democrats we interviewed. Nicole Cottrell, a forty-year-old lobbyist and liberal independent, had been involved in some political protests, including one that took place outside of a Donald Trump speech in Phoenix shortly before we interviewed her. In that speech, Trump had suggested that he might pardon former sheriff Joe Arpaio for his federal conviction for criminal contempt of court (an action that Trump ultimately took on August 25, 2017). Explaining why she attended the protest, Nicole told us:

> I felt very strongly and I just feel like it's my duty to go [protest]. Here are people that can't go or people that wouldn't be safe. But as a middle-aged, middle-class white lady, I'm pretty safe around the police, so I'll go. I call it "white people work." (*chuckling*) We have to go do that white people work for other people that maybe can't. . . . I consider white people work when my father-in-law is saying things like that and I'm trying to explain to him. I can use my mental energy on him to try to explain it and maybe someone who is living it can't. They don't have the mental energy. So if I can try to explain it to him a gentle way, "Your experience as a white man is not the same as a black woman. It's a little bit different." You try and lead them through it. I call that white people work.

When asked how often she does "white people work," Nicole laughed and replied:

> I try and do it if someone I'm friends with says something that's racist. Like my brother-in-law. We had some trees trimmed in our yard. My brother-in-law was like, "Oh, did you hire Mexicans?"

And I was like, "I didn't ask for their ethnicity, Jonathan. I just asked if they could do the job." Because it's not so personal for me, I can sort of gently explain, "That's not so cool. You probably shouldn't do that." And maybe get them to stop. But it's not going to hurt me emotionally to do that because I'm not the group that he's saying those things about. You just kind of have to gently lead the white people out. Kind of explain to them, "That's not okay." "Dennis, why do you care a woman is wearing a hijab? Relax about it." So I call that white people work, which sounds really stupid now that I say it out loud!

Rather than denying that whiteness confers benefits on those who can claim it, respondents like Nicole believed that they benefited from whiteness and had an obligation to call out and correct comments they deemed to be racist. Her comments reflected larger changes in white racial identity. There have always been variants of white racial identity by social class.[27] Varieties of today's white racial identity are patterned by partisanship. Among Democrats and liberals, like Nicole, white racial identity's salience manifests not as a source of pride, but as an object of critique. The political scientist Eric Kaufmann's analysis of American National Election Survey data for the *New York Times* shows that white liberals are more likely to see racism than black Democrats; whites who voted for Hillary Clinton in the 2016 presidential election also had more favorable views of diversity than any other ethno-racial voting group, and white Clinton voters were the only ethno-racial partisan group to view their own group *less* favorably than other ethno-racial groups.[28] In a similar vein, the liberal Democrats and independents we interviewed held up white racial identity, and the privileges that come with it, as a problem, the remedy to which was to fight racism in ways big and small.

Even if Arizona respondents believed that their whiteness gave them some privilege in their state, many also said that things were changing and that nonwhites and avowed antiracists might be slowly moving into a position of feeling most at home. This view resonated to some degree among Republican respondents. Some thought that time might have already arrived. When Elsa, quoted earlier, was asked who she thought felt most at home in Arizona, she told us:

The state has changed so much over time. I feel like you could have said "a Republican old white person" at some point, but I don't feel like that's the same anymore. . . . Well, there just continues to be the movement around the country. Most people in this city, in Phoenix at least, are from other places. They didn't grow up here. So demographically, as the U.S. gets more diverse from immigration from all over the place, outside the country or just different states coming here, I just feel like you end up with a lot of different people. So people are coming here for the opportunities of growth because the economy is good or our cost of living is low. And the weather is good. They like the sunshine. All different kinds of people from all backgrounds and religions and ethnicities like low cost of living and good weather. So you end up with a lot of people continuing to come. I hear the news that more and more of our demographic is Hispanic and it's going to be 50 percent soon if it isn't already. So that's just another changing thing, maybe with our proximity to the border or whatever. I think it's been changing over time and with people moving all over the place. So I don't feel like the particular kind of person that would be comfortable here is easy to pinpoint as maybe it would have been thirty years ago.

Elsa's sense that white dominance may be under challenge resonates with larger political trends in the United States. These trends, and the data we present here, reflect the splintering of white racial identity into two groups: those who see whiteness as a privilege and those who feel that whiteness is threatened by the growing minority population and the rise of immigration-driven diversity.[29] Arizona may indeed be ahead of the rest of the country in terms of immigration-driven demographic change. But our data show that this change may not be fully registering across the racial and political spectrum. Indeed, whites overall, and especially white Republicans in Arizona, exhibited the strongest sense of belonging and social identity connection with their state.

Do State-Level Patterns Look the Same at the National Level? American and Racial Identity

Does a state-level sense of belonging spill over into feelings of national belonging? In general, individuals' perceptions of their immediate environment, such as their state, may shape their perceptions of larger relevant contexts, such as the nation. While they readily distinguish the state and national contexts, because states represent some elements of the nation, people may generalize from their experiences in their state to how they feel about living in the United States.[30]

Arizona and New Mexico are clearly distinct political, territorial, and cultural places. The distinctiveness of each state, including their diverging approaches to immigration policy, shape whites' experience of living in them. But Arizona and New Mexico are also embedded in a larger political, territorial, and cultural unit: the United States. How whites experience the politics, policy, and culture of their state may color how they see themselves and other whites in the larger national context. We wanted to understand whether whites experienced any such spillover effects: did the state they live in affect their sense of American national identity, their racial identity, or their perception of whether their racial group experienced discrimination in the United States? In our examination of spillover effects, state residence and political party remained important predictors of identities and perceptions. But here we asked survey and interview respondents to think about these issues in the national context, starting with whether American identity was important to them.

ARE STATE OF RESIDENCE AND POLITICAL PARTISANSHIP RELATED TO WHITES' AMERICAN IDENTITY?

Overall, 86 percent of white respondents said that being American is very important to them (86 percent in both Arizona and New Mexico), the same level of importance we found among Latinos. Unlike the Latinos described in the previous chapter, however, whites were also quite likely to think that *other* people agreed that they belonged in the United States. Eighty-three percent of whites said that they thought that others felt like they belonged in the United States (83 percent in both Arizona and New Mexico), compared to only 57 percent of Latinos. Only 8 percent of whites said that they felt like an outsider in the United States (8 percent in both Arizona and New Mexico), and only 16 percent said that they felt like an outsider in their state (16 percent in Arizona; 17 percent in New Mexico).[31]

WHITES' SENSE OF BELONGING | 115

Figure 4.7 *My American Identity Is Very Important to Me: Predicted Probabilities among White Respondents, by State and Party*

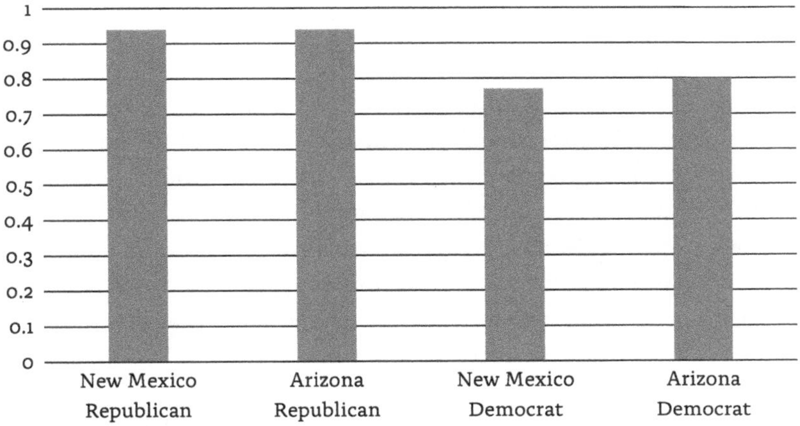

Source: Survey of Immigration and Belonging (Dovidio et al. 2016).

Although majorities in all groups agreed that being an American was important to them, Republicans were more likely than Democrats to agree strongly (see figure 4.7). The effect of state residence was minor.

We asked in-depth interview respondents what makes someone a true American and what it takes for immigrants to become American. Their responses show that even if white respondents from both states and both parties were strongly attached to an American identity, how they conceived of that identity differed, especially along party lines. In the abstract, respondents across the political spectrum agreed that American national identity has a nucleus characterized by *civic republicanism*: national belonging is defined by active participation in civic institutions.[32]

Republican respondents tended to emphasize this form of American identity in particular. For these respondents, belonging in the United States entailed contributing something for the sake of the national whole. Volunteering, joining the military, voting, even paying taxes were ways that everyone, immigrants and U.S.-born citizens alike, could be true Americans. Some respondents held out their own families as examples of Americans formed over generations from this ideal mold of American identity. Elaine Hatley, the nonprofit director and registered Republican quoted earlier, noted that her family's history of integration, and in particular her family's prominent military history, had formed her own sense of American identity:

> My mom and dad's family were very much American because they appreciated it so much and they loved America so much. So it's made me more patriotic. I remember being a kid and being very competitive about where my ancestors were from because I felt pretty special that my grandma was 100 percent Lithuanian and my [other] grandma was 100 percent French. And a lot of my friends, they were such mixes of things I thought that was really special. . . . So the patriotism I think was just naturally a part of that. Very much, "We love our country. We defend our country." Both grandparents were military families. Both granddads were in the army. And my mom especially, her dad was in the last cavalry with actual horses and everything. She took great pride in that and made sure that we knew that. Knew how much Americans did for Germany. She went over right after the war with her dad and mom and family, to help restore Germany. So I think she got to see a different side of the war, of World War II. Americans were the heroes, and so she really got to see that firsthand. And my dad was over there too, but my mom was more the one with the pride. You don't burn flags, you have a difference of opinion and that's great, but you still honor the president. That type of thing. She very much believed in the respect and honor of the country.

Elaine's account of American identity included hints of what Deborah Schildkraut calls "incorporationism," a model of American civic identity built on a celebration of immigration and the contribution of immigrant groups to the United States.[33] Here, Elaine offered a version of incorporationism in which European groups were the central protagonists. Those groups marched away from a sense of ethnic distinctiveness and toward an American identity premised on civic republicanism, which prioritizes collective forms of civic participation, like military service.[34] But the core of what made her family American, Elaine and others claimed, had more to do with what they had done to prove themselves as full members of the American polity.

If incorporationism was a side feature of Republicans' notion of American identity, it was the main event for Democrats. As our survey findings suggest, Democrats certainly felt attached to an American identity, and it was the incorporationist version that animated their image of American identity. Jack O'Grady, the Albuquerque film industry worker quoted earlier, grafted his vague sense of his own family's European immigrant origins onto an American narrative written by immigrants, then and now:

We're all immigrants. We all came here. I have English that came over on the *Mayflower*. And I have Irish that left Ireland, the Cape of Hope, during the potato famine. So I've got American history all in a row. . . . My Irish part, they definitely struggled. People in New York didn't want Irish people. And the Irish people were even the ones that competed with the free slaves down in the South. We're all immigrants! It's weird. I think, we're like, "All right, there's enough people, let's close the borders." That's not what we're founded on. This is the land of opportunity. "Bring us your cold or your weary." . . . In California I had a unique experience in that the Asian culture, the first generations that came from Asia, were very disciplined. "Gotta make it. Gotta do everything. Gotta save the pennies. Gotta send money back home. Gotta assimilate, get into this and be successful and hold on to our culture at the same time." The second generation saw how hard their first generation [had it], and they dominate the California school systems there. Higher education is like, "Wow! There's a lot of smart Asian people here." They worked a lot harder. By third and fourth generations, they become Americanized and they're like, "I don't need to work this hard, man!" It seems like the further you get away from that generation that immigrated, they settle into us lazy Americans. And then us lazy Americans, we're all about capitalism and that's all about competition. So, they look at immigrants and they're like, wow!

Like Elaine, Jack offered up his own family history as an example of the nation's immigrant heritage. But whereas Elaine implied that her family followed a different, more laudable trajectory compared to today's immigrants, Jack saw contemporary immigrants as keepers of a legacy of immigrant striving. Recall that we collected the survey

data months before Donald Trump's election as president. We conducted the in-depth interviews, however, during Trump's presidency.
The Democrats we interviewed saw Trump as a challenge to their
incorporationist notion of American identity and expressed a
diminished sense of pride in their American identity as a result. Susan
Clinton, a thirty-nine-year-old education administrator, registered
independent, and self-described political liberal, had lived abroad and
worked in advocacy organizations that assisted unauthorized immigrants. She said that she once felt like her views on American foreign
policy and immigration were a minority perspective. But in more
recent years, she had come to feel that her views were part of a growing mainstream trend toward decoupling American identity from
current U.S. policy:

> I have for a long time felt like counterculture. I was called the
> "gringa" when I lived in El Salvador (*laughing*) because I had strong
> critiques of the U.S. foreign policy and a lot of things. But now I feel
> different. I feel more mainstream. I feel like there's a lot of people
> like me who are not happy with the way that this country is being
> governed.

Contestation over immigration policy is a battle over the design of
the nation.[35] When the architecture of that design is in direct opposition to incorporationism, those who subscribe to the incorporationist
version of American civic identity see restrictive federal immigration
policies as anathema to contemporary, mainstream notions of what
it means to be American.

STATE OF RESIDENCE, POLITICAL PARTISANSHIP, AND WHITE RACIAL IDENTITY

Racial and national identities are informed by everyday lived experiences embedded in the local context.[36] But they are also constructed
by a larger set of historical and contemporary events that reverberate
nationally. Was our respondents' sense of their own white racial
identity and national identity inflected by state-level policy toward
immigrants?

When it comes to racial identity, the answer may not be so clearcut. It could be that living in an unwelcoming state immigration
policy climate shapes whites' racial identity by reinforcing their racial

group's dominant position. If the policy clearly signals that immigrants are unwelcome, then whites may draw the conclusion that belonging is reserved for people like themselves, who are white. Previous research suggests that living in a welcoming policy climate could produce a sense of threat to the status of whites, because welcoming policies ostensibly elevate the status of immigrants, threatening the place of whites at the top.[37] Recent research shows that the effect of those policies on whites may be inflected by party identification— that is, alignment between immigration policies and deeply held political orientations can have an independent effect on how whites feel about their racial identity.[38] Of course, there are immigrants who are white, and we do not assume that being a minority and being an immigrant are synonymous. In the two states we studied, however, and in the United States more generally, Latino immigrants are by far the largest group of newcomers, and there is a strong association between being Latino and being foreign in popular discourse.[39] Thus, it is safe to say that immigration policies and politics, whether at the national or state level, rarely, if ever, target whites. But even if whites are not the target, does living in a welcoming versus an unwelcoming state affect how they think about their own racial identity? Our survey data suggest not. Only 21 percent said that being white was very important to them (19 percent in Arizona; 22 percent in New Mexico). Putting this in context with the survey data we reported earlier, white survey respondents placed far more importance on being American than on being white, and there was a good deal of similarity across the two states in the importance they placed on being white. Figure 4.8 looks at these findings in the multivariate context, showing that whites in the two states placed a similar level of importance on their racial identity.

There were differences by party: Republicans said that white identity was more important to them than Democrats did, a finding consistent with other research on party identification and racial identity.[40] But importantly for the purposes of our study, we found no evidence in these data that the welcoming climate in New Mexico or the unwelcoming climate of Arizona enhanced white residents' attachment to their racial identity.

To further examine this question of whether living in a specific state-level immigration policy context heightens whites' attachment

Figure 4.8 *How Important to Me Is My Racial Identity? Predicted Probabilities among White Respondents, by State and Party*

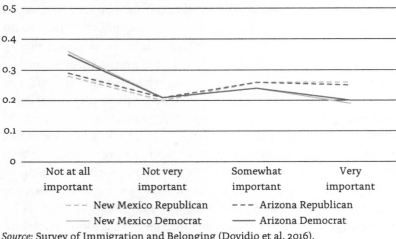

Source: Survey of Immigration and Belonging (Dovidio et al. 2016).

to their own racial identity, we explore the degree to which whites in our survey perceived discrimination against whites in the United States in general. Twenty-two percent of whites felt that there was "a lot" or "a great deal" of discrimination against their racial group in the United States (21 percent in Arizona; 23 percent in New Mexico). Similar to the responses about whether people perceived anti-white discrimination at the state level, New Mexicans were more likely than Arizonans to perceive discrimination against whites in the United States, but in this case the difference was small. Results from our multivariate analysis in figure 4.9 show that state residence was not a factor, but party identification was.

Once again, Democrats were far more likely than Republicans to say that there was no discrimination against whites in the United States, while Republicans were more likely to say that there was at least a moderate amount.

The way that in-depth interview respondents talked about their white racial identity, and about whiteness more generally, adds texture to these survey findings. In both states, white Democrats and Republicans assigned different meanings to their white racial identity, which helps explain why they had such divergent views of discrimination against whites in the United States. The white Democrats we interviewed explicitly articulated privilege as a key component of

Figure 4.9 *Are Whites Discriminated against in the United States? Predicted Probabilities among White Respondents, by State and Party*

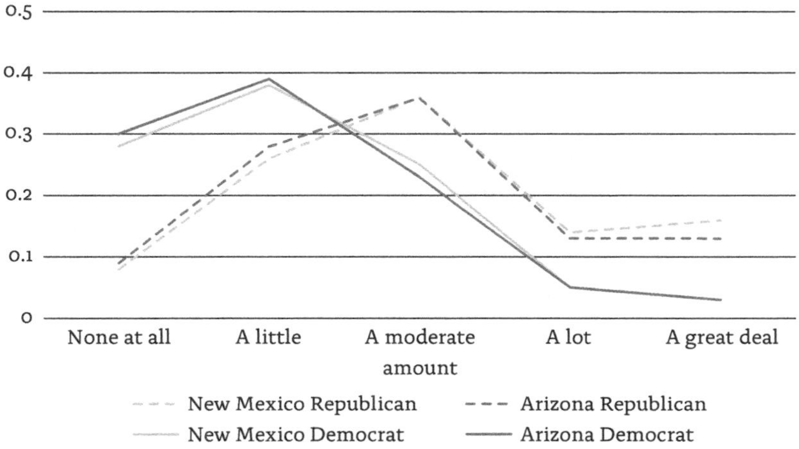

Source: Survey of Immigration and Belonging (Dovidio et al. 2016).

being white in the United States. Far from celebrating this privilege, like Nicole Cottrell whom we cited earlier, they viewed it as a problematic part of a racial system that confers material and psychological benefits on those who can claim membership in the white category. Roy Cottrell was a forty-five-year-old small-business owner, political independent, and self-described liberal (and husband of Nicole Cottrell). He put it in blunt terms: "I don't want to sound sexist or racist, but being a white man in America is like winning the lottery. It truly is, because life is just easier for you." That notion of whiteness as unearned privilege seemed particularly apparent because of the political moment—one defined by the politics of Donald Trump—in which recognition of white privilege seemed to have moved from academic conference panels to mainstream political discourse. For some respondents, it was this political moment, as well as their relationship with nonwhites, that spurred them to see their own racial identity as a privilege. Take, for example, the response of Bob McElroy, a white, sixty-one-year-old teacher, political independent, and self-described liberal from New Mexico, when we asked whether his background had ever been an advantage to him:

> I would say that as a white male, I have white privilege. I carry that white privilege with me everywhere I go. It's structural. It's institutionalized in our society, unfortunately. So the fact that I'm

Irish per se, or of Irish descent, other than interesting conversation, I don't know that that in and of itself gives me an advantage. When you look at the history of immigration in our country, the Irish of 1850 are the Hispanics of today. In 1850, nobody wanted the Irish to be here. And why were they here? Because of the potato famine in Ireland. Two million people died and two million more immigrated to the U.S. because Ireland was starving to death. So you came here because you could eat. They were the dishwashers and gardeners of the 1850s, and they started that cycle of education and social advancement. And we've seen every wave of immigrants do that. The immigrant wave of the late 1800s and early 1900s, the Irish and the Germans and all those, they came over and they were the grunts. They had to do all the crappy, manual labor jobs. So then they sent their kids to school and their kids get better jobs. We saw that after World War II. We saw this huge wave of Asians who were the gardeners and dishwashers. To me, right now it's the Hispanics' turn in the barrel, so to speak. Again, I have privilege by being a white male, but that doesn't have anything to do with being of Irish descent. I just carry that white privilege with me by being a white male, whether I recognize it or not. And that's structural.

Brody Faulkner, a forty-two-year-old web developer and registered Democrat in Arizona, used his best friend, who had Mexican ancestry, as a reference point for making sense of his own white racial identity and its concrete benefits:

White privilege to me, I feel like in a lot of cases if I were to go to an interview for something and I walk in, I would probably be more inclined to perhaps get a job. . . . And that's just one of those stereotypes [that minorities are not qualified] that some people believe. I don't think everyone does, but I think it's stupid to say, "Nobody does that anymore." My best friend is Mexican, and he said that he's had girlfriends—and this was in Texas in the Panhandle—that her parents made her break up with him or refuse to let her date him because he was Hispanic. So you see those things. I've run into homophobia absolutely. But as far as my appearance, I've never run into issues like that. But I'm sure every minority has at some point or another. That's what I would say is white privilege. I've never had a moment where I've said, "Man, being white has cost me this."

Brody's assertion that being white had never cost him anything captures the logical extension of recognition of white privilege, which is that there is no discrimination against whites in the United States. This form of white racial identity among white liberals—one wrapped in a critique of privilege and injustice—further reflects the patterns of a broader division in views of white racial identity as identified by the political scientist Eric Kaufmann, which we discussed earlier.[41]

White Republicans are on the other side of this divide. As our survey findings reveal, white Republicans did not see things the same way as white Democrats. Those we interviewed were aware of racial differences, but they did not use the language of white privilege that Democratic whites invoked when talking about their racial identity. Few were as explicit as Mark McEnery, a thirty-one-year-old lab researcher and registered Republican in Arizona, in articulating the connection between the Republican Party and white racial identity:

> I think just generally I feel like the Republican Party is kind of looking out for the average white person. So I'm like, "Well, that's me." Whereas when I listen to liberal politicians, I'll be honest: when I hear Hillary Clinton talk, I feel like, "I do not identify with you at all." I feel like what she's saying is she's looking out for the little guy. Which I can appreciate that, but I'm like, that's not what I am. You're looking out for the minorities, blacks, women, gay rights. I'm not gay, I'm not a minority. So, I feel like, in that sense, I feel the left is looking out for a certain demographic, and I'm not those things. I can appreciate those things, but I'm over here. And I feel like this party more represents what I am and they're looking out for my interests more. So, I naturally identify with what they're saying more often.

Other research shows that Mark's sentiments reflect a larger trend in racial identity and party identification. As the political scientists Marissa Abrajano and Zoltan Hajnal have shown, the Republican Party has become increasingly attractive to white voters in large measure because the party's stance on immigration makes it seem like a logical home for U.S.-born whites.[42] Even more than that, Mark suggested, the Democratic Party's explicit recognition of minority groups appeared to come at the expense of whites and made it seem a less welcoming political home for people like him.

And yet, where Democrats saw white privilege, Republicans saw their race as mostly a nonfactor in their lives. But when they did see their racial identity as salient, they saw themselves as victims of the critique-oriented version of white identity that animated the white racial identity of liberal Democrats and independents.[43] They saw whites as a group that experiences disadvantages in certain aspects of life, like college admissions and hiring. Mark McEnery's wife, Jennifer McEnery, a thirty-one-year-old homemaker and registered Republican from Arizona, told us, "I almost feel like when you're applying for college and things, it's better to be a minority. So being a typical white Caucasian girl, it's not necessarily a favorable [factor]." Asked whether that ever felt like a disadvantage for her, she said, "Yeah, so it would be like that. If you're Chinese and you're applying for college, they want a variety of people, so they're gonna have a leg up probably. So, therefore it would be a disadvantage."

Jennifer was seemingly unaware that Chinese ancestry generally does not qualify an applicant for most affirmative action programs at colleges and universities. But her comments capture the prevailing belief, especially strong among Republicans, that nonwhites may be unfairly getting ahead.[44] This belief is at the heart of racial resentment: the belief that racial minority group members make unfair demands and therefore violate traditional American norms like individualism and self-reliance.[45] What our survey and interviews reveal is that such resentment increases the salience of one's whiteness. Max Hellman was a forty-seven-year-old restaurant manager and conservative Republican in Arizona. He spoke glowingly about the diversity in his industry. But he echoed the view that being white posed potential disadvantages for whites in the United States today. Max told us that he believed that his father, a former engineer, was pushed out of his job because affirmative action policies mandated that his father's company hire minorities. Max added that he believed misplaced perceptions of widespread racism continue to put whites like him in an unfavorable position:

I feel like my grandparents' generation was probably very, very racist. I think that was the generation to me that was truly racist.

I remember my grandpa making racial jokes all the time. I feel that my parents' generation is where you had the '60s sort of evolution. You had Martin Luther King, you had Vietnam, all these things that happened in my parents' generation. . . . And I definitely felt like, as we had really started to make this full sweep of getting rid of racism, I really felt like we had turned that corner with my kids' generation. . . . And for some reason, the last five or six years, all of a sudden racism has just blown up on the world. And I feel that being a white male is almost a negative right now in some social circles. You're considered, whether you are or not, to be . . . I don't know. Things should be easier for you or something like that. And I don't think they are. I almost think because of that, they've become more difficult. When you go into job interviews, some people are just like, "We're looking to hire a female." Or someone from another country or another skin color or whatever. I almost feel like it's almost made this reverted process back to almost 1950. So yeah, I don't feel that being a white male is necessarily a great thing right now.

In many ways, what we heard about the nature and perceived significance of white racial identity is reflected in larger political trends that have been under way in American society for decades. For precisely the reasons Max stated, some whites see their own racial identity as a disadvantage.[46] Over time, a growing number of whites, particularly those who identify as conservative or Republican, have said that there is significant discrimination against whites in the United States, and whites increasingly display resentment toward minority groups for what they believe are unfairly obtained economic gains.[47] Max's comments mirror those trends and give voice to our survey finding showing that white Republicans are more likely to see discrimination against whites in the United States.

Conclusion

Even though whites in Arizona and New Mexico are not the targets of immigration policies that materially and symbolically shape the lives of immigrant and U.S.-born Latinos, the policies may still impact whites symbolically. The key question here is, to what degree does living in these policy contexts shape their sense of belonging in their state, and in the United States as a whole?

We find that the immigration policy climate is one ingredient in a mix of factors that shape a sense of belonging. Although we find that there can be some cost to feelings of belonging, we also find that this cost is not uniformly associated with one type of climate; that the cost itself still leaves most whites in both places exhibiting high levels of belonging; and that the state immigration policy context does not affect whites' sense that they belong in the United States. Further, we find that the impact of the state immigration policy climate is sometimes conditioned by partisanship; for example, white Arizona Democrats feel a diminished sense of belonging because of anti-immigration policies as well as other conservative measures in the state. Unwelcoming immigration policy is incompatible with their party identity, which is increasingly built on a version of white racial identity that is partly defined by more accommodating views on immigration and race.[48]

On the whole, the welcoming immigration climate in New Mexico does not appear to support the notion that it threatens the status of the state's white residents. Although we found that white Republicans in New Mexico perceived more anti-white discrimination than other groups in the state, it was our *one* finding of that nature across fifteen dependent variables. Indeed, whites in New Mexico generally took pride in being from their state and often relished drawing favorable comparisons with their neighbor to the west. If anything, we conclude, Arizonans pay a price for their state's unwelcoming policy climate. Not only did we find in the previous chapter that Arizona's Latino residents felt alienated, but our findings in this chapter show that white Democrats in the state felt the same way.

There is reason to believe that welcoming policies may have similar impacts in other places as well. New Mexico certainly has attributes that make it stand out from other states. But its welcoming immigration policies, and the responses to them of white and Latino residents, are attributes that the state shares in common with other states, cities, and counties across the United States that have implemented welcoming policies. Even though New Mexico clearly has a history that sets it up for success when the goal is to have people of all backgrounds feel included, there are good reasons to believe it is not unique. There are plenty of other places in the country that have similar histories of comfortableness with diversity, as well as once homogeneous places that have found ways to welcome immigrants and at the same time defuse alienation among members of the host community.[49]

Nonetheless, there is still a question of whether the history of New Mexico is such that residents would be immune to changes in the policy climate. What would happen to their sense of pride and belonging if their state switched gears and opted to become more like Arizona? And given the degree of comfort we found among Republicans in Arizona, it is reasonable to wonder how much their sense of belonging might be affected negatively if leaders there decided to shift toward a more welcoming approach. Or perhaps, like the rural residents whom Lay studied, they would ultimately feel at home and comfortable even if they lived in a place that welcomed immigrants. Thus far, we have made the case that states have a lot to gain and not much to lose if they pursue a welcoming approach to immigration, but our examination has focused on current conditions in states with very different histories. How would white and Latino residents of Arizona and New Mexico respond if there were a shift in their state's approach to immigrant reception? We turn to that question in the next chapter.

5 WHAT IF THE IMMIGRATION CLIMATE WERE CHANGED?

Our survey findings and interviews, discussed in chapters 3 and 4, point to state immigration policy as a key influence, though not the only factor, in the different experiences of Arizona and New Mexico residents. While those data are informative in their own right, they stop short of addressing an important question: Does living in an environment that is welcoming or unwelcoming to immigrants *cause* individuals to feel a greater or diminished sense of belonging? To answer this question, we turn to data from an experiment embedded within our telephone survey that permits us not only to examine how Latinos' and whites' perceptions of a welcoming or unwelcoming immigration context *relate* to their feelings of belonging but also to determine whether a welcoming or unwelcoming context *causes* those feelings. Because immigration policies are cues from which individuals draw inferences about whether they belong, the experiments allowed us to present respondents with that cue and to assess its effect on their perceptions of their place within the state.[1]

Our experimental findings demonstrate that the type of state-level immigration policy—either welcoming or unwelcoming—has a causal effect on belonging that is independent of other influences. Hearing that state policymakers were considering the adoption of welcoming state-level immigrant policies led to a greater sense of belonging among a large swath of respondents. Notable exceptions included U.S.-born Latino and white Republicans; both groups showed depressed feelings of belonging as a result of welcoming state immigration policy. These patterns were similar for both Arizona and New Mexico residents. We replicated these findings in a separate experiment with U.S.-born white and Latino respondents recruited from across the United States.

Our in-depth interviews further explored how respondents thought about state immigration policies. Notably, differences in people's views were more closely linked to their political ideology and partisanship than to their ethno-racial background. The interviews showed that, regardless of their state of residence, Democrats and Democratic-leaning independents saw welcoming policies as a way to integrate immigrants and reap the full economic benefits of immigration and diversity. Among Republicans, we heard concerns that welcoming policies might attract more immigration. And yet, in explaining their position, these same respondents also voiced support for policies that would make it easier for unauthorized immigrants already here to legalize their status. The interviews illuminate the complex thinking that underlies attitudes toward policies intended to welcome immigrants.

Together, findings from the two experiments and from the interviews reveal that the adoption of statewide policies that welcome immigrants may have broader support across constituent groups than public discourse suggests. In contrast, states' adoption of unwelcoming immigration policies may alienate a significant segment of the population—not only Latino immigrants but also Democratic and Democratic-leaning U.S.-born Latinos and whites. It appears that the conventional wisdom about the polarizing and ethno-racially divisive effects of immigration policies is overstated. With a majority of whites nationally identifying as either Democrats or independents, welcoming immigration policies are likely to have direct and spillover effects that can promote, rather than deter, national unity.

Testing the Power of Policy Experimentally

For all of their demographic similarities and entwined statehood histories, Arizona and New Mexico differ across many dimensions beyond their prevailing immigration policies. Even though insights from our survey and interviews all point to each state's policy approach to immigration as the key factor in respondents' differing experiences, they do not establish whether state immigration policies directly *cause* differences in people's sense of belonging. It could be that individuals prefer to live in states where the climate for immigrants aligns with their personal views. If that is the case, then the differences we observed might be due to self-selection. People who feel more warmly toward immigrants and who might themselves benefit from more welcoming immigration policies may choose to reside in New Mexico because of its history of greater tolerance toward immigrants, whereas those who are more reluctant to embrace immigrants and who have less to gain from welcoming immigration policies may opt to reside in Arizona. If this is the case, our evidence describing differing responses may have more to do with respondents' choice of state of residence than with the influence of enacted state policies.

Because these multiple possible interpretations have very different implications for social policy, we conducted controlled experiments aimed at exploring whether state-level immigration policies and the discourse that accompanies such policies can *cause* differing feelings of belonging like those we observed across the two states in the cross-sectional data presented in chapters 3 and 4. The power of an experiment is that because the intervention that describes a policy as welcoming or unwelcoming is the only element that varies between groups when it is introduced, it isolates the effect of the intervention on how people respond. This is not to say that culture and history are unimportant, but that an experiment of this type can establish that the welcoming or unwelcoming nature of the immigration policy independently influences people's responses—and particularly their sense of belonging, the focus of our research.

We embedded the first experiment at the end of the survey. We randomly assigned respondents to read information about proposed state policies that varied in how welcoming they were to immigrants. Because the survey and embedded experiment drew from people who resided in just the two states of Arizona and New Mexico, we conducted a second, similar experiment with a sample of people recruited from across the United States. Although the national sample was not representative of the national population, it included Latinos and whites from a large number of states. In addition to observing the effects of different immigration policies in these experiments, we considered the effects of respondent characteristics, including ethnoracial identity, state of residence, country of origin, and political orientation.

In other research that used convenience samples of participants from different parts of the country, we found that people's attitudes toward immigrants and immigration policies are influenced by what they think others in their community feel about immigrants.[2] Learning how others feel about immigrants communicates a norm—that is, a social standard within a community—about how immigrants *should* be treated. In that work, we constructed fictitious headlines that suggested state residents were rallying in support of state-level policies that either supported immigrants (a welcoming climate) or discouraged immigrants (an unwelcoming climate). We found that whites who read in a newspaper headline that residents of their state were rallying in favor of supporting immigrants subsequently displayed more favorable attitudes toward immigrants generally, and toward Latinos specifically, than did those who read a headline about a rally discouraging immigrants.

Can Immigration Policy Context Determine How Residents Feel about Their State: An Embedded Experiment in the Survey with Arizona and New Mexico Residents

We used a similar experimental approach to study whether the immigration policy context in Arizona and New Mexico was a cause of Latinos' and white residents' feelings about their state.[3] We conducted the experiment when the Trump administration was adopting national policies to deter immigrants and to slow immigration. These policies included a zero-tolerance policy that resulted in the separation of migrant children from their parents. One of our core theses is that even within a context of draconian, unwelcoming national policies, state policies can have a robust impact both on the immigrants directly targeted by the policy (the target population) and on U.S.-born Latinos (a collaterally affected group) and whites (a symbolically affected group). Given the proliferation of a range of welcoming and unwelcoming state policies, the specific effect on these groups should vary according to a state's overall policy approach, either welcoming or unwelcoming.

Besides its direct administrative functions, state-level immigration policy can have broader symbolic effects on state residents.

Of particular relevance to our investigation, it can influence the way people think about themselves in relation to their state—their sense of whether they belong in the state. The process of instituting a policy and the politics and media attention that surround it communicate and shape both current and future public opinion, through "bottom-up" influences as well as "top-down" ones. Simply learning that a large percentage of the population in a state feels a particular way constructs what individuals see as normal and normative, how they perceive different groups, and how they feel about themselves. As we discussed in chapter 1, restrictive U.S. citizenship laws in the late nineteenth and early twentieth centuries reinforced an ethno-racial hierarchy that favored people from northern Europe and defined citizenship as a right for individuals classified as "white." These laws conveyed who belonged and who did not as a function of their national origins and ethno-racial group membership.[4]

Even when public opinion remains divided, immigration policy endorsed by political and social leaders carries particular psychological meaning and impact. Leaders have unique influence because they signal a common purpose to followers who define themselves and their group in the image of the leader.[5] Leaders influence not only perceptions of what is, but also beliefs about what should be.

Our experiment involved the representative samples of residents in Arizona and New Mexico (630 U.S.-born Latinos, 324 foreign-born Latinos, and 906 U.S.-born whites) whom we recruited for our survey, as described in chapters 3 and 4. After completing the relevant survey items, these same respondents read descriptions of proposed state policies written to reflect either a welcoming or unwelcoming context for immigrants and then were asked questions that gauged their emotional reaction and sense of belonging in the state. Because participants may have had different understandings of what their state's *actual* policy was, we introduced people to a *proposed* policy that varied in how welcoming it was to immigrants. Random assignment of respondents to the welcoming or unwelcoming condition allowed us to infer whether reading about differences in state context produces different sets of psychological responses, a causal relationship that only experimental data can address.

In the "welcoming" immigration policy condition, half of our total sample of whites (all U.S.-born) and Latinos (a mix of foreign-born and U.S.-born) were assigned to read that lawmakers in their state were considering new policies that would provide noncitizens with more social services, require bilingual government documents, and create state-issued identification cards. Those in the other half of the sample were assigned to consider "unwelcoming" state policies being considered by state lawmakers that would restrict noncitizens' access to social services, emphasize English-only laws, and require employer verification of immigration status. (See the online appendix for details about the experimental stimuli and the post-experiment questionnaire measures.) Immediately after participants read the welcoming or unwelcoming proposal, we asked them to report how they felt in response to the proposal.[6] We also asked respondents how the policies would affect their sense of belonging.[7]

In this experiment, respondents' state of residence did not systematically affect the results: respondents in Arizona and New Mexico reacted to the two proposed immigration policy reforms in similar ways. While at first glance this result appears inconsistent with our findings from the survey showing substantial differences by state, it is actually conceptually consistent with our main thesis that state-level policies significantly shape individuals' responses to immigration. That is, residents of Arizona and New Mexico learned the same information about the proposed position on immigration by lawmakers in their state, and they responded in the same way, demonstrating that the proposed policy affected their in-the-moment response, independent of existing state, federal, and local positions. Despite their vastly different approaches to immigrant policy, the immediacy of a new proposal may override residents' prior views regardless of the status quo in their respective states. Our findings suggest that by enacting policies, even ones that depart from current practice, leaders can influence how residents respond to immigrants in their state.

The results of this experiment demonstrate the power that states have to construct policies that can powerfully shape how residents feel about their place within the state. The information we provided about the impending policy affected respondents in similar ways, regardless of whether they were residents of Arizona or New Mexico. Because key findings are similar for those who reside in Arizona and those who reside in New Mexico, we present these findings combining both states. Specifically, we discuss the responses of foreign-born Latinos, U.S.-born Latinos, and whites to welcoming compared to unwelcoming policies, as well as any differences that might occur within these groups related to their political preferences.[8]

Overall, exposure to information that state leaders were thinking about adopting welcoming state-level immigrant policies produced more positive feelings and generated a greater sense of belonging than did learning that state policymakers were formulating unwelcoming policies. Thus, people in both Arizona and New Mexico generally found the possibility of a welcoming policy for immigrants more satisfying and appealing. Because this study used an experimental design, we can conclude that learning about the welcoming policy, compared to the unwelcoming policy, *caused* a more positive reaction.

However, not all groups of respondents embraced the welcoming immigration policy equally. Our large sample allowed us to look at the effect of learning about a welcoming versus an unwelcoming policy separately for foreign-born Latinos, U.S.-born Latinos, and whites. Within each of these groups, we were also able to break down the findings by political party identification (Democrat, Republican, independent). Doing so reveals distinct trends by political party, and our interviews uncover even more nuance regarding partisanship and responses to proposed policies. Some of our in-depth interview respondents espoused views and policy preferences that did not necessarily align with those articulated by the political party they identified with. Other interview respondents were comfortable calling themselves liberal or conservative but were reluctant to claim an affiliation with a political party.

FOREIGN-BORN LATINOS: SUPPORT ACROSS THE BOARD

The results from our embedded experiment suggest that the unwelcoming policy regime in Arizona and the welcoming context in New Mexico may indeed have caused the types of reactions we heard among Latinos in the two states in earlier chapters. The response of foreign-born Latinos bears out their position as the target group of immigration policy. They felt more positive and displayed a greater sense of belonging after learning that their home state might adopt

Figure 5.1 *Effect of State Immigration Policy Manipulation and Party Identification on Foreign-Born Latinos' Positive Feelings about Their State (Arizona/New Mexico Sample)*

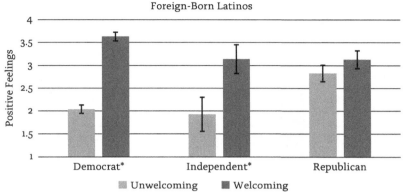

Source: Survey of Immigration and Belonging (Dovidio et al. 2016).
* Indicates meaningful differences for each group across the two experimental conditions (statistically significant at $p < .05$).

a set of new policies designed to welcome immigrants. Figures 5.1 and 5.2 show how foreign-born Latinos felt about the possibility of more welcoming or unwelcoming state policies.

Specifically, foreign-born Latinos reported more positive feelings about the welcoming proposal relative to the unwelcoming proposal (figure 5.1). This is perhaps not surprising, as foreign-born Latinos are the group that would be most directly affected by any immigration policy regime. Breaking down the responses by party identification did little to change the overall picture. How foreign-born Latinos felt about the proposed policies was consistent across the political spectrum, with those reading about welcoming policies consistently displaying more positive feelings than those reading about unwelcoming policies. This pattern held whether they identified as Democrats (mean = 3.63 versus mean = 2.04), independents (mean = 3.14 versus mean = 1.93), or Republicans (mean = 3.13 versus mean = 2.83).

As illustrated in figure 5.2, foreign-born Latinos also displayed a greater sense of belonging in their state when they learned about the welcoming policy, compared to their reaction to the unwelcoming policy. This effect of welcoming policies leading to a greater sense of belonging than unwelcoming policies occurred across the political

Figure 5.2 *Effect of State Immigration Policy Manipulation and Party Identification on Foreign-Born Latinos' Sense of Belonging in Their State (Arizona/New Mexico Sample)*

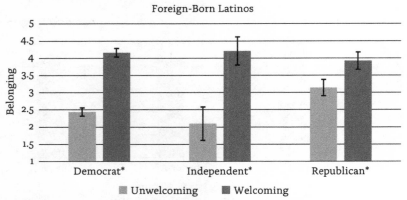

Foreign-Born Latinos

Source: Survey of Immigration and Belonging (Dovidio et al. 2016).
* Indicates meaningful differences for each group across the two experimental conditions (statistically significant at $p < .05$).

spectrum: Democrats (mean = 4.16 versus mean = 2.44), independents (mean = 4.21 versus mean = 2.10), and Republicans (mean = 3.92 versus mean = 3.14). While not surprising, these results perhaps reveal the practical and symbolic impact on foreign-born Latinos of political rhetoric about immigration policy. Among the ethno-nativity groups in our sample, it is this group that was most likely to feel the consequences of both welcoming and unwelcoming policies. The findings lend further credence to the notion that Latino immigrants see themselves as direct targets of immigration policies.

U.S.-BORN LATINOS: DIVIDED BY PARTY IDENTIFICATION

Legally speaking, U.S.-born Latinos are American citizens. However, their family backgrounds can vary substantially. Among U.S.-born Latinos in Arizona and New Mexico are those whose parents immigrated to the United States as well as those whose families have been in the United States for multiple generations—in some cases

Figure 5.3 *Effect of State Immigration Policy Manipulation and Party Identification on U.S.-Born Latinos' Positive Feelings about Their State (Arizona/New Mexico Sample)*

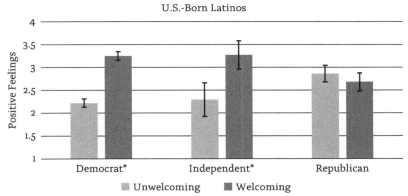

Source: Survey of Immigration and Belonging (Dovidio et al. 2016).
* Indicates meaningful differences for each group across the two experimental conditions (statistically significant at $p < .05$).

(especially in New Mexico) back to a time when the Spanish crown claimed authority over what is now the U.S. Southwest. Immigration policy generally has less direct effect on individuals the further away they are from the original immigrant generation.[9] U.S.-born Latinos thus respond to immigration policy as a collaterally affected group.

In chapter 3, we showed that U.S.-born Latinos perceived Arizona and New Mexico as different contexts when it came to how immigrants were received, and that state immigration policies played a part in shaping their sense of belonging, although Democratic and Republican Latinos differed some in their reactions. The experiment largely supports that picture. Figures 5.3 (positive feelings) and 5.4 (belonging) show how U.S.-born Latinos responded when they learned about proposed state policies that were either welcoming or unwelcoming to immigrants.

Much like foreign-born Latinos, U.S.-born Latinos when presented with a welcoming policy generally had more positive feelings and reported a greater sense of belonging than those presented with an unwelcoming policy. However, within this group, unlike foreign-born

Figure 5.4 *Effect of State Immigration Policy Manipulation and Party Identification on U.S.-Born Latinos' Sense of Belonging in Their State (Arizona/New Mexico Sample)*

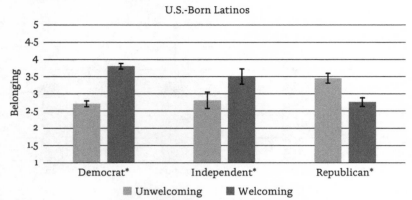

U.S.-Born Latinos

Source: Survey of Immigration and Belonging (Dovidio et al. 2016).
* Indicates meaningful differences for each group across the two experimental conditions (statistically significant at $p < .05$).

Latinos, the pattern of findings across the two experimental conditions differed depending on party identification. As figure 5.3 shows, all U.S.-born Latinos, except for Republicans, who saw the welcoming proposal reported noticeably more positive feelings compared to those who saw the unwelcoming proposal. This pattern held among Democrats (mean = 3.25 versus mean = 2.22) and independents (mean = 3.27 versus mean = 2.29). U.S.-born Latinos who were Republicans showed the opposite pattern of response by reporting *less* positive feelings after seeing the welcoming proposal, in contrast to their reaction to the unwelcoming proposal (mean = 2.68 versus mean = 2.86). This difference, however, was small in magnitude and not statistically significant.

Similar findings emerged when we examined how the two policy proposals affected U.S.-born Latinos' sense of belonging in their state (see figure 5.4). Once again, among Latino Democrats and independents, welcoming policies generally produced a greater sense of belonging compared to unwelcoming policies (Democrats mean = 3.80 versus mean = 2.71; independents mean = 3.50 versus mean = 2.81). In contrast, U.S.-born Latino Republicans reported *less* of a sense of belonging when they saw the welcoming proposal compared to when they saw the unwelcoming proposal (mean = 2.76 versus mean = 3.45).

In contrast to Latino immigrants who responded to immigration policies as a target group, political orientation plays a large role in shaping how U.S.-born Latinos who are socialized in the United States respond to policies. As was the case among foreign-born Latinos, U.S.-born Latinos who identified as Democrats or independents displayed responses consistent with that of a collaterally affected group, reporting a greater sense of belonging when the policy was welcoming than when it was unwelcoming (but not as great a sense of belonging as among Democrats and independent Latino immigrants). In contrast to this belonging boost, U.S.-born Latinos who identified as Republicans reported a decline in their sense of belonging when the policy was welcoming versus unwelcoming. In contrast to foreign-born Latinos across the political spectrum and to U.S.-born Latinos who identified as Democrat or independent, the sense of belonging among U.S.-born Latinos who were Republican did not benefit from a proposal that was welcoming to immigrants. In fact, this group expressed a slightly *higher* sense of belonging when the proposal was *un*welcoming to immigrants. If Latino immigrants are targets of immigration policies and U.S.-born Latinos were collaterally affected, Republican U.S.-born Latinos were collaterally affected not because of their ethno-racial origins but because of their political orientation.

WHITES: VIEWING IMMIGRATION POLICY
THROUGH A PARTISAN LENS

Our survey data and in-depth interviews, in combination with recent political science research, indicate that there are significant ideological divides in how whites view immigration.[10] As we saw in the previous chapter, Democratic and independent whites in Arizona responded as a symbolically affected group, expressing a diminished sense of belonging because of the state's historically right-leaning politics and policies, including the spate of unwelcoming immigration policies of the last two decades. Conversely, Republican whites in New Mexico reported a weaker sense of belonging in a state that has historically welcomed immigrants, a pattern that surfaced more

Figure 5.5 *Effect of State Immigration Policy Manipulation and Party Identification on U.S.-Born Whites' Positive Feelings about Their State (Arizona/New Mexico Sample)*

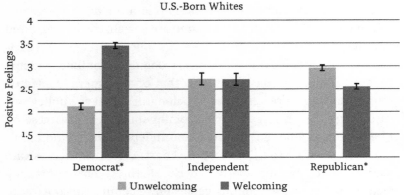

Source: Survey of Immigration and Belonging (Dovidio et al. 2016).
* Indicates meaningful differences for each group across the two experimental conditions (statistically significant at $p < .05$).

strongly in the interviews than in the survey data. Findings from the survey and interviews suggest that when individuals' preferences match the state's immigration policy context, they feel a greater sense of belonging. In contrast, when there is a discrepancy between personal preferences and the state context, people experience a diminished sense of belonging. We saw this especially in Arizona, where many people who supported welcoming immigrants felt more alienated by living in an unwelcoming place than did those who preferred a more restrictive environment did by living in a welcoming place.

But do state-level immigration policies *cause* those different feelings among whites in the two states? Data from the embedded experiment suggest that the answer is yes. Figures 5.5 (feelings) and 5.6 (belonging) show the results of the experiment for U.S.-born whites in our sample. In contrast to the findings for foreign- and U.S.-born Latinos, the effect of policy type (welcoming versus unwelcoming) yielded notably different effects among whites across the ideological spectrum. Among white Democrats, the findings are similar to those among foreign- and U.S.-born Latinos: those who read about a welcoming policy reported more positive feelings than did those who

Figure 5.6 *Effect of State Immigration Policy Manipulation and Party Identification on U.S.-Born Whites' Sense of Belonging in Their State (Arizona/New Mexico Sample)*

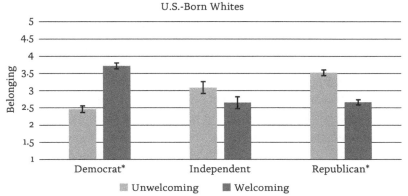

Source: Survey of Immigration and Belonging (Dovidio et al. 2016).
* Indicates meaningful differences for each group across the two experimental conditions (statistically significant at $p < .05$).

read about an unwelcoming policy (mean = 3.45 versus mean = 2.12). This finding is significant both statistically and substantively. It runs contrary to the prevailing message of some recent social scientific analyses of whites' attitudes toward immigration, which suggest that whites as a group will display more negative feelings and a lower sense of belonging in response to a context that is more welcoming of immigrants.[11] It is further evidence that Democratic whites, and to some degree independent whites, are symbolically affected by immigration policy, in that they are affected by whether policies align with their identity as partisan Democrats.

However, as the previous chapter suggests, whites are not uniform in how they see immigration. Whites who identified as Democrats resembled both foreign-born Latinos and most U.S.-born Latinos, in that welcoming proposals elicited more positive reactions than unwelcoming ones did. However, as was the case with U.S.-born Latino Republicans, white Republicans reported *less* positive feelings toward the welcoming policy compared to the unwelcoming policy (mean = 2.53 versus mean = 2.96) (see figure 5.5). Among white independents, there was no observable difference in how they responded to the welcoming versus the unwelcoming policy (mean = 2.71 versus mean = 2.72).

Among whites, the pattern of findings for a sense of belonging, presented in figure 5.6, is similar to the pattern for feelings. Once again, whites' sense of belonging in response to the policies varied by party identification. Democrats who read about the welcoming policy reported a greater sense of belonging than those who read about the unwelcoming policy (mean = 3.72 versus mean = 2.46). In contrast, Republicans who read about the welcoming policy reported *lower* levels of belonging than did Republicans who read about the unwelcoming policy (mean = 2.66 versus mean = 3.52). Independents showed a similar response to Republicans, but the magnitude of the effect was smaller (mean = 2.65 versus mean = 3.09).

Among whites, Democrats and Republicans reacted to our experiment in opposite ways. This finding challenges the conventional wisdom that whites uniformly oppose more immigration. Moreover, contrary to the image dominant in the media, a large subgroup of whites, those who self-identify as Democrats, are receptive to and respond positively to policies that welcome immigrants. And another important subgroup, independents, appear to be less affected by the policy proposals in our experiment.

Can Immigration Policy Context Determine How Residents Feel about Their State? Replication in a National Convenience Sample

In addition to the experiment embedded within our survey of residents in Arizona and New Mexico, we conducted a separate experiment to examine whether the effects found in the two southwestern states would generalize to Latinos and whites nationwide. (For details about our methodology and sample characteristics, see the online appendix.) The procedure we used was identical to that of the experiment embedded in the telephone survey. As in the state-level experiment, participants read that state lawmakers were proposing either a welcoming policy (for example, requiring bilingual government documents, creating state-issued identification cards) or an unwelcoming policy (for example, emphasizing English-only laws, requiring employer verification of legal work authorization). The main

Figure 5.7 *Effect of State Immigration Policy Manipulation and Party Identification on U.S.-Born Latinos' Positive Feelings about Their State (National Sample)*

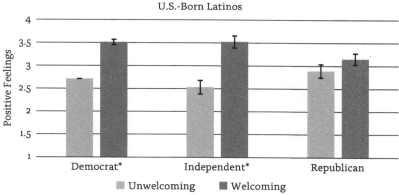

Source: Survey of Immigration and Belonging (Dovidio et al. 2016).
* Indicates meaningful differences for each group across the two experimental conditions (statistically significant at $p < .05$).

outcomes of interest were, again, positive feelings in response to the policy proposal and sense of belonging. (See the appendix for details about the experimental stimuli and post-experiment questionnaire measures.) Following our approach in analyzing the findings from the two-state experiment, we looked at how welcoming and unwelcoming proposals were viewed by U.S.-born Latinos and U.S.-born whites and whether these views varied according to respondents' political party identification.

Findings for U.S.-born Latinos who self-identified as Democrats, independents, or Republicans are depicted in figure 5.7. The findings were largely consistent with those from the Arizona–New Mexico samples. While U.S.-born Latinos, regardless of their party identification, responded with more positive feelings when presented with the welcoming than the unwelcoming proposal, the degree of difference was larger among Democrats (mean = 3.51 versus mean = 2.71) and independents (mean = 3.52 versus mean = 2.53) than among Republicans (mean = 3.15 versus mean = 2.89). As was the case with the first experiment, the difference in reactions to the proposals among Republicans was not statistically meaningful.

The results for a sense of belonging (see figure 5.8) were similar, but with one difference. As we saw elsewhere, U.S.-born Latinos in

Figure 5.8 *Effect of State Immigration Policy Manipulation and Party Identification on U.S.-Born Latinos' Sense of Belonging in Their State (National Sample)*

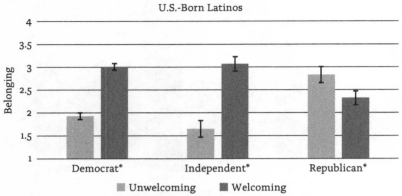

Source: Survey of Immigration and Belonging (Dovidio et al. 2016).
* Indicates meaningful differences for each group across the two experimental conditions (statistically significant at $p < .05$).

the national sample who were Democratic (mean = 3.01 versus mean = 1.93) or independent (mean = 3.07 versus mean = 1.65) reported a substantially stronger sense of belonging when presented with welcoming proposals versus unwelcoming proposals. In contrast, U.S.-born Latinos who identified as Republicans experienced less of a sense of belonging when reading about welcoming policies than they did when reading about unwelcoming ones (mean = 2.32 versus mean = 2.83), and the difference is statistically significant.

Findings for U.S.-born whites' affective response to unwelcoming and welcoming immigration policies are presented in figure 5.9. As in our two-state experiment, the welcoming and unwelcoming policy proposals had divergent effects on U.S.-born white Democrats and Republicans. In the national sample, U.S.-born whites who identified as Democrats responded more positively to welcoming policies than to unwelcoming policies. In contrast, U.S.-born whites who identified as Republicans responded more positively to unwelcoming policies than to welcoming policies. A key difference between the findings from the two-state sample and the national sample is among U.S.-born whites who identified as independents. In the Arizona–New Mexico sample, independents' feelings toward the two proposals were similar, and whatever difference appeared was not statistically significant. In contrast, in the national sample, U.S.-born whites who were independents responded much like those who were Democrats,

Figure 5.9 *Effect of State Immigration Policy Manipulation and Party Identification on U.S.-Born Whites' Positive Feelings about Their State (National Sample)*

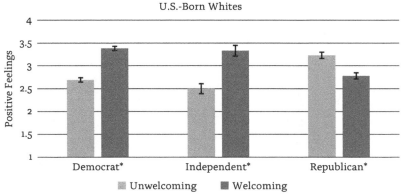

Source: Survey of Immigration and Belonging (Dovidio et al. 2016).
* Indicates meaningful differences for each group across the two experimental conditions (statistically significant at $p < .05$).

with more positive feelings toward the welcoming proposal compared to the unwelcoming proposal (mean = 3.33 versus mean = 2.50).

We found similar patterns when we looked at how reading about welcoming versus unwelcoming policies affected respondents' sense of belonging in their state (see figure 5.10). U.S.-born white Democrats in the national sample reported a stronger sense of belonging in response to welcoming proposals than when presented with unwelcoming proposals (mean = 2.85 versus mean = 2.16). White independents similarly reported higher levels of belonging in response to welcoming policies compared to unwelcoming policies (mean = 2.79 versus mean = 1.91). But, as illustrated in figure 5.10, white Republicans experienced less of a sense of belonging in their state when they considered welcoming proposals than they did when considering unwelcoming proposals (mean = 2.09 versus mean = 3.04).

Findings from the national sample largely replicated the results from the Arizona–New Mexico sample. Political orientation shapes how both U.S.-born Latinos and whites respond to policy proposals designed to either welcome or deter immigrants. Our experimental replication with a national convenience sample thus shows that the effects revealed in the first experiment are not limited to the two border states, Arizona and New Mexico, where immigration issues are particularly salient. Rather, similar psychological and political responses appear to drive both Latinos' and whites' responses to

Figure 5.10 *Effect of State Immigration Policy Manipulation and Party Identification on U.S.-Born Whites' Sense of Belonging in Their State (National Sample)*

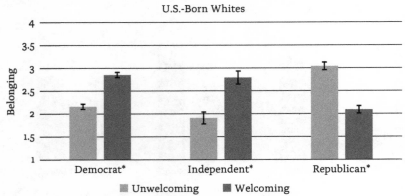

Source: Survey of Immigration and Belonging (Dovidio et al. 2016).
* Indicates meaningful differences for each group across the two experimental conditions (statistically significant at $p < .05$).

policies that shape the context for immigrants across a larger number of states.

The pattern of responses we observed indicate that U.S.-born ethno-racial groups do not have monolithic responses to proposed immigration policies, be they welcoming or unwelcoming.[12] The overall preference appears to be for welcoming policies, which elicit more positive emotional responses and greater feelings of belonging for a large segment of the population. But there are notable differences within the sample, the most important of which fall along partisan lines: Democrats respond more positively to welcoming policies and U.S.-born Latino and white Republicans respond less positively. Nonetheless, the overall picture is that welcoming policies produce a greater sense of belonging for a majority of Latinos and whites in the United States.

Making Sense of Immigration Policy Contexts and the Impact of Policies on the Sense of Belonging

A consistent finding from our survey and experimental data is that political orientation plays a major role in how both Latinos and whites respond to immigration policies. The in-depth interviews we conducted in Arizona and New Mexico offer further insight into why political orientation matters so much. We asked residents whether they would support either a more welcoming or a less welcoming approach to immigration in their state. Interview respondents' reactions added depth to the survey results presented in earlier chapters and the experimental results presented in this chapter.

In line with our survey and experimental findings, the clearest divide in our interview sample was not between whites and Latinos or between foreign- and U.S.-born individuals. Instead, political orientation marked the largest differences in views among interviewees. In general, foreign-born Latinos, Democratic and independent U.S.-born Latinos, and Democratic and independent whites tended to favor more welcoming state-level policies. U.S.-born Latino Republicans, especially those from New Mexico, and white Republicans were not as keen on welcoming policies, and they were more tolerant of unwelcoming policies. However, Republicans' perspectives were characterized more by ambivalence than by unqualified support for or opposition to any given policy approach. Although we asked respondents about welcoming and unwelcoming policies at the state level, most saw state-level policies as entwined with laws set at the federal level. They thus offered views and policy prescriptions that included both state governments and the federal government.

DEMOCRATS AND INDEPENDENTS: SEEING THE BENEFITS AND RESPONSIBILITIES OF WELCOMING POLICIES

Most respondents, much as we observed in the survey and in the experiments, were warm to the idea of state policies that were more welcoming to immigrants. Democrats and independents were especially vocal on this front, regardless of ethno-racial background or national origin. This group of respondents tended to see welcoming policies as positive instruments of integration.

However, we did see some subtle differences in how members of different ethnic groups explained this view. For Latino immigrants and U.S.-born Latinos with close ties to immigrant family members, who viewed themselves as direct targets of immigration policies, those policies resonated personally and often provoked an explicitly emotional response. The responses of Latino immigrants from Arizona were especially poignant, living as they did in a place where the prospect of more welcoming policies ran counter to reality. Take, for example, Catarina Cortez, the school administrator, registered independent, and self-described moderate quoted earlier. Catarina was born in Mexico and became a naturalized U.S. citizen when she was twenty. Her father came to the United States as an unauthorized immigrant and legalized under the Immigration Reform and Control Act (IRCA) of 1986.[13] When we asked her how she would feel if Arizona lawmakers instituted policies that would make things more welcoming for immigrants, she responded:

> I mean, the first thing is, just happy. You know, I feel like it's just treating people with respect, right? It's like everyone has their human rights, and just because someone is born outside of the U.S., that doesn't mean that they deserve a second-class education or second-class treatment or second-class access to health or second-class anything. I think when it comes down to it, it's like we're all human beings and it's our basic human rights. So when we have all these policies that affect people and their access to education or their access to health care, to me, those two things are basic human rights.

Mario Mendoza, the construction worker quoted in chapter 3, was an unauthorized Mexican immigrant in Arizona who identified with Democrats. He spoke for other immigrants in his home state when he reported that more welcoming policies "would be the difference; everyone would feel calmer. I think we could do more things, get a new car, buy a house; the state would have more economic movement."

U.S.-born Latinos also expressed explicitly positive feelings in response to the possibility of more welcoming policies, particularly those with interpersonal networks that included a substantial number of immigrants. Claudia Alejo was a twenty-year-old Democrat and third-generation Mexican American college student from Arizona who came from a socially conservative family. However, she, unlike most of her family, was a registered Democrat and self-described liberal. She was passionate about DACA and immigration policy. Claudia's passion for immigration reform came from having grown up around Mexican immigrants, the children of immigrants, and young people who would become Dreamers. She echoed the emotional response we heard from immigrants: "I would be happy because, like, I feel like it finally, like . . . justice would finally be served, like, in a portion. But just because, like, it would give everyone the same opportunities and stuff like that." Asked how a welcoming policy would affect her personally, she replied: "I don't feel like it would affect me negatively. Like, it would make me feel, like, happier that those things are finally being put in place."

In the experiments, we assessed respondents' emotional reactions to policy proposals that either welcomed or deterred new immigrants. The interviewees' responses lend further support to our assumption that consideration of immigration policy contexts evokes a strong emotional response for our respondents, especially Latinos with connections to the immigrant community. For them, thinking about immigrants' place in their community was not just a theoretical exercise—it was personal. The respondents also showed the power of immigration policies to shape a sense of belonging, not just for the groups explicitly targeted by the policies but also for the collaterally affected groups created by immigration policies.

The support we heard for welcoming policies among Latino immigrants and U.S.-born Latinos with immigrants in their networks was rooted in more than emotional resonance. They saw such policies as offering larger societal benefits in the form of both economic advancement and social integration. When we asked Catarina Cortez what things would be like if Arizona instituted more welcoming policies, she immediately mentioned the economic benefits she thought they would bring for the children of immigrants with whom she worked:

> I feel like our economy would be better. And I feel like there's this talk about the economy and how we need to raise the education levels of Arizonians because by, like, 2020, X amount of jobs will require more than a high school degree, whether it's vocational or associate's or higher. And so, I think that's the rhetoric. . . . We need to make sure that native Arizonians, their education is increased, because that's what we need economically. So, speaking in money and numbers, that's what we need.

Catarina went on to note that welcoming policies would open up greater economic possibilities for the students she worked with, many of whom were DACA recipients—opportunities that would benefit themselves, their families, and the entire state.

For Enrique Saldívar, an immigrant Latino, thirty-seven-year-old warehouse worker, naturalized citizen, and registered Democrat, more welcoming policies would benefit his family, including his wife, an unauthorized Mexican immigrant. When we asked his opinions on specific welcoming policies, Enrique touted the benefits of work permits and driver's licenses:

> Well, I think they should do something where these people can be able to work. I understand there's work permits, which is [what my mother-in-law] has, a work permit. . . . I think they should be able to give a license if you're driving, you should have a license no matter if you're legal or not legal. Whatever, you're already here, might as well just have a license to drive, right?

Enrique noted that driver's licenses offer not just the ability to drive legally but also a sense of comfort and safety for those who possess them:

> They will be able to get status, be able to feel safe. I think that's the biggest thing—just being able to feel safe. . . . I'm pretty sure when they drive from their house to their job they're scared that they get pulled over and then: "Your license, where's your documents?" "I don't have documents." "Well, let's go, I'm taking you with me." They will feel more safe, and we will feel more safe knowing that, you know.

Driver's licenses are one way in which states straddle the line between immigrant and immigration policies. Although most state-level documents determine access to rights, resources, and institutions, driver's licenses as a form of identification mark membership in a state. As the sociologist John Torpey argues, documents issued by governments signal the state's embrace of those who possess the document.[14] Indeed, licenses have both practical and symbolic value. In Arizona, the practical value was abundantly apparent the infamous "crime suppression sweeps" in immigrant neighborhoods conducted by former Maricopa County sheriff Joe Arpaio, who often used an unauthorized immigrant's lack of a driver's license as grounds for arrest, detention, and eventual deportation.[15] Arizona now offers driver's licenses to DACA recipients, a move forced upon the state by a federal court ruling. Still, widespread access to licenses is nowhere on the horizon for Arizona's unauthorized immigrants.

Across the eastern state line, however, driver's licenses for all residents, regardless of legal status, have been a reality since 2003. Although, under Governor Susanna Martinez, the state began issuing licenses bearing markings that distinguished licenses for unauthorized immigrants from other licenses, the state nonetheless continues to provide licenses to all residents regardless of their immigration status.[16] Latinos in New Mexico who supported these policies saw them as consistent with the state's more welcoming culture and as one of the structural pillars that upheld that culture.

The Democratic and independent whites we interviewed could be just as supportive of welcoming policies as the Latinos we heard from, if not more so. However, their relationship as peripheral targets of immigration policy were clear in that they were less likely to provide personal or emotional justifications for their position. Instead, both Democratic and left-leaning independent whites described welcoming policies in terms of improving the economy and reducing social tension. Take the comments of Bob McElroy, the retired teacher and liberal Democrat quoted earlier: he believed that more welcoming policies would be an economic boon by allowing more of Arizona's population to fully participate in the economy:

> I think Arizona could be an economic powerhouse if we took advantage of it. I think, again, it's hypocritical to talk about trade with Mexico when we want to close the borders. . . . If you really opened the door and say, "We want you in because we know you can bring something to us. What is that? What are you gonna bring?" You're bringing your culture. If we're so concerned about immigrants, then why is it that when you go to L.A. or New York on vacation, you say, "Let's go to Chinatown. Let's go to Little Italy." Why? Culture! It's different. It's exciting. It's interesting. So bring that closer. Granted, again, rule of law. Everybody has got to be treated the same. But I really think that if we truly said, "Look, we want you here because we know you can contribute. If you come,

we just ask you to contribute. But come legally and make a contribution to society." We could be an economic powerhouse because
we're vastly overlooking a substantial percentage of our population
in terms of what they could contribute. And if we gave them that
opportunity . . . I mean, if every kid in South Phoenix was educated
the same way that every kid in North Scottsdale is educated, what
could our society be? That's the way I look at it.

Daniel Colbert, the retired military officer and liberal Democrat from
Arizona quoted in chapter 4, echoed Bob's economically driven ratio-
nale for supporting more welcoming policies: "This economy would
boom, number one, just from the pure economics standpoint. This
economy would boom. We could draw people who would then create
opportunities because we gave them access. Then they'll create their
own opportunities."

For these interviewees, welcoming and integrating immigrants
into the community was a fiscal issue. Unlike Latinos, who saw welcoming policies as likely to have an immediate impact on themselves
or their families, white Democrats and independents, as peripheral
targets, had less skin in the game. As a result, they tended to foreground economic concerns. And for the most part, they did not see
welcoming policies as having a negative economic effect on them
personally; immigrants put neither their jobs nor the jobs of their
loved ones in peril. Rather, interviewees' reasoning was focused on
the broader issue of the economic fortunes of the state.

Democratic and independent whites believed that more welcoming policies would not only bring about economic benefits but also
lead to greater social cohesion. These respondents saw welcoming policies not so much as a magnet for immigrants as a means of
facilitating integration for immigrants already in the community—
and they viewed that integration as beneficial not just for immigrants and their descendants but for the state as a whole. Lena Bell
Gladstone, the young entrepreneur, occasional libertarian voter, and
self-described liberal from Arizona quoted earlier, supported more
welcoming policies:

In my experience of being fully welcoming and working to integrate anybody into anything, it's always a win-win situation. If
we come to it with that perspective and the tools that we'll all

communicate and figure it out. Because I think most people are good and most people want to be happy, and they want their family to be happy and they want to live a good life. And that's true for people who are already residents of Arizona and immigrants coming in. So if we were able to find a way for policymakers to make it a more welcoming environment, we have to build some really, really cool communities that will absolutely thrive. And work together without losing the heritage and without losing these really cool customs and things like that, that both sides do. So I actually think it would be a huge winning situation for all of us if that was able to take place and communication was strong, and we had mediators and people to help us integrate in a way that really makes sense for everybody.

While findings from our two-state survey experiment showed no differences across states in residents' reactions to the different proposed policies, the interviews revealed some nuances in how Arizona and New Mexico residents thought about policies that welcomed immigrants. For Democratic interviewees from New Mexico, welcoming policies represented an opportunity to burnish the state's image as a tolerant and open place. Even if they could not identify specific policies already in place, they knew that New Mexico was culturally welcoming and that more welcoming policies would likely reinforce that tradition. Christina Davis, a white, eighteen-year-old college student, registered independent, and self-described liberal from New Mexico, favored more welcoming policies, seeing them as consistent with New Mexico's general stance. She viewed such policies as an opportunity to make the state a national leader in setting the tone for welcoming immigrants:

> New Mexico as a whole already is pretty diverse, but I think it would just get even more diverse. We're such a melting pot of people in New Mexico, and I love that about us. But I'm assuming we'd get mostly Mexican immigrants, because depending on where you live in the world, you get certain types of immigrants. So I would assume we would get Mexican immigrants. I think that more people would learn Spanish and there would be a lot more Spanish spoken around New Mexico. We already do a pretty good job of celebrating certain holidays or bringing notice to different

cultural events. But I think that would just escalate from where it is right now. There's a huge population of these people who celebrate this one thing or who believe in something. . . . So I think their culture is assimilating into what we already have and it would just grow. You would only benefit from growth like that.

We asked her how much she would support a move like that. "I would support a move. On a scale of one to ten, probably an eight. Because I think that a change in policy and going from hate to welcome is a good thing. And I think that would also start movements in other states, even if it was just in the states around us." Rick Schmitz, a white, thirty-two-year-old small-business owner, registered independent, and political liberal from New Mexico, similarly remarked:

> I think it would be great. I think it would be fantastic. I think communities flourish when you have that mindset of, "Hey, let's learn from one another." There's opportunities for growth and relationships and those type of things. I think in that regard, hopefully they do make it more welcoming for people to come here and experience it. I think it's what makes New Mexico beautiful.

This idea that more welcoming policies may prove integrative may not be far from the mark. As the sociologist Abigail Andrews found, when local policies take on a more welcoming hue, immigrants become more civically engaged locally and see incentives to cast themselves as "good immigrants" who deserve the welcome that local governments have rolled out for them.[17]

The Democratic and independent Latinos we interviewed strongly supported welcoming policies. However, they also displayed a civic republican strain in their responses. Recall that civic republicanism emphasizes an engaged polity, one invested in the responsibilities of citizenship.[18] In maintaining that there should be limits to how welcoming any policy was, respondents argued that if the state was going to be welcoming, then immigrants had to offer something in return. This view was especially common among U.S.-born Latinos, but also among Latinos who were naturalized citizens. Both drew on their position as American citizens and members of the ethno-racial group at the center of the debate to articulate their desire to set perimeters around state-level welcoming policies. Consider what we heard from Lara Aguiano, the naturalized U.S. citizen and liberal Democrat quoted in chapter 3, in response to our question about whether she would support policies that would make things more welcoming for immigrants in her home state of New Mexico:

> I think that it would be, it would be good and bad in ways, I think. Because there's only so much work and so much . . . you know, because you have to support these people. They're going to support themselves as much as they can, but they don't have the education. I mean, I'm sure they can work, right, but they don't have degrees, they don't have any, you know. They're coming in without much, just bare minimum-wage jobs, getting by doing whatever odds and ends types of things they're going to be doing. We need people like that if you think about it, right. It's crazy to say, but Americans aren't going to go work in the fields, they're not going to go clean the motel rooms or the hotel rooms, do the yard maintenance at the big corporate, whatever it is, the Chili's, the Applebee's, that these Latinos, Mexican immigrants, come in and do because they're willing to do whatever it takes to earn a dollar.

Adrian Hernandez, a seventy-four-year-old Latino small-business owner, registered Democrat, and self-described moderate, similarly offered support for welcoming policies, while noting that there needed to be limits to the generosity, lest New Mexico experience what he considered the negative consequences of overly welcoming immigration policies seen in California:

> I see policies here like the driver's licenses that are issued for the immigrants that are here that are doing the . . . you know, we . . . we get it. They're here; they're working hard. We're not talking about the criminals, okay? . . . Unfortunately, one cannot exist without the other. But what we do want is that the majority be of working class, not bringing in the illegal drugs or . . . or cri—. . . or criminalization, you know? We don't want that. I see the policy here, here in New Mexico as [favorable] for the immigrants, which I like. . . . There's still gotta be some guidelines. . . . Like everything else, positive cannot exist without negative. . . . The yin-yang kind of effect. . . . You can't abuse the system. You got to respect the system. Look at California, what it did to California, put them

billions of dollars [in] debt; because of that abuse. So there's gotta be guidelines. . . . It still doesn't reject them . . . there has to be limits to everything. You can't abuse the system.

Adrian went on to offer his own family's experience as a reference point, lauding his ancestors for making their way in the United States, he claimed, without any assistance. When considering their support for welcoming policies, Democrats and independents reasoned that welcoming policies needed to be good for the state as a whole, not just for immigrants, and that if immigrants were going to be the beneficiaries of more welcoming policies, then they had to do their part to contribute socially and economically to the state and the country.

Tracy Ryan, a white, forty-seven-year-old education administrator, registered independent, and self-described political moderate from Arizona, similarly offered:

> I think being welcoming, but also it needs to be a balance. To be welcoming also means that our communities support all of that in a good way. So we're not disadvantaging one group over the other. I think to try to strike a balance there. I certainly wouldn't be comfortable being in a state where we had policies that weren't welcoming. Like, "Nope, we're closing up. You're not allowed." I absolutely am opposed to that. I would want something that's welcoming. But again, we have to think about how we can sustain that. What's an orderly and appropriate way to do that, that doesn't put lives in jeopardy, that doesn't compromise the quality of humanity? But also allows our communities to have a sustainable solution in place too? I think that's obviously much more difficult to achieve than just to say it. There's a lot of considerations, but I would certainly want Arizona to be a state that we want diversity, inclusion. We want you to have a home here. But how are we going to support that? I think that's where people get tied up on that too, because they feel like it's pitting one against the other. And [that's] where we get to the divisive aspect.

Democrats and independents were willing to expand rights to immigrants, extending even to citizenship, and they felt that the community should expect to reap some benefit from doing so. As they reasoned, those rights were beneficial not only to the individuals who received them but also to the economic and social well-being of their state. And yet for these respondents, citizenship was not simply a matter of rights—it also entailed responsibilities. If more rights were to be extended to immigrants, they said, not only should those rights have some reasonable limitations, but immigrants would have to embrace the responsibilities that went hand in hand with those rights.

REPUBLICANS: SEEING DRAWBACKS OF WELCOMING POLICIES WHILE LEAVING THE DOOR OPEN TO THE NATIONAL CLUB

Whereas Democrats and liberal-leaning independents viewed welcoming policies as tools of social and economic integration, Republican interviewees saw the same policies as economically and socially costly. Their views reflected a strong version of civic republicanism in which the political community ought to exist for the sake of its members and immigrant nonmembers have no claim to the benefits of membership.[19] The costs they perceived arose primarily from a belief that welcoming policies would attract more unauthorized immigrants who might further deplete community resources. Hardly seeing himself as part of a group that immigration policy targeted directly, collaterally, or otherwise, Dennis Amaya, the Latino small-business owner and conservative Republican in New Mexico quoted earlier, warned against what he saw as the perils of more welcoming policies. While Adrian Hernandez, the moderate Democrat, favored welcoming policies so long as they did not go as far as they did in California, Dennis held up California as an unequivocally negative example in making his case that states should not have welcoming policies at all:

> I'm an American citizen. Thank you, God, for me being born on this side of the border, I guess, okay? Even though the border changed. The border changed on me. I didn't come across, I was already here. . . . But I had to work for everything that I have. I don't think it's fair that people come in and all of the sudden they get a driver license, that they get public assistance. California is a good example. . . . If they are going to get public assistance, well, where

does that public assistance come from? Think of it in the simplest sense. Where does it come from? Does this magic bag of money drop into the coffers of the state to pay for this? How does it come? What's government's role? Government's role is to provide protection and services to its citizens. And in turn the citizens shall be taxed— the taxes. And so, that's how we, meaning the people that have a job, people that are living the American dream that are paying their taxes, are paying for public assistance.

Dennis, unlike Adrian, saw no good reason for adopting any more welcoming policies, no matter how limited. Individuals like Dennis, whose family roots in the United States dated back multiple generations, expressed a strong sense that they had a special claim to political membership in the United States, and that the rights and responsibilities of citizenship should be restricted to legitimate members. Their view that welcoming policies might encourage nonmembers to claim rights that should be reserved for members meant that they could not support welcoming policies that benefited individuals outside the national "club." For the Republicans we interviewed, immigration policy was supposed to be about limiting immigration, and efforts to create a more welcoming context interfered with that aim.

In answering our question about how she would feel about a welcoming policy, the response of Jennifer McEnery, the white homemaker and conservative Republican in Arizona quoted earlier, was typical of the view expressed by other Republican respondents:

I think then everybody would come. I think we'd have even more people come if there was not a stamp [or] trying to make a wall or whatever. I think there would be even more people trying to get in if there was no policies or very lenient policies. . . . I probably wouldn't [support that move]. I'd feel like there's policies and protections for us for a reason. And sometimes they come over and sometimes they're criminals and this and that. I'm okay with pumping the brakes and letting people in but making sure they go through the process. . . . Because if we get tons of people here, then there will be a lot more people and I do feel like that affects the crime.

Among our respondents, a lack of support for welcoming policies did not necessarily mean enthusiastic support for unwelcoming policies. We conducted the bulk of the in-depth interviews during a time when the Trump administration was instituting a "zero-tolerance" immigration policy, which included separating parents from their children and even locking children in fenced cages in detention facilities. That federal response weighed on interviewees as they considered their support for unwelcoming state policies. Later in the interview, when we asked Jennifer whether she would support unwelcoming policies, she temporized at first but eventually talked herself around to saying that she would:

> I guess I'm pretty neutral. I don't want them to be less welcomed, but I don't want them to be more welcomed either. And in Arizona, especially being a border state, we're getting the brunt of it. So if they made it less welcoming? I guess I wouldn't be opposed to it, and I think Arizona obviously would be affected too, and it would be less people because they're filling our schools and stuff too. I don't know. So I would be okay with that too. . . . We'd probably have less Latinos in our neighborhood and our state. So I guess that's how it would affect me. I don't have anything against them. They're good people too, and as long as they can speak my language . . . (laughing)

Jennifer's support for unwelcoming policies revolved around concerns about population and cultural change. As research has shown, fear of cultural change is the main driver behind a desire for more limited immigration, and perceptions of a growing nonwhite population stoke negative attitudes about minorities.[20] If welcoming policies attract more immigrants and unwelcoming policies repel them, then those who have concerns about cultural change—who tend to be Republican—favor the latter.

For interviewees who self-identified as Republican, and for some Republican-leaning independents, the jurisdictional layers of immigration policy were intertwined. They articulated concerns about welcoming policies attracting more immigrants while also voicing at least some support for legalizing the unauthorized immigrants already here. They generally linked state and national policies, reasoning that people whom the federal government determined were unauthorized should not be entitled to any welcoming policies from the state. At the same time, however, they maintained that unauthorized immigrants ought to be given a chance to become legal residents and even citizens. In other words, Republicans opposed welcoming state-level policies and simultaneously endorsed measures that would make it easier for immigrants already in the United States to gain citizenship. Felipe Gastelum, the registered independent and self-described conservative from New Mexico quoted in chapter 3, offered an emblematic perspective:

> We should be unwelcoming to people who are breaking the law and getting in illegally. . . . You just get flooded. That's what's happening in Europe right now. There's just an influx of immigration that is destroying their own culture, and also, you need to go through a certain process to find that. And granted, it's hard. I think the question should be, how do we make it easier to and shorter period of time to get a legal immigration status?

Linda Jones was a seventy-one-year-old white Republican business owner in New Mexico. She also supported unwelcoming policies in New Mexico while simultaneously voicing support for legalizing unauthorized immigrants already in the country. Her remarks highlight how she and other Republican respondents mixed together seemingly opposing views on immigration policy:

> I think the bulk of the state would rise up against [unwelcoming policies]. I don't think it would ever happen. The politicians could never do that. . . . I would support it, depending on how it was done. I don't want people rounded up. I don't think anybody really does, no matter how they characterize it even nationally. I don't think it's appropriate to go round up people that are here for a certain period of time. I'd like to see it done more like if you've been here for a number of years and can show proof of residency and proof you've got a job, you should be able to walk into an office somewhere and sign up for the road to citizenship. And get a legal card immediately. . . . I've seen some houses where they've got fifteen, twenty people in one home. They just rotate in and out as they come across the border. It's like these state houses where they stay.

I've seen them. There's all those people who are not working, they just get on the dole.

As we show in the next chapter, a majority of our sample—and indeed Americans as a whole—support legalization of unauthorized immigrants already in the country, provided there is strict screening to filter out criminals and other undesirables. Respondents opposed to more welcoming policies argued that it was not supposed to be easy for immigrants to make their way into American society, and that the state should not make migrating to the United States unduly attractive through misguided generosity. But migrants already here, they believed, should be given opportunities to overcome the obstacles associated with their legal status that derail their full integration into U.S. society.

Conclusion

The different immigration policy regimes in Arizona and New Mexico have a profound impact on the lives of the people who live under them. Our survey and interview data suggested that Latino immigrants, and most U.S.-born Latinos and whites, feel a greater sense of belonging when state-level immigration policies are more welcoming, but one question lingered: Did differences in state-level immigration policies *cause* differing feelings of belonging among residents of the two states? The experimental data from this chapter have provided further evidence not only that immigration policies shape belonging but that immigrants respond as targets, U.S.-born Latinos as a collaterally affected group, and U.S.-born whites as a symbolically affected group. We also show that the effect of different immigration policy contexts on belonging is largely determined by party identification, an increasingly central part of social identity.

Our findings affirm well-established social science research demonstrating that an unwelcoming or discriminatory climate can diminish feelings of belonging in a community.[21] Our results also affirm that Latino immigrants see themselves as targets of immigration policy who benefit or suffer depending on whether those policies are welcoming or unwelcoming. We find that when foreign-born Latinos were asked to consider the adoption of welcoming policies for immigrants, they exhibited greater positive feelings about their state and a greater sense of belonging than when asked to consider unwelcoming policies. Among Latino immigrants, the results were robust and held up regardless of the state of residence. This is perhaps unsurprising given that state policies directly target and impact Latino immigrants. U.S.-born Latinos, by contrast, are legally protected from state-level immigration policies because they are U.S. citizens by birth. Yet for the most part, U.S.-born Latinos exhibited the response of a collaterally affected group, showing similarly greater positive feelings about their state and a greater sense of belonging when considering welcoming policies.

There were some differences by political party in this group. Democratic and independent U.S.-born Latinos reacted positively to welcoming policies. Republican U.S.-born Latinos responded differently, expressing somewhat more positive reactions to unwelcoming policies than to welcoming policies. Overall, however, most U.S.-born Latinos expressed more positive feelings about their state and felt a greater sense of belonging when considering welcoming policies than they did thinking about unwelcoming policies. These findings support other research, including our survey findings, that show that U.S.-born Latinos, as a collaterally affected group, can feel the sting of unwelcoming immigration policies, especially when their skin color and surname leave them vulnerable to the negative stereotypes related to the nativity and legal status of Latino immigrants.[22] Our findings for U.S.-born Latinos reflect the anticipated collateral effects of proposed immigration policies specifically targeting foreign-born noncitizens.

Most noteworthy are our data regarding U.S.-born whites. Research and public discourse focus on the political rightward turn among whites, which is in some measure attributed to their views on immigration.[23] Following the 2016 election of Donald Trump, who ran on calls for aggressive restrictions on immigration, the public narrative centered on his support from whites. The conventional wisdom began to suggest that whites, as a group, would oppose welcoming immigration policies and that any consideration by political elites of such policies would spur negative feelings and a diminished sense of belonging among whites. Our evidence contradicts this expectation, demonstrating that partisanship divides whites. Democratic whites, a group symbolically affected by immigration policies, consistently exhibited *more positive* feelings about their state and felt a *greater* sense of belonging when they believed that political leaders were considering making their state more welcoming to immigrants. This effect was also evident among independents in the national sample (but not in the Arizona–New Mexico sample). The only consistent deviation from the pattern was among Republicans, who showed *less* positive feelings about their state and felt a *diminished* sense of belonging when primed to believe that policies welcoming immigrants to their state were being considered.

The interviews added to the evidence that welcoming policies have largely beneficial effects on the people who live under them. Democrats and liberal independents, regardless of ethno-racial background, believed that welcoming policies would be an economic and social boon for their state. And yet even those who supported more welcoming policies believed that there should be limits and that the beneficiaries of those policies should be expected to make a positive social and economic contribution. Republicans—both white and Latino—opposed more welcoming policies, fearing that they would attract more unauthorized immigrants and thus have a negative social and fiscal impact on their state. At the same time, however, they called for legalizing unauthorized immigrants who were already in Arizona and New Mexico. They reasoned that if illegality was a problem, it could be solved by making deserving immigrants legal, provided that those immigrants could prove that they did not pose a threat and that they could prove their ability to make an economic contribution.

Not only are welcoming immigration policies likely to receive broader support than public discourse suggests, but they can also have a profoundly positive effect on both immigrants and the established populations that receive them, including a significant proportion of U.S.-born whites. Although it is true that a segment of whites have made a rightward turn in response to immigration, a majority of whites identify as either Democrat or independent.[24] As we have shown, these Democratic or liberal-leaning independent whites, in addition to foreign-born Latinos and most U.S.-born Latinos, are likely to have positive responses to welcoming immigration policies in their state.[25] Such policies proposed by political elites could appeal across groups that vary in nativity, ethnicity, and even ideology to create greater unity in immigrant-receiving communities and could even be scaled up to changes in federal policies that inform the content and welcoming bent of state policies.[26]

Is a sense of unity a long way off? We take up that question in the next chapter by looking at attitudes about federal policy. Our finding that there is a surprising consensus of views about federal immigration policies adds to the conclusion that Latinos and whites in Arizona, New Mexico, and nationally share considerable common ground in their views about immigration.

IMMIGRATION POLICY PREFERENCES IN A DIVIDED UNITED STATES

6

All of the jurisdictional layers of immigration policy in the United States are interconnected: federal policy informs the policies that state and local governments enact, and state measures either extend or restrict rights and access to resources and institutions based on a legal status defined by the federal government. As the findings from the last chapter hinted, when Arizonans and New Mexicans consider potential changes to a state-level immigration policy, their reactions are informed by their attitudes and feelings about federal policy. This chapter offers a closer look into respondents' views about major federal immigration policy debates, including border security, offering a path to citizenship for unauthorized immigrants living in the United States, and offering legal status to people who were brought to the United States without authorization as children. By examining respondents' views on these federal questions in the context of state-level policies, we can gain deeper insight into the immigration debate and the political divide at work within it. The analysis in this chapter also suggests that more welcoming policies at the federal level may be politically viable.

In recent years, media accounts (and some academic discourse, as well) have rendered the contemporary national immigration debate largely through caricatures: on one side white Republicans who are anti-immigrant and pro-border enforcement, and on the other side nonwhite Democrats who are pro-immigrant and advocate open borders.[1] Broad as they are, these caricatures have some basis in reality. In recent years, attitudes about immigration have coalesced around party identification and race. Republican identification, white racial identity, and restrictive views about immigration have become more entwined, and Democratic identification, nonwhite identity, and a preference for more open immigration policies have become more closely aligned.[2]

Drilling down further, however, it appears that whites hardly hold uniform views about immigration. Whites who identify as Democrats tend to favor accommodating immigration policies and efforts to achieve racial justice; whites who identify as Republicans are far more likely to support restrictive policies, though even they are divided.[3] The findings we have presented already and those that we offer in this chapter bear out the existence of strong political divisions. At the same time, our interviews and survey data also reveal that the way individuals grapple with federal immigration policy questions belies the stereotypes on which the contemporary immigration debate relies.

Among our respondents, it is true that white and Latino Democrats, and especially the immigrants among them, wanted more generous immigration policies. But they also thought that border security was necessary. White and Latino Republicans tended to oppose unauthorized immigration and wanted more aggressive immigration enforcement. But they also believed that unauthorized immigrants who had been here for a while and displayed the behaviors of good citizens deserved a chance to legalize. White and Latino Republicans favored a path to legalization for unauthorized immigrants, including Dreamers, provided that they were sufficiently screened and proved their ability to contribute economically and socially. White and Latino Democrats, including immigrants of all legal statuses, voiced similar views (although they were more enthusiastic about legalization and put a bit less weight on screening and demonstrating an ability to contribute).

A similar pattern emerged when it came to the question of border security and immigration enforcement. White and Latino Republicans supported a more muscular immigration enforcement regime, but they also believed that there were practical limits to how far enforcement could go. White and Latino Democrats were less in favor of stricter enforcement, but they also saw a need for border security— a view that was prominent even among respondents who were themselves undocumented.

Taken in sum, there appears to be significant overlap in views about immigration across the political and ethno-racial spectrum. The differences we saw were generally a matter of degree, not of kind. A theme running through what we heard from both Arizonans and New Mexicans was a desire for unity, defined by a shared political status that would allow everyone to participate more fully in civil society. In keeping with the themes of this book, we found little evidence that people wanted to make immigrants feel unwelcome. Put simply, there may be more consensus on immigration policy than current and past national debates imply.

Including the Outsiders Already Here?

As we have noted several times, the layers of U.S. immigration policy work reciprocally in their implementation and enforcement. But they were also entwined in how our respondents articulated their views. Federal policy informed how they thought about policy at the state and local levels, and their experience and perception of policy at the subfederal level influenced how they made sense of immigration policy nationally. Attention to the national policy debate was especially strong during the interview phase of the research because the flurry of policy activity undertaken by the Trump administration was well under way at that time.

The federal policy preferences of whites and Latinos in Arizona and New Mexico hinged on what is perhaps the most perennially pressing issue in immigration policy: unauthorized immigration and the presence of unauthorized immigrants. While some subfederal jurisdictions, including at the state level in Arizona and New Mexico, have established policies that affect the lives of unauthorized immigrants, the most determinative policies are set at the federal level. And yet subfederal jurisdictions have gotten deeply involved in immigration policy because so little has been done to resolve the status of the estimated 10.5 million unauthorized immigrants currently in the United States.[4]

We asked our survey respondents to identify what they thought government policy should be toward unauthorized immigrants now living in the United States. Respondents were offered three choices: (1) "Deport all unauthorized immigrants and send them back to their home country"; (2) "Have a guest worker program that allows unauthorized immigrants to remain in the United States in order to work, but only for a limited amount of time"; or (3) "Allow unauthorized immigrants to remain in the United States and eventually qualify for U.S. citizenship, but only if they meet certain requirements like paying back taxes, learning English, and passing background checks."[5]

Figure 6.1 compares the results from our state-level representative survey with our national, nonrepresentative MTurk survey. Respondents in both of our surveys, whites and Latinos alike, overwhelmingly preferred that the U.S. government offer undocumented immigrants a path to citizenship (a pattern that matches national survey data). Among Latinos, 79 percent in Arizona and 80 percent in New Mexico favored a path to citizenship. Among whites, 62 percent in Arizona and 66 percent in New Mexico were in favor of such a policy.[6]

Our in-depth interview data are consistent with these findings. Indeed, they suggest that consensus around legalization might be even stronger than the survey data indicate. We asked each of our in-depth interview respondents what they thought the federal government should do about unauthorized immigration. Unlike in the surveys, we left it to respondents to give us their views without offering them a menu of fixed responses from which to choose. As in our survey findings, Republican whites and Latinos took a harder line on unauthorized immigration than their independent and Democrat counterparts—and these differences across ideological lines were greater than those associated with ethno-racial origin. Even so, what we heard in our interviews complicated any sort of clean division by party or ideology.

Republicans often stated that unauthorized immigrants had broken the law and that the consequences of breaking the law should be enforced. They thought that unauthorized immigrants who had committed crimes once they were in the United States should be deported, and they were mostly unconcerned about enforcement efforts going too far. However, they also felt that unauthorized immigrants who displayed the right behavior deserved the chance to become members of the American polity. While few offered specific policy prescriptions, the Republicans we interviewed were clear about the principles upon which any legalization should be based: learning

Figure 6.1 *Should the Government Offer a Path to Citizenship for Undocumented Immigrants Living in the United States?*

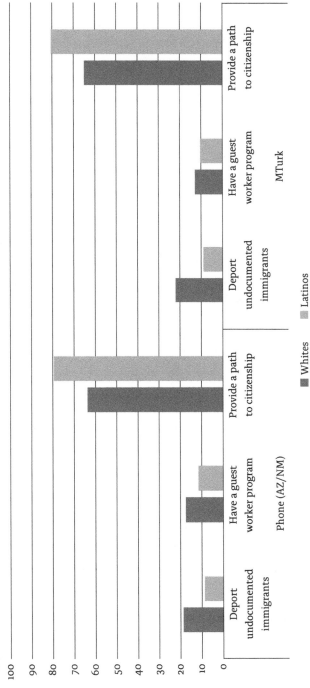

Source: Survey of Immigration and Belonging (Dovidio et al. 2016).

English, paying taxes, having a clean criminal record, making a contribution to U.S. society, and having been in the United States for
some period of time. The first three of these criteria are the backbone
of comprehensive federal immigration reform legislation that has
been debated in Congress for nearly two decades. The fourth criterion
(making a contribution to U.S. society), which was offered by respondents from across the political spectrum but emphasized by Republicans, echoes the notion of civic republicanism discussed in chapters 3
and 4. This tradition emphasizes the participatory responsibilities
of citizenship as the keystone of American identity.[7] If immigrants
could prove their ability to make contributions to U.S. society, respondents reasoned, then they were worthy of citizenship. Interviewees
also saw the fifth criterion—time spent in the United States—as a
key factor in whether unauthorized immigrants ought to be made part
of the polity. Being in the United States for a long time, they explained,
had given immigrants the opportunity to make demonstrable economic and social contributions. As the political scientist Elizabeth
Cohen has documented, time in the United States—*jus temporalis*—has
been a central principle of immigration and citizenship policy going
back to the nation's founding.[8]

For Republicans, *jus temporalis* amounted to a probationary period
during which unauthorized immigrants could prove themselves
worthy of citizenship. Max Hellman, the Arizona hotel manager and
conservative Republican quoted in chapter 4, summarized what we
heard from other Republican white respondents:

> I'm actually okay with [offering citizenship], based on the caveats
> of you've gotta learn the language, or at least the basics of it. From
> an employment standpoint, being able to converse. Paying back
> taxes is important. Taxes is what pays for your streets, it pays for
> your infrastructure. It's been paying for whatever sort of benefits
> you've been receiving up to this point.[9] So it's definitely important
> to do that. . . . You're here, we can deport you and you can come
> back again illegally, or we can deport you and you can begin the
> process. But you're here. You've been here for however long. You've
> proven that you're not a criminal, you're not running drugs. You
> are working and doing all these things, so you are attempting to
> be a fruitful member of society. So let's fix the retro part with your

taxes. Let's make sure we do a background check. With technology it's quick. Yeah, I'm actually okay with something like that.

Some Republican respondents injected economic pragmatism into their reasoning. They believed that the economy relies on unauthorized labor and that any effort to remove these immigrants en masse would be too great an economic disruption for the country to bear. In spite of taking this view, Republicans did not see themselves as going easy on unauthorized immigration. Take, for example, Linda Jones, whom we heard from in chapter 4. Linda had been a New Mexico restaurant owner for the last three decades. By her own admission, she employed unauthorized immigrants, though she had no definitive proof because they showed documents that allowed her to hire them in compliance with federal law.[10] In praising the work ethic and the character of her immigrant employees—in particular a cook who had been working for her for twenty years—she offered a policy solution based on *jus temporalis*:

> I know now that one of them is illegal, but I don't care. If they're there that long, they should have some way to get sponsored by an employer or something, to be made legal. So it's not the immigrants at all, it's just not. I just want them to do it legally and I want the system to be fair so that they can do it legally. But being productive when you get here.

Just minutes after laying out what was virtuous about her employees, she articulated strong support for President Trump and her belief that a wall along the southern border to keep out immigrants she perceived to be taking more from the system than they put in was essential to national security.

Linda was not alone in relying on personal experience with unauthorized immigrants to formulate views on legalization. In chapter 4, we heard from David Kahn, a white retiree and registered independent who said that he leaned liberal but held conservative views on immigration. He recalled families that he knew who were deported under Operation Wetback, a deportation program that sent more than a million mostly Mexican immigrants back to Mexico in the 1950s and early 1960s.[11] He argued that legalization would be good for the economy and lead to greater economic justice for immigrants, whom he believed were often abused by employers. He supported a quasi-legalization program, even as he argued that the United States ought to end birthright citizenship (the policy in the Fourteenth Amendment of the U.S. Constitution that states: "All persons born . . . in the United States . . . are citizens of the United States and of the State wherein they reside"):

> I don't see too many young white folks saying, "Oooh, I want to pick corn." So we needed those people to come in. But the problem was because our work visa, our whole visa system is understaffed, underfunded, so in order to get a visa, you've got to jump through so many hoops. . . . That $25 billion to start a border wall? Complete waste of money. I would rather take that $25 billion, hire new staff to streamline the visa process . . . maybe we need to eliminate the automatic citizen thing for being born here. Just because you're born here, you're an automatic citizen. No. I think it should be if your parents are here legally and you're born here. So whether they're citizens or they're here on a national visa, they have a legal reason to be here, then you become a citizen. I think it will end some of the "birther tourism" that the far right is crying about. . . . They're here, they've got families, they have jobs, many of them own property. So they're paying sales tax, they're paying property tax. The only thing that separates them from me is that I've got a birth certificate. That's it. And I make a little more money because I'm not being abused by an employer.

The desire to extend legal status was mixed in with a desire to restrict some rights, like birthright citizenship, in the views that virtually all respondents expressed about immigration. Far from articulating either pure restrictionist or pure accommodating views about immigration, our respondents' perspectives reflected the ambivalent quality of American attitudes about immigration more generally.[12]

If a hard economic calculation led some white Republicans to favor legalization, others rested their views on softer, but still influential, religious principles. Take, for example, Lorraine Young, a white, thirty-year-old homemaker, moderate Republican, and devout Mormon in Arizona. The breaks she took from the interview to tend to her baby seemed to underscore her tacit ambivalence about immigration and the federal government's treatment of children. On the one hand, she was a conservative Republican who believed that immigration laws had to be followed. On the other hand, her own family's immigrant history and her religious beliefs summoned her to welcome the stranger, a call that rang louder to her because of the Trump administration's child separation policy, which was dominating national headlines at the time of the interview:

> I don't know. It's so hard. I do feel like people should be given a chance to live a better life, 100 percent. . . . Spiritually, I feel like we are all God's children, we are all loved. We should be given a place to feel safe. And I feel for those who are not. I know that it's difficult to let everybody who wants to come to America come to America. It's difficult to distinguish those who want to come to America to do bad things and those who want to do good things. And honestly, I would rather give the benefit of the doubt. I don't agree with how they're handling it now, but I do agree with making the border safe. I do agree making it an easier process that people can apply to be Americans and go through the process. And for it not to be such a treacherous and scary and awful journey for these families that are coming over. I don't have a solution, though! I guess I would just say make the process easier. I wish I had a solution for this, because I was thinking about this this morning. I don't know what the best way is to handle it, but I know that the way we're handling it now [by separating children from their parents] is not.

It was not that Republican whites were opposed to getting tough on immigration. But they counterbalanced that support with the view that unauthorized immigrants, provided that they showed themselves to be good potential citizens, should eventually be brought into the citizenship fold.

The views of Republican Latinos lined up with those of Republican whites. While research confirms that in general Latinos tend to display more accommodating views about immigration, their views are hardly monolithic. Distinctions among them are defined by country of origin, language, region of settlement, and generation since immigration.[13] Many of our Latino respondents, and especially those in New Mexico, had generational roots in the Southwest that reached back to a time before that region was part of the United States, and even before the nation's founding. These Latinos saw their family history as grounds for making claims to membership in the national club that is the United States. That sense of membership enabled them to evaluate any legalization program from the perspective of national insiders. Dennis Amaya, the small-business owner quoted in chapter 5, had a black-and-white view of legal status. For him, unauthorized immigrants had done things the "wrong" way, whereas an authorized immigrant had done things the "right" way. After he laid out that dichotomy, we asked Dennis whether he would favor legalization: allowing undocumented immigrants to stay in the United States and qualify for citizenship if they complied with certain requirements like paying taxes and fines, learning English, and passing background checks. His response highlighted his black-and-white view of legal status, on the one hand, and his support for a path to citizenship for individuals who followed the law, on the other. "I don't have a problem with that either. It's the same. It falls into the same thing that I've been saying. There's rules and there's laws. Follow the rules and the laws. That's what I'm saying. And I think that most of them would be willing to do that. Yeah."

Republicans clearly took a hard line on unauthorized immigration. Nevertheless, their willingness to consider a legalization program seemed to permeate that line.

It was not just Republicans who belied stereotypes of their views on immigration. Whites and Latinos on the left of the political spectrum also displayed views that did not quite square with the stereotypes of Democrats' views on immigration. As our survey data indicated, Democrats were more likely to favor legalization (see online appendix), a pattern that echoed in our in-depth interviews. In those interviews, Democrats indicated that they supported a legalization program not only because they believed that it was the just thing to do, but also because such a program seemed consistent with the country's immigrant legacy.[14] And yet, even as they offered strong backing for legalization, they also supported a screening process that would allow the government to exclude immigrants who might seek to harm the United States. Take the comments of Dustin Agnew, a thirty-five-year-old white advertising specialist and liberal independent from Arizona. Dustin's support for a legalization program rested on similar principles as those espoused by Republicans like Max Hellman: potential recipients needed to contribute to U.S. society.

> Amnesty? I am totally for it. I think if somebody has been through the struggle to uproot their lives and their family to come here and to work in a shadow system, then they absolutely deserve to come out of the shadows and be part of our society. I think anyone that's willing to take the risk and the effort to do something better for their family is absolutely American, no matter what. And so people that come here, it really sucks that somebody has to come here and work on a fake ID or be paid under the table. So yeah, anyone that comes here that's willing to put forth the effort to be a positive member of society deserves to be here. I think that's what we were founded on and that's something we lose sight of.

Even the most liberal Democrat respondents offered caveats when expressing their support for legalization. Ann Myers, the young, white graphic designer quoted earlier, who described herself as very liberal, had worked in restaurants all over the United States. That experience gave her a firsthand look at the lives of the many unauthorized immigrants she worked with:

> I support a very strong path to citizenship. I think that most American citizens probably couldn't pass the citizen test that most people have to take when they come to this country. That's more than enough. I think you should come here and you should be offered a path to citizenship when you come. If we wanted to set up those boundaries and decide that somebody who doesn't, can't be a citizen because of a criminal record, I think those are really valid concerns—that the people that come over aren't a danger to our society. But I think if there's no real giant reason like that, they should just let them come and let them find a place. I don't think we're suffering from a huge overpopulation problem.

Latino Democrats saw eye-to-eye with white Democrats, and also with Republican whites and Latinos to some degree. They supported legalization for unauthorized immigrants, believed that there should be some screening, and also thought that those receiving lawful status should be required to demonstrate an ability to make an economic and social contribution. Independent and Democrat Latinos differed from whites with similar ideological views when it came to the personal nature of a potential legalization. For respondents like Hugo Garcia, a thirty-one-year-old Latino sanitation worker and liberal Democrat whose wife was a DACA recipient in the process of applying for residency, legalization could be life-changing. Echoing what we heard from other Latinos with close ties to the immigrant experience, Hugo reported:

> I feel like they are working and they're contributing. If they break the law, okay—that's one thing. . . . I'm for border security. Yeah. We can't let everybody . . . we can't . . . we can't just . . . it sucks, you know. . . . It's a long process, but let them be here. Let them work to be here as long as they follow the laws and everything. . . . Let's help them out, [the people] that are here, 'cause they've gone through hell to get here and they're going through hell to stay here. Why not let's alleviate it and work on the problem? As a politician, as anybody.

The unauthorized immigrants we interviewed spoke to legalization's benefits for themselves and for the larger unauthorized population. Take Francisco Olmos, a twenty-five-year-old unemployed DACA recipient who was brought to the United States by his parents when he was a child and who identified with the Democratic Party. Although he personally stood to benefit from a legalization program, he saw the larger issue of unauthorized immigration and legalization as thorny for both lawmakers and unauthorized immigrants. He emphasized the need to observe immigration laws while also stating that those who had broken them but were otherwise contributing members of society deserved a chance to be formally included as citizens. Francisco wrestled aloud with the puzzle when he told us:

> This is something that I struggle with every day on how to kind of work this, and I'm sure politicians in Washington and in the states struggle with [it] as well. But I think people that are here and that are working already and that are contributing to social programs with their taxes and stuff like that should be given a chance to have a pathway to residency, citizenship. But they should be legally. Immigrants that want to come to this country should do it legally, because laws are still in place. But as for myself, I didn't really have

a choice whether to come here or not. It was up to my parents. And because of their choices, now I'm stuck with this big kind of like sticker on me where . . . you know, "He's unauthorized. Should he go back because of his parents' actions?" If you want to send me back and that's how you feel, then okay. But I feel like I've given enough to this country, and I've shown that I'm a good enough citizen to be here by working, by going to school, by not committing crimes. There are gonna be a few black sheep in these immigrants that have come here. They've dealt drugs. They've carjacked. They've committed murders. I understand that part. But because of that it shouldn't affect all of the immigrants. The majority are hard-working, honest, and they just want to provide for their families; same as people that grew up here, that were born here. And so, it's a little tough to decide it. But I feel like if you're honest and you're hardworking, you pay your dues, you pay your taxes, you should be able to stay here.

Clearly there were political, ethno-racial, and nativity divides in how respondents viewed a potential legalization program. But for all the divides, there was a fair degree of overlap in how respondents from across the sample made sense of the idea. That overlap was defined by support for a legalization program in general, support for some screening of potential recipients, and, to varying degrees, a desire for the recipients to show that they were willing and able to fulfill the responsibilities of citizenship.

Support for a Dream?

Respondents in our research applied similar logic when they considered the possible legalization of certain subsets of the unauthorized population. The general category of unauthorized immigrants encompasses a wide range of circumstances, including distinctions by mode of entry (for example, avoiding inspection when entering the country versus entering legally and overstaying a visa), country of origin, and even the social circumstances of entry.[15] The legal terms of entry are heavily implicated in the distinctions that respondents made about both legal and social belonging in the nation as a whole.[16]

"Dreamers" are perhaps the highest-profile subset of unauthorized immigrants; most of them were brought to the United States by their parents. Several of our interview respondents were Dreamers, and their comments showed how state-level immigration policies shape the experiences of immigrants. This group of the unauthorized population is also at the center of national policy debates. When in June 2012 President Barack Obama announced the executive directive Deferred Action for Childhood Arrivals (DACA), the fate of unauthorized immigrants who had been brought to the United States by their parents had already been debated in Congress for more than a decade as part of the Development, Relief, and Education for Alien Minors Act, or "DREAM Act." That measure included many of the same provisions as DACA, but went further, offering a pathway to legal permanent residency. The DREAM Act has been introduced in each Congress since 2000 but has never found its way into law. DACA, which granted temporary legal status to undocumented young people brought to the United States as children, was a stopgap. Even so, most assumed that it would remain in place even with a change in the administration. The election of Donald Trump changed that assumption. Candidate Trump promised to rescind DACA, and President Trump did just that in September 2017. Most national polls show that Americans overwhelmingly support the program, even a majority of Republicans.[17] In June 2020, the U.S. Supreme Court ruled that the Trump administration had acted on capricious and arbitrary reasoning and could not terminate DACA. As of this writing, DACA is still active. President Joe Biden signed an executive order on January 20, 2021, his first day in office, to preserve and fortify the program.

Our survey asked each respondent, not about DACA, but about the DREAM Act: "There is a proposal from the federal government to allow people who were illegally brought into the U.S. as children to become permanent U.S. residents under some circumstances. Would you say you strongly favor, somewhat favor, somewhat oppose, or strongly oppose such a proposal?" The results, shown in figure 6.2, are quite similar across both surveys, even though one was administered by phone and confined to Arizona and New Mexico, while the other was online and included a national sample. Figure 6.2 also shows that Latinos and whites alike expressed significant support for the DREAM Act. In both surveys, support among whites exceeded 60 percent while support among Latinos exceeded 75 percent. This

Figure 6.2 *Support for Permanent Residency for Children Brought to the United States Illegally by Their Parents*

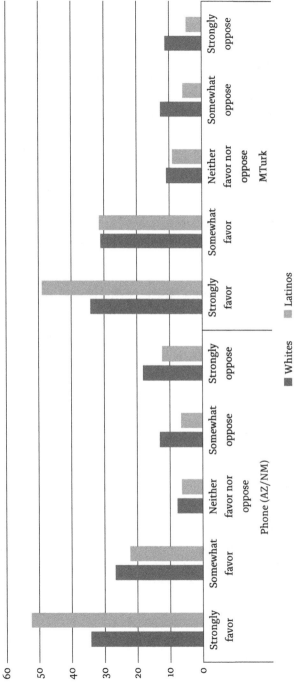

Source: Survey of Immigration and Belonging (Dovidio et al. 2016).

question received majority support among both groups regardless of their state of residence.[18]

In our interviews, support for the DREAM Act generally mirrored respondents' support for a broader legalization program. Whites and Latinos across the political spectrum understood the plight of immigrants, and they believed, by and large, that there should be some allowance for Dreamers to be brought into the legal fold. They also asserted that there should be a process for screening out those who had not followed the law, distinguishing between them and potential citizens. In expressing their support for efforts like the DREAM Act and DACA, white and Latino Republicans mixed empathy with an emphasis on the need for immigrants to fulfill a civic obligation. Take, for example, the comments of Lori Jansen, a white twenty-nine-year-old homemaker and Republican from Arizona. Lori supported DACA, but also believed that legalization should come with the requirement that recipients give something in return. In voicing her qualified support for a larger legalization program, she focused on DACA:

> You get into the DACA situation where families, or their children, what do you do? You can either say, "Well, you were from Mexico, we're sending you back." They don't know anything about it. So, you have to find a way for them to make them legal. What are the ways? Be a member of the armed services. Provide some civil service. I'm just reflecting back. . . . There's a real value in giving to somebody else—helping people to do that. Maybe they've never been in a situation where they could do that. If they can work to help support the community that they're in, then they can give back to somebody else. That's the way it works.

For Republicans like Lori, citizenship was not something that ought to be handed out freely: it needed to be earned. These respondents were concerned that a legalization program, even for the Dreamers, violated a fundamental principle of the civic republican model of citizenship, which centers on citizens doing something for the national whole.[19]

Republican respondents also believed that the line between legal and illegal had gotten too blurry. They reasoned that accommodating people who were already in the country without legal documentation, regardless of the circumstances of their entry, was a slippery slope that could result in unqualified immigrants achieving legal citizenship. While some felt that, in principle, any unauthorized person should be deported, this view was tempered by their evaluation of the practicality of such an undertaking. Jennifer McEnery, the homemaker and registered Republican quoted in chapter 5, was disappointed that so many unauthorized immigrants had made it into the United States in the first place. She favored the DREAM Act with limits, a stance driven in part by the sheer logistical difficulty of mass deportations:

> There again I would be thinking, "Okay, if you do all this and your parents are still illegal, then what happens if they get deported and you stay here? Then you're tearing the families apart again." But that sounds like one way to try and get people to stay. To have those guidelines that they can fulfill. I guess I think we have maybe gotten too far. . . . This whole Dreamer thing. These kids came over when they were little and now they're doctors, lawyers, they're professional people, which is wonderful, but maybe to have something where you can draw the line of who would be acceptable to stay and who wouldn't. . . . I can see both sides of it. But I kind of wish that since the beginning that the U.S. should have been on top of all of this and not let it get so far gone. We should have been more on top of people coming in and are they on visas, are they legal, are they giving their pathway to citizenship.

Republican Latinos were no less protective in their views of citizenship as they weighed support for legalizing Dreamers. Just like white Republicans, they saw Dreamers as an admirable group deserving of a chance to become citizens. However, they also believed that the government should not offer any special benefits beyond a shot at citizenship. Dennis Amaya supported a legalization program so long as the potential beneficiaries had proven themselves to be net contributors to the social, political, and economic whole:

> So, if they're paying taxes and they are buying homes, and they are ingrained in the American dream, I think they should be given an opportunity to become an American citizen. And I think that at some point they themselves would feel that they were Americans. I think they would say, "I'm an American." 'Cause you know, I have

friends that are Mexicanos and they feel they are American. But you know what? They have businesses. They have kids that were born in the United States. They are ingrained in the communities. And deep down inside I really think that's what they want to do.

Some Latinos, like Dennis, did not identify with an immigrant origin at all. But their contact with contemporary Latino immigrants and their political ideology led them to support the DREAM Act. New Mexico Latinos were especially likely to present a family and ethno-racial narrative constructed without immigration as a center-piece. In spite of the sense of "big-tent" Latino identity in the state, New Mexico's multigenerational Latinos tended to stake a stronger claim to an American national identity, and thus they tended to be more protective of what they saw as the benefits of citizenship.[20] Such a protective stance was common among Republican Hispanos. Felipe Gastelum, whose family had been in New Mexico for centuries, saw the Dreamers as an emblem of perseverance and self-determination. He told us he would support their legalization so long as the government did not step in with special help, which he thought would corrupt the rugged individualism that was Dreamers' greatest asset:

> I think the Dreamer thing is a problem, but it's also kind of nice. I would love to see more data on Dreamers. Because, talk about having to hold yourself accountable for shit. . . . They might feel bad, their friends might feel bad for them, but anyone that feels bad for them is actually hurting them . . . strengthen yourself, is what you should encourage in other people and in yourself. . . . I think the military's great. Amazing. That's perfect. That's the best way to assimilate. Because you learn values through discipline. . . . I don't think [I could support the program if college was paid for], because I think you're competing against Americans, and you're oversaturating the college, you're oversaturating people with educations that you're losing the demand, the value within the economy. So you're actually taking money away from other people. But if you want to compete just like everyone else, then why not [pass the DREAM Act]?

New Mexico has, in fact, offered in-state tuition and financial aid at its public universities for unauthorized students since 2005. But for Felipe and other Republicans, a federal effort to offer these education benefits to Dreamers, no matter how unlikely, was a bridge too far. In a way, their comments embodied a principled conservatism based on individualism and limited government. While the government should step in to legalize Dreamers, they said, that was as far as it should go. Dreamers who benefited from a legalization program should have to contribute something to the national whole.

For white and Latino Democrats, the fact that the Dreamers had been in the country for so long was enough for them to favor legalization. Democrats echoed some of the sentiments expressed by Republicans, but felt that more types of "national service" should count as a contribution, and that more people should be eligible for legalization. Bob McElroy, who supported broader legalization, also voiced strong support for the DREAM Act:

> I'm comfortable with the thought of allowing them to become permanent residents. I would even see that they should be given a path to citizenship. I guess I'm uncomfortable with the specific requirements of an education or military. I don't know that I would require that they do *only* those things. There might be other things that we could say they could do in lieu of those things. What if they served in Vista or AmeriCorps or the Peace Corps for two years? That's the equivalent of military service. So yes and no to your question. I'm open to the opportunity. I'm not sure I agree with the constraints of that.

In a similar vein, Daniel Colbert preferred legalization with fewer barriers:

> I think that makes sense for some of them. I would probably expand on that. Make those time lines a little broader so that it affects more people. So you don't have to go through the same thing over and over again. . . . I don't think we should be setting up so many barriers. Let's make it easier for them to do well. Go to school, get a job, go to the service. Those are all things that we should be doing anyway. If you do those things and you came here as a kid, you came here illegally, then you're an American now. You speak the language, you wear the clothes, you sing the National Anthem, you say the Pledge of Allegiance. What else is there here? (*laughing*)

Democrats and liberal independents had more contact with Dreamers than Republicans did, often in school. Their experience affirmed the prediction of the "contact hypothesis" that under the right circumstances contact between members of different groups can improve intergroup attitudes and opinions generally, and toward immigrants specifically.[21] In interviews, respondents who had more contact with Dreamers seemed to have more favorable views of them, offering unqualified support for their legalization. Their contact with Dreamers was proof to them that Dreamers were already fulfilling the obligations of citizenship. Julie Mazer, a white, thirty-nine-year-old education program coordinator and registered independent who described herself as very liberal, had been part of a protest movement called "DREAM Army" that occupied the Arizona offices of Senator John McCain. For her, participating in that event highlighted the ways in which she saw Dreamers already participating in American democracy:

> To me, the highest ideals of this country are around liberty and equality and opportunity. And so I actually remember being at DREAM Army, being in a tent encampment outside of McCain's office when they were voting on the [Department of Defense] bill and if they would include the DREAM Act [in] it. And here you have like ten [people], a bunch of people, all Dreamers, and they had this American flag there. . . . Just this sense of integrity, honor, sense of purpose, all of that that I saw in the Dreamers and then they voted down the [Department of Defense] bill. And they were so disillusioned with their idea of America. I remember them having a conversation afterwards that like, "Well, what does America really stand for?" And that's what I saw represented in the Dreamers. That's what, to me, is like, "proud to be American."

Julie stood out among whites because of her activism on behalf of immigrants. But the principle that undergirded her activism echoed what we heard from other Democratic whites for why they supported a legalization program for the Dreamers. There was little daylight between white and Latino Democrats and liberal independents on this issue. Both groups saw Dreamers as deserving of citizenship because they had already been in the United States for so long and had shown themselves to be Americans in all ways except their legal documentation. For some Latinos, a recent family history of immigration informed their support for legalization programs. For U.S.-born Latino Jaime Saenz, a twenty-eight-year-old sales representative and moderate Democrat from New Mexico, his view of Dreamer policies was shaped by his Mexican immigrant father's experiences with the immigration bureaucracy:

> The process is too long. It shouldn't have to take that long. When my dad tried to become a citizen of the United States back in the fifties and sixties, he had to learn English. He was in his forties, and he couldn't do it. Also, he had only gone to part of third grade when he had to be pulled out of school to help at home, so he was not very educated. By trying to learn another language to become a citizen was never worth it to him. . . . So my dad maintained his legal status in the United States, but he was always a resident [not a citizen]. I think there needs to be a certain amount of filtering; there has to be a process. . . . The Dreamer—that child that was brought here from another country illegally with parents and that kid doesn't know any other culture but this one or any other place to live but here—grant him citizenship. What is the deal? Grant him citizenship as soon as he graduates from high school so that he can do what he needs to do. There is a lot of goofiness that goes on, but also I don't know all of the nuances, I really don't. I would hate for someone to make a rule about my family when they don't know all the rules about my family, all the nuances. I get that. I think it's a process that has way too many steps.

The picture that Democrats and some Republicans drew of Dreamers came to life in interviews with Dreamers themselves. Our Dreamer respondents' support for the DREAM Act and DACA was rooted in their own experiences and those of their friends and family members. Cindy Rubio, the health care representative and Mexican-born DACA recipient who identified with the Democratic Party and was quoted earlier, told us:

> I consider it a home because this is where I grew up. Of course, I don't remember Mexico when I left. I was three years old, but this is pretty much where I grew up, where I learned a different language, where I met people, where I attended school, where my parents, where we met the people we know now. So, pretty much

this is all I know. Mexico, I hardly have any memories because I wasn't there. . . . When I go to California or to Vegas with friends, it's not the same thing. I get homesick. I want to go home. This is where my home is. . . . I understand when people talk about illegal immigrants, "this is not your home." But I, I feel like they don't know what other people go through, so it's easier for them to judge in a way because they were born here. (*translated from Spanish*)

We highlighted in chapter 3 how state policies in Arizona excluded Dreamers like Cindy from state benefits, such as in-state tuition and financial aid at Arizona's public universities. But the legal protections provided by DACA had a tangible impact on recipients' lives, and respondents cited this in voicing support for the program. Take Nelia Torres, the construction manager and Mexico-born DACA recipient quoted in chapter 3. In stating why she supported the DREAM Act, Nelia noted just how much her life had changed after DACA was put into place:

Because of DACA, I was able to continue to advance in my career and step into that leadership role that allowed me to earn more income. And, of course, having a Social Security number allows you to build credit, which makes loaners definitely more comfortable to loan you a good sum of money for a home. . . . [The possible expiration of DACA is] definitely scary. My husband is a citizen, so I will be taking a different path to getting a more permanent residency. So, I feel like regardless of which way I go, I should be okay. But that still doesn't change a lot [for] friends . . . I know that have DACA. . . . I believe myself and probably every other Dreamer out there feels that they are American. I don't have many ties to my birth country. I know where I'm from. I know who I am, but I don't have ties to [Mexico]. This is my home. And, you know, a lot decide to ignore that part. It is very frustrating.

The Dreamers we interviewed considered more than their own personal situation in their supportive comments about DACA and the DREAM Act. Notably, they echoed the calls of other respondents, white and Latino alike, for screening and civic participation, saying that sifting out individuals who may do harm to the United States was a necessary part of any legalization program.

Our respondents recognized that although DACA falls well short of full legalization, even its limited protections have afforded recipients a much better life. That view has been confirmed by other research: the program has boosted the education, job prospects, income, wealth, and mental health of its recipients.[22] Similarly, respondents across the ethno-racial and political spectrum appeared to recognize the potential payoff of the DREAM Act for recipients and for the United States as a whole. Given the broad support for the bill and the fact that it has been stalled in Congress for nearly two decades, it is perhaps no wonder that our respondents, and especially the Dreamers among them, voiced such profound frustration.

Border Security and Immigration Enforcement

Legalization programs are principally about changing the rules about who is eligible to become a citizen and how. Enforcement efforts, however, deal with implementing existing law—in particular, on keeping immigrants out or removing those already in the United States. As our survey did not address the question of enforcement and border security, we rely on data from other nationally representative samples to understand public views on the issue.

National polling as of this writing indicates that Americans in the aggregate think that border security is inadequate, are opposed to open borders, and are divided over the need for a wall on the U.S.-Mexico border.[23] Importantly, national surveys show large differences on these questions according to respondents' party identification and stated political ideology. Republicans are more likely to see current levels of border security as inadequate and to favor less immigration, and they are more apt to express support for building a wall. Democrats are more likely to see current border security efforts as adequate, are more inclined to favor more immigration, and are less likely to support a wall. These surveys also show differences by ethno-racial background. Latinos are less inclined to favor closed borders, and they are divided in their views about the adequacy of current levels of border security and the need for a wall. Whites, in contrast, are overall much more apt to see a need for more border security.[24]

We used our in-depth interviews to understand how individuals in our target states, Arizona and New Mexico, made sense of federal enforcement policies. This topic was particularly salient at the time of the interviews because the Trump administration was implementing highly restrictive policies, including child separation and detention, and was fighting for funding to build a wall along the U.S.-Mexico border. Across the ethno-racial and political spectrum, our respondents agreed that there was a need for border security. As with the other policies discussed in this chapter, respondents' differences were a matter of degree, not of kind: no Democrats or Latinos argued for completely open borders, and no Republicans or whites argued for shutting down immigration into the country entirely. This is not to say that there was perfect agreement across the interview sample. The interviews in many ways reflect what our survey data and other survey data show: that there are significant partisan and ethno-racial differences in views about immigration and immigration policy. But the caricatures drawn by partisans—which paint Democrats, and especially Latinos among them, as advocates for "open borders," and Republicans, and especially whites among them, as anti-immigrant border-security hawks—were not borne out in our interviews.[25]

For the Republican whites and Latinos, concerns about safety were at the heart of their attitudes about border security and enforcement. They endorsed the long-standing Republican view, championed at the time by President Trump, that the streams of migrants to the United States contained a criminal element that needed to be screened out. Such screening, they said, ought to be the focus of American immigration policy. And yet, even as they emphasized the need for strong border security, they also recognized the difficulty of implementing it. Take, for example, what we heard from Nancy Goldbloom, a white, seventy-seven-year-old retired teacher and moderate Republican from Arizona:

> I really do feel we need a wall, mostly I'd say for safety reasons. We don't know what's coming over the border. Maybe we could have a thing where we let more people in the regular way. Or if we partnered with Mexico, so they did part of the screening before the people were coming over that way. But we have the gangs that have come over. In the old days, they had the Italian gangs. The Italian

mafia, and a lot of Jewish people joined those gangs too! Anyway, but it doesn't feel safe. This janitor and his wife who are in school I taught in most of the years, they were always going back, like every other week—going back to Mexico and bringing back a grandchild. Nobody had this many grandchildren! . . . But I think when I see droves like that, that's frightening to me. Only because they need to be vetted, you see. We don't even know that they're coming from Mexico. They may be coming from Iraq or anywhere over there. . . . I mean, it's very hard to vet the amount of people that just came in now. How do you vet them? . . . We border each other, just like Canada. And the U.S. is supposed to get along. If Mexico, Guatemala, and all those places, if there was a way of making sure the criminals are not the ones getting through, I don't know how to do that. But if they did a better vetting and if their economy was better, maybe not.

Nancy cited U.S. immigration history, noting concerns about the criminality of previous waves of immigrants, like Italians. The security threats she saw might have come from all over the world, including Iraq. She used this history not as a justification for maintaining past immigration policies, but rather to argue that the United States ought to do now what it did not do in the past: screen immigrants more thoroughly. In making that case, she did not argue for American isolationism but instead explained that the United States should work with its neighbors to make immigration less attractive.

Respondents offered views like these in the context of a heated national political debate, stirred up but hardly originated by President Trump and his administration's policies. The Obama administration set records for the number of deportations it initiated. Although stated policy was to prioritize criminals, under Obama the federal government removed most deportees for immigration violations, not criminal violations. (This changed somewhat in the later years of the Obama administration, when immigrants with criminal violations made up a larger share of deportees.)[26] But under Trump, *anyone* who was unauthorized was subject to deportation. That sort of policy suited some Republican Latinos we interviewed just fine. Take, for example, the comments of the Latino Sergio Diaz, a thirty-two-year-old banker and conservative Republican from New Mexico whose family had been in the region for seven generations. Sergio believed that anything short of full enforcement attracted the wrong kind of immigrants:

> So the truth about immigrant labor is that it's low-wage, we know that statistically, and when you attract a large supply of low-wage labor, it drives all labor wages down and so it hurts. . . . That's the thing. If you make all these things available to people that are not Americans, it hurts Americans. And I'm totally about America first. I mean, there's however many hundreds of countries out there; we can't help everyone. We're Americans first, and we're only Americans because we assimilate together. We can't give everybody a job, we can't give everybody political asylum, we can't give everybody an economic opportunity. You just can't.

Jomara Salas, a twenty-two-year-old Latino college student, was a political independent and self-described moderate with conservative views on immigration. Her opinions were based partly on her own experiences. She was born in Costa Rica, came to the United States legally with her family, and eventually became a citizen. Deportation, she said, was a necessary step to take against people who had violated immigration laws. And yet, she felt that deportation should be part of a larger policy framework that would also make it easier for immigrants to arrive legally so that they did not have to be in the United States unauthorized:

> I don't really know all the details that go into deportation or anything like that. But definitely if it comes down to deportation, then that's what needs to happen. I just feel like if you know that you want to live here, there's the legal ways to do it. So, if you don't do it, then you get reprimanded for what you do wrong. . . . So, definitely not be treated like they're not people, but have some sort of repercussions to what they did. They focus on, "Oh, yeah. All these people are getting deported. Like, we're being treated like we're illegal. No person is illegal," all these things. While they're focusing their energy on that, there's other things that could be helpful. How about organizations that help people that are in those situations or, like, lawyers that help people file the papers? Education on how to do things the right way to avoid those situations. . . .

There are steps to take before that can change the whole situation. So I feel like instead of focusing so much on the after fact, maybe focus on what you can do before to help people, so they are not put in those situations where they're separated from their families and stuff like that.

Democratic and independent whites also supported some degree of immigration enforcement and border security. But they were much more inclined to emphasize a need to keep the doors open to immigrants. Bob McElroy made the case for making borders more open than they currently were, noting that previous waves of immigrants had faced far less scrutiny when they came to the United States. For him, making border crossing easier would be consistent with the historical approach to immigration taken by the United States and with the economic needs of the country:

Within reason, I'm for open borders. We are a nation of immigrants, and so to me, first of all, it's hypocrisy to basically get in the door and then want to turn around and close the door behind you. That's kind of an analogy of when I look at what's going on. Trump's an immigrant. His father came from Germany in the 1800s.[27] Now he wants to close the door behind him. To me, that's the height of hypocrisy and cruelty. I think again, what does it say on the Statue of Liberty? "Give me your tired, your poor, your huddled masses," and so on. I think it's a struggle because a lot of the initial waves of immigration came out of Europe. So you had white people coming here, even though they were Hungarian or Slovakian or Eastern European, Irish, and Italian, and German. But they were white, and so now we're seeing a much greater shift of Hispanic, Mid-Eastern, things like that population. But I think again, there's an economic argument for it. Want to grow your workforce? You've gotta bring them in. They're taking jobs that nobody wants. That's just the facts. . . . And I guess I would prefer that we take a much more welcoming attitude of, "That's great. We're glad you're here. We're glad for what you bring to America, to our society. What are you gonna contribute?" Let's ask them that. "What are you gonna contribute? Why are you coming?" "I want to get a job, take care of my family. And I see opportunity here that I don't have anywhere else." That's fine. So I guess from that standpoint, I would argue more for open borders. Again, you have to vet people in terms of we don't want terrorists and criminals, but there's a lot of arguments that go the other way too. If we're so concerned about bringing in terrorists and criminals, why is it that the vast majority of mass shootings are conducted by white males? So people say we don't want to let criminals in. We already have the criminals here, and they're part of the majority of society. So that's hypocrisy to me.

Even with his stated support for some form of "open borders," Bob still believed that people who are coming in must be screened to protect the United States from terrorist attacks. For Bob and other Democrats we interviewed, "open borders" did not mean an unchecked flow of migrants. Instead, it meant a greater allowance for legal immigration, so long as the immigrants who come to the United States contribute economically and socially.

Latino Democrats' and independents' discussion of immigration enforcement during our interviews similarly subverted popular caricatures. Even as they articulated more accommodating views, they picked up some of the same threads of concern about security and the importance of contributing to the country socially and economically. Unauthorized immigrants were especially likely to raise such themes. As we mentioned previously, these immigrants saw themselves as having honored the informal responsibilities of citizenship—like playing by the rules once in the United States and contributing socially and economically—and thus as having distinguished them from immigrants whose behavior made them undeserving of being part of the American polity. Abigail Andrews found that some undocumented immigrants in Southern California saw themselves as occupants of a moral high ground relative to deportees who broke criminal laws.[28] Some of our undocumented immigrant respondents made similar insinuations, folding that perspective into their views of border security. Evan Chávez, the hairdresser and unauthorized immigrant quoted in chapter 4, expressed sympathy for the Republican viewpoint, even as he argued elsewhere in the interview that law-abiding unauthorized immigrants deserved the chance to regularize their status:

I understand when people say that there's a lot of bad from certain groups; a lot of people come and do a lot of bad things and whatever. But it's not everyone. It's not all of us. There's a lot of people that come here to actually have a better life, and not just for us, but the people that we leave behind. . . . I've had friends from high school or just a different part of my life that I've heard it from. A lot of them just come here, and they find an easy way to make money, which is drugs, selling drugs, or doing a lot of things that I don't necessarily agree with. Or stealing stuff to go and resell it, or things like that. I feel like those are things that give us a bad reputation. They are not just earning a bad reputation for themselves, but it gives a bad reputation to everyone. (*translated from Spanish*)

Lidia Luna, a fifty-six-year-old Latina retail manager in Arizona, came to the United States on a visa that lapsed in 2005. In spite of her legal status, her identification with the Democratic Party, and her opposition to a border wall, Lidia echoed Evan's view that strong border security was necessary:

Well, it's good that there's control, right? Because, sadly, there are a lot of bad people that come who are running away for punishment, or something, and they come in, right? But I think they shouldn't generalize, because that money [they spend on the wall] they could use on so many things that the country needs. Yes, there should be control, but not excessive. The expense shouldn't be so big that— because in the end, I think people will continue coming anyway. It will be hard, but they will. And that has consequences, because it's more money to the people that bring them, more risk to their lives, more everything. (*translated from Spanish*)

It is indeed the case that added border security, including physical deterrents like a wall, do not appear to prevent people from coming. Instead, migrants take more dangerous routes to evade detection. Those routes require the help of smugglers, who charge soaring fees to assist with the passage. Because clandestine migration has become more dangerous and expensive, unauthorized immigrants have become more prone to staying permanently once they arrive in the United States, rather than going back and forth.[29] The response by the federal government, however, has been to double down on border enforcement.

Lidia hinted at a larger theme that we heard from Latino immigrants regardless of their legal status: their concern that immigration enforcement was overly aggressive. But far from arguing that there should be no enforcement, they instead were concerned that aggressive enforcement tactics were sweeping up the wrong people—those who were contributing to American society, even if they were unauthorized. The threat of deportation weighed on noncitizen respondents heavily. There was a sense that they, too, could find themselves on the receiving end of more aggressive immigration enforcement.

But their concerns were about more than just legal status; they were also disturbed by the ethno-racial aspect of immigration enforcement. The U.S.-born Latinos we interviewed saw the Trump administration's tactics not only as an effort to aggressively enforce the law, but also as a move to relegate all Latinos to a subordinate status and, as we saw in chapter 3, to write Latinos out of the national narrative. Veronica Gomez was a fifty-one-year-old Latina information technology specialist and liberal Democrat of Puerto Rican ancestry who was born on the East Coast. Now an Arizona resident, she believed that aggressive immigration enforcement in her state was an attack on all Latinos, and that U.S.-born Latinos needed to join in solidarity with immigrants. Veronica responded to our question about enforcement by noting the effect it had had on her personally and by making the case for a more expansive notion of citizenship based on local civic engagement:

It affects you psychologically, and in a lot of ways. It affects you directly or indirectly, but it does affect you. . . . If people don't follow the rules, I agree: they have to deport them. But not people that didn't do any harm and are good citizens. Because everyone who lives in a certain place, in any country, are citizens of that country even if you weren't born there. You are a citizen of that country because you follow the rules of that country, you work to have a good life, and you contribute to the economy of that country. You do a lot of stuff. You try to have a good life, so you are a citizen of that country, of that city, of that state, someone who makes a difference, a nice difference, a good difference. So, even though that person isn't your brother by blood, it's your brother of race. We all are sons of the same God, so everyone should—it should affect you, it should affect you what's happening or when things like that happen. You cannot be indifferent to someone's pain. (*translated from Spanish*)

Veronica captured the essence of what it means to be part of a collaterally affected group: to experience the social-psychological repercussion of immigration policies that target Latino immigrants because of a shared ethno-racial origin with that target population. As a U.S.-born citizen, Veronica and other U.S.-born Latinos were not subject to the letter of immigration enforcement laws, but as a Latina, she was subject to the spirit of the policies and politics that targeted Latinos.

Looking at the range of responses across the ethno-racial and political spectrums, it would be hard to say that a consensus emerged. There was considerable overlap in the opinions we heard, however, and the differences related more to the degree of enforcement that respondents favored than to the question of whether there should or should not be enforcement at all. On its face, this observation might not seem surprising. But in light of the prevailing narrative about American attitudes toward immigration (reinforced to some degree by polling), which tends to promote those attitudes as a binary ("for" or "against"), the fact that we heard such complex discussions of immigration enforcement is significant. As with other immigration policy issues, respondents seemed to take the full view of a thorny issue, even if their view emphasized different approaches to enforcing immigration laws.

Conclusion

While the previous chapters examined perceptions and feelings of belonging at the state level, this chapter has explored how our Arizona and New Mexico respondents made sense of the relationship between policy and belonging at the federal level. The findings suggest that their views of immigration policy at the federal level overlapped to some degree with their views of policy at the state level. Although their emphasis on the welcoming or unwelcoming aspects of the federal policy was largely dictated by their political ideology, they showed some common ground in favoring moves that would create a sense of legal belonging in the American polity for immigrants. These findings further suggest that there may be a large belonging dividend from enacting what would be the most welcoming federal policy of all: mass legalization.

A glance at the national media at this time would suggest that the nation was deeply divided on immigration. A near-daily drumbeat of news reporting on increasingly restrictive immigration policies and the political backlash to those policies evoked a nation divided by race and political party, and survey research on the politics of immigration echoes this portrayal to some degree.[30] This portrait of a nation divided was reflected in some ways in our respondents' attitudes. Certainly, our survey data revealed some polarization along ethno-racial and political lines. Whites, and especially white Republicans, were more likely to favor unwelcoming state policies, less likely to support a large legalization program or the DREAM Act, and more in favor of muscular immigration enforcement. Latinos, and especially those who identified as Democrats, were more likely to favor welcoming state policies, more strongly in favor of smoothing the path to legalization and passing the DREAM Act, and less inclined to support strict enforcement. But our survey results also show that ethno-racial background and political party are imperfect predictors of immigration policy preferences. A substantial share of whites supported more accommodating immigration policies, legalization programs, and less draconian border enforcement. And a significant number of Latinos showed support for unwelcoming policies, were not especially supportive of legalization programs, and wanted stricter immigration enforcement. In many ways, our survey data subvert the caricatures of the immigration debate that pit Republican, anti-immigrant whites against pro-immigrant nonwhites.

Our in-depth interviews challenged that portrait as well. The most pronounced divide we saw was defined by political orientation, but we nonetheless uncovered significant overlap in the ways in which respondents from across the political and ethno-racial spectrum came to their views about immigration policy. Republicans were more opposed to welcoming state-level immigration policies, fearing that they would attract more immigrants. And yet these same respondents also wanted immigrants already here to have more opportunities to enter into the polity. Democrats saw welcoming policies as a way to better integrate immigrants socially and economically, and they simultaneously emphasized the need for careful screening and border enforcement. There were differences in the emphasis that respondents placed on national policies but still significant overlap on the policies themselves. Across the in-depth interview sample, we heard a call for the legalization of unauthorized immigrants, and especially Dreamers, provided that they were screened and demonstrated good citizen behaviors. We heard support for border and interior enforcement, though Republicans and Democrats differed in how strict they felt that enforcement should be.

As we examined our survey findings and listened to the voices of Arizona and New Mexico residents, the preferences they expressed regarding immigration policy revealed a larger longing for unity defined by shared citizenship. Calls for legalization and greater civic participation among immigrants were also calls for a greater sense of belonging—one rooted in the idea that everyone living in the United States could share the same set of rights, responsibilities, and commitment to the nation.

Why are these preferences not reflected in current policy? Our interviews provide a partial answer. Recall that Latinos with some connection to immigrants, and especially Latino immigrants themselves, were invested in immigration policy because it had a direct effect on their lives and the lives of the people in their network. Noncitizen Latinos, who have the most to gain from more accommodating immigration policy, are also the very people who have no formal say in the policy process, and it is thus difficult for them to translate their policy preferences into reality. It is also difficult for U.S.-born Latinos, who, because of their lower average level of education and youth, are much less likely to vote.[31] This is not to say that Latinos have been quiet. Some of the largest mass political demonstrations of the last generation were led by Latinos in response to restrictive immigration policy proposals.[32] And there has been an impressive growth in the number of Latino elected officials.[33] Yet Latinos' formal political voice still does not match their numbers.

Whites, while offering strongly stated opinions about immigration policy, are not nearly as invested in it. As our white respondents often told us, the policies that we asked them about would not directly affect their lives all that much. There was thus little at stake for them. Even though our study suggests that the share of whites inclined to support a more welcoming approach to immigration is larger than the share that is opposed, they tend to be drowned out by the voices of whites who passionately oppose any immigration reform that includes legalization. The difficulty white Democrats and independents have in seeing how their lives are directly affected by immigration policy stunts their commitment to this issue. Moreover, any sort of mass legalization is still seen as more politically costly than rewarding for too many elected officials. The result is a federal immigration policy that fails to reflect the policy preferences of the people who live under it.[34]

CONLUSION   7

The United States does not have one overarching immigration policy. It has a patchwork of immigration policies at the federal, state, and local levels. While the federal government has not significantly over-hauled its immigration policies since 1986, subfederal jurisdictions—cities, counties, and states—have been heavily engaged in creating and implementing their own policies. Measures at both the federal and local levels, such as county and city, also can significantly shape individuals' responses. We focus on state-level policies because such policies can have profound effects and are easier to enact than fed-eral policies.

Activity at the state level has been especially feverish in the last two decades, resulting in a range of immigration policy regimes that can be placed on the spectrum of welcomeness. At one end of the spectrum are states with policies that are decidedly unwelcoming to immigrants: these states enthusiastically cooperate with federal immigration enforcement and restrict immigrant access to state-sponsored services and support. At the other end of the spectrum are states with policies that are welcoming to immigrants: these states seek to protect the rights of immigrants and grant them access to government-sponsored services and support. While many states have instituted a mix of these policies, the states most active in immigration policymaking have tended to institute mostly either unwelcoming or welcoming policies. Once in place, those policies reinforce the view of immigrants, and potentially other groups, that informed the policy in the first place.

The absence of federal legislation and the resulting patchwork of state-level immigration policies have made states laboratories for immigration policies that provide an opportunity to understand how different kinds of immigration policy contexts affect the lives of people living under them. Our laboratory contexts were mainly Arizona and New Mexico, adjacent states in the U.S. Southwest that are interconnected in their historical origins and demographically comparable, but that differ substantially in their immigration policies (see chapter 2). Their immigration policies do not necessarily reflect a consensus view of who belongs and who does not.[1] Nor do they serve only an administrative function, dictating what is permissible under the law and what is not. Immigration policies profoundly shape the sense of belonging felt and experienced by both the groups explicitly targeted by the policies and those who are *not* explicitly targeted but may nonetheless feel the effects of immigration policy.

We focused on individuals' sense of belonging—a basic psychological need—in their state of residence as our core outcome of interest.[2] A sense of belonging affects the way people think and feel about themselves and others; their relationship to their ethnoracial group, their state, and the nation; and the way they act toward other ethno-racial groups. Because of belonging's foundational role in social life, closely examining it offers insight into a broad range of specific behaviors that have often been studied in isolation but may all be traced back to some degree to their roots in the human desire to be accepted and welcomed.[3]

Practically, a number of different approaches can be adopted to integrate newcomers into societies in general and into the United States in particular. Some of these approaches are designed to force assimilation (for example, English-only language policies, as in Arizona); others are aimed at signaling inclusion (such as providing bilingual education, as in New Mexico). Punitive actions require significant resources for surveillance and often have negative collateral consequences, while supporting and encouraging a sense of belonging fosters engagement and is more likely to reap the benefits of diversity.[4] We set out to study how these contexts relate to and causally influence belonging, which is a "general inference, drawn from cues, events, experiences, and relationships, about the quality of fit or potential fit between oneself and a setting."[5] Belonging may seem like a "soft" outcome, but it encapsulates the emotional drivers of views about immigration and immigration policy in the United

States today.[6] We examined the effect of immigration policies on the sense of belonging of the group they target most explicitly—Latino immigrants—and also the impact of these same policies on the sense of belonging of those *not* explicitly targeted—U.S.-born Latinos (a collaterally affected group) and U.S.-born whites (a symbolically affected group). We also investigated the role of political party affiliation (Democrat, Republican, or independent) in this process.

We addressed this issue from sociological, political science, and psychological perspectives. We also employed a range of behavioral science methodologies, including representative surveys, experiments, and in-depth interviews. The survey and interviews showed that state-level immigration policies do have a systematic effect on people's sense of belonging and how they feel about themselves and others. Our experiments suggest that state-level policy can *cause* differences in a sense of belonging, not only among residents of Arizona and New Mexico but also among people in other states. Our data triangulate on a common conclusion: while both federal and municipal (for example, city) policies matter, state-level policies are independently important.

In this final chapter of the book, we identify what we learned from our deep dive into the feelings, beliefs, and experiences of whites and Latinos in Arizona and New Mexico—the two similar states in our case study that exemplify, respectively, unwelcoming and welcoming immigration climates. Our investigation revealed policy's pervasive influence on people's sense of belonging. State-level immigration policies are not simply based on constructions of groups; policies in and of themselves send signals about who belongs. As we have shown, the individuals who live under those policies internalize signals that, in turn, profoundly shape their sense of belonging. The specific ways in which immigration policy influences the sense of belonging depends on the ethno-racial background and political party affiliation of the individual.

Our research reveals that even as the federal government seems paralyzed in its efforts to enact sweeping immigration reform, states still have substantial leeway in the kinds of policies that they enact. When states create measures aimed at welcoming immigrants, the result is a greater sense of belonging, not just for the immigrants who are directly targeted by such policies but also for groups not targeted by those policies. For the foreseeable future, states may be the best hope for instituting immigration policies that foster the very sense of belonging this multiethnic, immigrant-receiving nation so desperately needs.

Lessons from Arizona and New Mexico

Political leaders have a particularly strong influence on how the community responds to immigration policies. They personify the standards of a community, and their actions communicate who belongs and who does not.[7] Political leaders thus communicate social norms—the unwritten rules about what people should think and do in relation to others—and laws and policies further formalize and enforce these social norms.

Our examination considered the target population of state-level immigration policy (foreign-born Latinos), a collaterally affected group (U.S.-born Latinos), and a symbolically affected group (U.S.-born whites) in Arizona and New Mexico. With Arizona, an indisputably unwelcoming state, and New Mexico, a welcoming state, as real-world laboratories, we used a telephone survey of representative samples of Latinos (U.S.- and foreign-born) and whites from each state to examine differences in feelings of belonging between these two state policy contexts; experiments to show that these differences caused diverging feelings of belonging; and interviews to understand how individuals made sense of living in a particular state-level immigration policy regime.

We learned that a state's policy established a context of reception that does indeed affect the sense of belonging.[8] We also learned that the effect is refracted into the lives of individuals by nativity, by ethno-racial background, and especially by political orientation. A mix of history, culture, and policy informed our respondents' perceptions of Arizona as an unwelcoming state and New Mexico as a welcoming state. In our survey and interviews, respondents in Arizona, regardless of nativity or ethno-racial background, agreed that their state was unwelcoming to immigrants, and they pointed to the state's policies as the primary culprit; respondents in New Mexico, in contrast, viewed their state as welcoming to immigrants. These states' different policies had the most direct effect on the targeted

Latino-immigrant population. However, the policy context also affected the sense of belonging felt by U.S.-born Latinos and U.S.-born whites.

The sense of rejection felt by Latinos in Arizona, especially the foreign-born, was profound. They felt the impact of administrative and symbolic exclusions facilitated by the state's unwelcoming policies as they navigated daily life. U.S.-born Latinos likewise felt targeted by these policies. Importantly, the rejection of Latinos in their state did not feel like an embrace to white Arizona Democrats. Instead, many felt a diminished sense of belonging in their state because the cues sent by its policies, including those related to immigration, cut against their identity as Democrats. White Republicans in Arizona, by contrast, saw immigration policies as cues that enhanced their belonging because they lived in a state whose policies and politics reflected their political identity.

In New Mexico, both U.S.- and foreign-born Latinos reported a deep sense of belonging because of a generally welcoming culture. Latino immigrants loosely connected this feeling to policy, noting that they could operate in daily life without concern that the state was attempting to exclude them. The generally positive immigration context in New Mexico probably obscured the specific impact of New Mexico's immigration policies on the experiences of Latino residents in their daily lives. It was when New Mexico respondents compared the situation in their state to the notoriously hostile context of Arizona that New Mexico's welcoming immigration approach became more apparent. Whites in New Mexico also felt embraced in their home state, but they noted that it was multigenerational Latinos in New Mexico who were on historical and cultural home turf more than any other group. Nonetheless, these same whites still cited a general culture of openness in New Mexico.

Whatever differences in feelings of belonging respondents had connected to their state, our survey did not pick up any impact of these feelings on their feelings of belonging in the national context. We conducted our survey while President Obama was still in office. The in-depth interviews, which we conducted after the 2016 election, suggest that President Trump's restrictionist, enforcement-first immigration policies changed the national context, shaping how our interviewees made sense of the relevance of national immigration policy in their lives. In particular, the changed federal context challenged the deeply held notion among Democratic and some independent respondents that the civic identity of the United States rested on incorporationism—the idea that the national self-understanding was rooted in an immigrant heritage.[9]

While our survey and interview data indicate that immigration policy was connected to respondents' feelings of belonging in their state, our experimental data, described in chapter 5, showed that immigration policy can be a *cause* of those feelings. In experiments with the representative samples of respondents in Arizona and New Mexico and with a nationwide convenience sample, we led participants to believe that their state was considering adopting markedly unwelcoming or welcoming immigration policies. Among residents of Arizona and New Mexico, responses to those potential policies were patterned by political affiliation more than anything else. When we told respondents that their state lawmakers were considering more welcoming immigration policies, Democratic and independent Latinos, regardless of their nativity, had highly positive emotional responses. Foreign-born Republican Latinos were not affected, nor were white independents. It was only Republican U.S.-born Latinos and Republican whites who did not have positive emotional responses. We found a roughly similar impact on respondents' feelings of belonging: learning that their state was considering welcoming policies led Democratic and independent Latinos, both foreign- and U.S.-born, and Democratic whites to feel a stronger sense of belonging. Republican whites, Republican U.S.-born Latinos, and, to a lesser degree, white independents felt a weaker sense of belonging. We uncovered this same general pattern of results with a nationwide sample of U.S.-born Latinos and whites.

Similar patterns showed up in the in-depth interviews in Arizona and New Mexico. But amidst the division, a degree of consensus about what it means to belong emerged from responses to interview questions about the possibility of state lawmakers fashioning policies to be either more or less welcoming to immigrants. Latino Democrats and independents supported such policies because they stood to benefit directly and because they believed that welcoming policies, in promising to integrate immigrants, would realize the economic benefits of immigration. White Democrats and independents saw welcoming policies in much the same way. Notably, Democratic and independent Latinos and whites alike qualified their views, asserting that immigrants should have to prove themselves as social and economic contributors if they were to reap the benefits of more welcoming policies.

Republican whites and Latinos saw welcoming policies differently. They largely opposed such measures out of concern that these policies would attract even more immigrants, who might take more from the system than they deserved. Even while voicing these opinions, however, Republicans asserted that there ought to be a pathway to legalization for unauthorized immigrants. The same ideological divisions and logic respondents displayed when reacting to different policy measures appeared when we asked them to describe what kind of state-level immigration policies they preferred. And, here again, respondents supported, to varying degrees, legalizing unauthorized immigrations, a move that only the federal government could make.

When it came to federal policy, our survey and interview data revealed similar political divides, but also even more explicit consensus around legalization and border security. On the one hand, Democratic and independent whites and Latinos, both U.S.- and foreign-born, were far more supportive of providing a pathway to citizenship for unauthorized immigrants and offering legal status to individuals brought to the United States without authorization as children. On the other hand, white and Latino Republicans were more inclined to prioritize support for stricter enforcement of immigration laws. As familiar as these political divisions seem to be, we also uncovered significant overlap in respondents' views, regardless of ethno-racial background or political orientation. Even as they articulated their preference for more accommodating state and federal immigration policies, Democrats and independents belied their popular reputation as advocates of "open borders," saying instead that immigrants had an obligation to display behavior that demonstrated good citizenship. Although they did not think the federal government should prioritize immigration enforcement, Democrats and independents argued that border security was necessary. Republicans also challenged popular stereotypes of them as unbending opponents of immigration and immigrants. In general, they wanted more immigration enforcement and less emphasis on policies that accommodated immigration. But they also voiced support for legalizing unauthorized immigrants who had been in the United States for an extended period and who had a proven track record of contributing economically and socially.

These results both affirm existing findings and hold new lessons for social science. Our investigation confirms that ethno-racial origin and political affiliation are powerful organizing categories that shape how individuals inhabit and interpret the contexts in which they live. Our results also indicate that the alignment of these categories in contemporary U.S. society leads respondents to interpretations that current evidence in the research literature does not necessarily anticipate. Existing social science research has shown, as do we, that unwelcoming policies have a detrimental impact on the material and psychological outcomes of immigrants.[10] However, welcoming policies at the state level, which have become more pervasive in recent years, and their effects were something of a black box before our studies. We demonstrate that welcoming policies have a net positive impact on Latino immigrants' feelings of belonging. The finding is perhaps not surprising on its own. But the way it positively affects Latino immigrants' sense of belonging is significant. Welcoming policy contexts do not necessarily appear to them as a tight embrace. Instead, the sense of belonging comes from their more equal footing with citizens when accessing rights, institutions, and resources. That equal footing translates to a sense of normalcy that seems remarkable only when compared to a less equal situation in another context, like Arizona.

Our data also offer insight into how different kinds of policy contexts shape belonging for nontargeted populations. We studied two such populations: U.S.-born Latinos and whites. We show that a welcoming policy context has a collateral effect on U.S.-born Latinos who share an ethno-racial origin with the immigrant target population. The effect owes to family ties between some U.S.-born Latinos and immigrants and to their response to political rhetoric that connects foreignness, illegality, and Latino-ness.[11]

Even less clear before our study was how whites would respond to welcoming and unwelcoming policy contexts. Past research might lead us to anticipate a zero-sum reaction—that is, whites seeing unwelcoming policies as an embrace of white belonging and welcoming policies as a rejection of white belonging.[12] Our work tells a different story. Whites were divided in how they responded; the differences had less to do with being white and more to do with political party identification. Democratic and, to a lesser degree, independent whites displayed a benefit to their sense of belonging from more welcoming policies. Republicans showed diminished feelings of belonging in response to the same policies.

Changing intersections of party identification, ethno-racial origin, and views about immigration drive this pattern. Political party identification is a salient social identity, and one tied to ethno-racial background.[13] The Republican Party is not just descriptively white; it is also associated with whites' political interests.[14] Yet, a substantial share of whites identify as Democrats or Democratic-leaning independents. Indeed, party identification divides whites. So do attitudes about immigration and race. Race-relevant policies, especially immigration policies, have become more partisan issues now than at any time in modern history, with Democrats lining up behind more accommodating views about race and immigration and Republicans staking out a restrictionist stance. But the divergence between the two parties on immigration is mostly driven by a dramatic increase in more accommodating opinions among Democrats, and especially among white Democrats, and less so by increasingly restrictionist views among Republicans, whose outlooks have remained mostly unchanged in recent years.[15]

The growing salience of party identification as a social identity, the way party identification divides whites, and the tight connection between accommodating attitudes about immigration and the Democratic Party have given unwelcoming policies a larger target population than just immigrants. Immigration policies do not affect white Democrats as directly or intensely as they do immigrants, but because they violate the core principles that Democrats hold dear, white Democrats are affected symbolically by these policies. As a result, welcoming policies facilitate a sense of belonging among white Democrats, and unwelcoming policies dampen it. More generally, these patterns suggest that a policy positively affects nontarget populations' sense of belonging when the policy affirms other kinds of identities not directly associated with the group targeted by the policy, like party identification.

Considering the effect of immigration policies on the target (Latino immigrants), the collaterally affected (U.S.-born Latinos), and the symbolically affected (whites), our findings also bear out the substantial social-psychological benefits of more welcoming policies for a broad swath of these populations. Among our respondents on average, all of these groups exhibited a greater sense of belonging when living under or being asked to consider living under more welcoming immigration policies. It is not just that the majority reacted positively to welcoming immigration policies. The majority also agreed that these were the kinds of immigration policies they wanted.

Can the United States Become More Welcoming?

Our analyses hold lessons for how the United States might become more welcoming. If welcoming policies have such a clear payoff, and if there is some consensus around certain aspects of immigration reform, is there any hope that such policies would become more widespread? We believe there is. Our hope comes from our reading of the views of our respondents, and of the American public more generally, as well as from what many states, cities, and counties have already done to foster a more welcoming context for immigrants.

Our assessment comes with caveats. We could not capture all of the variation in subfederal immigration policy at not only the state level but also the city and county levels. In New Mexico and Arizona, the tenor of immigration policies at the state level largely lined up with the tenor of these policies in each state's metro areas. Our respondents tended to collapse differences across jurisdictions to form an overall view of their state. But state and municipal immigration policies are not aligned everywhere. Even within a state, individuals can live under a county immigration policy approach that differs from the state and federal approaches.[16]

This is not to mention differences between cities within counties, which have implications for the legal and administrative implementation of policies. Federal law takes precedence over state law, and state law takes precedence over municipal law. When immigration approaches collide, there is often a legal tussle over which jurisdiction's immigration policy prevails. These jurisdictional differences almost certainly have implications for individuals' sense of belonging as well. Although we could not capture these granular jurisdictional differences, our findings and what we know from psychology suggest that the most unwelcoming policies, whether at the state or municipal level, prevail in the minds of individuals as they form a sense of belonging.[17]

Recall that our respondents from both states drew attention to the unwelcoming policies in Arizona, while the influence of the welcoming policies in New Mexico tended to recede into the background. Welcoming policies allow immigrants to go about their lives mostly unrestricted in their access to the rights, institutions, and resources provided by the state. The sense of normalcy provided by welcoming policies simply does not register as powerfully as the feelings engendered by unwelcoming policies that deny access to rights, institutions, and resources. We have no reason to believe that the tendencies we uncovered would be different in other states.

ARIZONA, NEW MEXICO, AND THE NATIONAL PICTURE

Our data on the opinions of respondents from Arizona and New Mexico, as well as data on U.S. public opinion more broadly, show broad support for more welcoming policies.[18] It is important to acknowledge that political divisions across the country are significant. If there is a perceived truism about the United States today, it is that the nation is as politically divided as it has ever been, if not more so. Leaders of the two major parties can hardly find consensus on any issue. It would seem that the division is spilling out of Capitol Hill and statehouses and saturating everyday life in the United States. Rank-and-file Democrats and Republicans are clearly divided on a host of issues ranging from abortion and education to foreign policy and race relations.[19]

It is not just that people with different political orientations see the issues differently; there is evidence to suggest that they occupy different cultural worlds.[20] Broadcasts of President Trump's political rallies—which regularly featured crowds chanting some of the president's favorite slogans, including "build the wall!" and "send her back!" (in reference to Representative Ilhan Omar, a U.S. citizen who arrived in the United States at age ten with her family)—gave the division a dramatic and visceral resonance. The divisions have become so pronounced that a leading magazine, *The Atlantic*, dedicated a December 2019 special issue to analyses aimed at avoiding another civil war ("How to Stop a Civil War").[21]

Nevertheless, our findings, along with national data, also show that Americans share considerable common ground even on an issue as seemingly divisive as immigration.[22] Notably, this common ground extends across ethno-racial categories, with white Democrats in our study responding nearly as positively to welcoming immigration policies as did foreign-born Latinos and most U.S.-born Latinos. There are differences, to be sure, depending on the particular aspect of immigration individuals considered. Although there were clear political divisions in the degree to which individuals wanted policies to be more welcoming, we found general consensus in support of arguably the most welcoming policy of all: legalizing unauthorized immigrants who were already in the United States.

Our results dovetail with findings from national polls. Over time, the U.S. public has become more accommodating and inclusive in its views about immigration. A growing share of Americans say that immigration should either be kept at its present level or increased; a declining proportion says that they would like fewer immigrants. In fact, in the summer of 2020, during the heat of a contentious presidential election campaign, the Gallup Poll found that the share of Americans wanting increased immigration (34 percent) was greater than the share desiring less immigration (28 percent).[23] That trend holds for both Republicans and Democrats, though the share of Democrats saying that they would like immigration to be kept at its present level or increased has increased dramatically.[24] The same national polling also shows that Republicans are split in their views about unauthorized immigrants and legalization. Roughly half have sympathetic views toward unauthorized immigrants, and an equivalent share favors legalization.[25] When it comes to granting legal status to unauthorized immigrants who were brought here as children, a slight majority of Republicans favor doing so, and more than nine in ten Democrats support that policy move.[26] And during the Trump presidency, a period of tremendous social and political turmoil that emboldened white nationalists, anti-black and anti-Latino prejudice declined.[27]

National polling also dovetails with our findings about the primacy of political party identification, even more than ethno-racial origin, as an attitudinal lens through which Americans view immigration. While the Republican Party has increasingly become a home to white voters, divisions between white Democrats and Republicans on key social issues, including immigration and race relations, have grown.[28] White Democrats have increasingly moved left—even further left than nonwhite Democrats—in their policy positions on race and immigration.[29] In the spring and summer of 2020, a diverse coalition of protesters that included a substantial number of whites took to the streets in the United States proclaiming that "Black Lives Matter" in response to police violence against African Americans. Amid the protests, surveys revealed spikes in support for greater racial justice across a wide swath of the population.[30] It remains to be seen whether support for addressing racial justice will spill over to immigration. What is clear from our data and from national polling, however, is that a large segment of the white population is becoming more liberal in its views about immigration and race. That pattern may bode well for the adoption of more welcoming immigration policies.

It would be naive to think that welcoming federal immigration policies would magically follow public opinion. Federal policy has been out of step with public opinion on immigration for some time. Under the Trump administration, the federal government shifted immigration policy further away from the center of public opinion on immigration. From a travel ban that excluded immigrants from Muslim-majority countries and the attempted rescindment of DACA to mass deportations and separation of children from their asylum-seeking parents, the Trump administration's federal government sent a message that was more than unwelcoming to immigrants: it was hostile to them.

Even with a Democratic president, Joe Biden, there still may not be significant movement at the federal level on immigration. There was a two-year window from 2009 to 2011 when Democrats controlled the White House and Congress. No significant immigration reform emerged from that time, owing in part to the Senate filibuster. The new Biden administration, with a narrow majority in both houses of Congress, has its hands full responding to the pandemic and related economic recovery. These are inauspicious circumstances in which to enact immigration reform, including more welcoming policies for immigrants already here. Just as threatening to prospects for policy change is that the American public is politically polarized in ways that dwarf differences in policy preferences. This polarization is "affective," in that Democrats and Republicans see each other as socially different, morally lacking, and even the enemy.[31] With the American public viewing the social and political landscape through such polarized lenses, it is difficult for them to see eye-to-eye on policy, even when there is agreement on the substance.

And so, for the foreseeable future, the best hope for more welcoming immigration policies rests in subfederal jurisdictions, which tend to be less infected by polarization.[32] States, counties, and cities have already moved in the direction of more welcoming immigration policies. Since 2012, subnational immigration policies have taken a notably welcoming turn that has become even more prominent.[33] Our findings from Arizona and New Mexico suggest that these welcoming policies are likely to have created a stronger sense of belonging for a large share of the population in states that have implemented them.

In subfederal settings that have not yet embraced a welcoming approach, officials might be reluctant to adopt such policies out of fear that immigration policymaking is a zero-sum affair—that a gain for one group would mean a loss for another group. Leaders who believe that they are operating in a zero-sum environment see themselves as caught in a dilemma: they can create a policy climate that is welcoming to immigrants but risk alienating whites, or they can establish a policy climate that is unwelcoming to immigrants and risk alienating the growing nonwhite population. But our research and that of other social scientists suggest that welcoming policies have a strong payoff in the form of greater cohesion among different groups. For instance, in an expansive study of four small cities in different U.S. regions, the political scientist Abigail Williamson shows that even in places where welcoming policies produced an initial negative backlash among established residents, those policies ultimately resulted in more harmonious integration between immigrant newcomers and the established populations.[34]

Similarly, in her study of ethnic change in rural Iowa towns, J. Celeste Lay finds that "people adjust, and over time natives and immigrants create a new normal in these small communities."[35]

Lay notes that the process takes time and that the decisions of local officials—for example, refusing to enforce an English-only ordinance—can help ensure that group harmony is the eventual outcome. "It would be a good idea for [welcoming] communities to be more vocal about their positive experiences with immigration," she writes, adding that leaders in these places "could help people in other communities learn that, even though there were difficult periods in the beginning, immigration has been mostly a positive experience for their towns."[36] Thus, a zero-sum assessment that treats welcoming policies and white belonging as mutually exclusive misses the mark. Welcoming policies not only reflect the will of a sizable proportion of the population but also present an opportunity to foster a greater sense of belonging for a large and diverse segment of the U.S. population.

That segment of the population must also include populations that we did not study: Asian Americans and African Americans. Asian Americans are part of the multigenerational population in the United States, but the immigrant and second-generation populations predominate. So, too, do perceptions of Asian Americans as "forever foreigners."[37] Much as in the past, today Asian Americans find themselves on the receiving end of blame for what ails American society. Because the COVID-19 virus is believed to have come from Wuhan, China, political leaders in the United States have made China and people of Chinese descent scapegoats and blamed them for the pandemic. A dramatic increase in hate crimes in large U.S. cities against people with Asian ancestry has ensued.[38] Although it is difficult to know for certain whether the rise in hate crimes is related to the scapegoating, the result, even if coincidental, has been a dramatically less welcoming context for people of Asian descent. As they relate to our study, these events illustrate the need to enforce basic civil rights protections alongside welcoming policies that benefit immigrants regardless of their origins. These events also suggest the need to understand how welcoming policies affect the sense of belonging among foreign- and U.S.-born people of Asian descent.

The other segment of the population for which a greater sense of belonging must also be fostered is African Americans. Our examination does not consider how immigration policy affects African Americans. We focused our research on Latinos and whites in Arizona and in New Mexico because, together, they add up to most of the population—currently 86 percent—in each state. Ethnographic research demonstrates possibilities for solidarity between Latino immigrants and African Americans when it comes to defending Latinos against unwelcoming immigration policy.[39] Furthermore, as the political scientist Niambi Carter shows, African Americans' attitudes about immigration need to be understood through the lens of white supremacy.[40] Black Americans, Carter finds, are neither anti-Latino nor anti-immigrant in the way that some whites are. Rather, African Americans' sense of belonging and sense of national identity are shaped by a long history of exclusion, and their attitudes reflect a recognition that new immigrants may further entrench anti-black structures in the United States. Polling suggests that African Americans are likely to react positively to more welcoming immigration policies given that they have largely accommodating views of immigration.[41] How policies are framed, however, not only legally but also in public rhetoric, would probably shape African Americans' responses to welcoming or unwelcoming immigration policies. If African Americans perceive an unwelcoming state-level immigration policy as a signal of a general discriminatory pattern, they will tend to respond negatively to the policy and be supportive of a welcoming policy because of the minority identity they share with Latinos.[42] If, instead, the policy is accompanied by rhetoric that pits being American legally and culturally against having a different national identity, African Americans may be inclined to respond more favorably toward an unwelcoming policy while experiencing a greater sense of belonging locally and nationally.[43]

In reality, there is no zero-sum policy trade-off: policies that benefit immigrants can and should be advanced alongside those that address inequalities stemming from systematic racism against African Americans. The imperative for both is clear. The Black Lives Matter protests during 2020 invigorated explorations of anti-blackness in the Latino community and also highlighted the potential for solidarity in the fight against the overpolicing that subjugates both groups.[44] When policies have been more welcoming to immigrants, future U.S.-born generations and American society as a whole benefit.[45] Historically, the intergenerational progress of immigrant groups broadened the ethno-racial and religious segment of the population with a sense of belonging in the U.S. mainstream.[46] But that expansion only marginally included people of African heritage, who were undeniably excluded from enjoying the full benefits of belonging in multiple aspects of American life.[47] Today the mainstream appears to be expanding once again, yet it once again stubbornly excludes African Americans.[48] That exclusion is unacceptable. Welcoming immigration policies can be part of a larger imperative for institutional changes that achieve greater belonging for marginalized groups, and especially for African Americans.[49]

STATES CAN CHANGE THEIR STRIPES

Our hope for more welcoming policies is also rooted in the history of state-level immigration policy change, which serves as a reminder that states that are welcoming or unwelcoming can and do change their stripes. Perhaps no state serves as a clearer example than California. A generation ago, California was arguably the most unwelcoming state in the nation. During the 1990s, California voters passed a series of ballot initiatives that were a direct and hostile response to the growing Latino population.[50] In 1994, voters passed Proposition 187, better known as the "Save Our State" initiative. Had it survived legal challenges, Proposition 187 would have made unauthorized immigrants ineligible for publicly funded social services, health care services, and public education. Proposition 187 would have also required state and local agencies, including teachers, to report individuals whom they suspected of being in the United States without legal authorization.[51] Just two years later, in 1996, California voters approved Proposition 209, which amended the state's constitution to bar any consideration of race, sex, or ethnicity in public employment, contracting, and public education. In effect, Proposition 209 banned state affirmative action programs. In 1998, California voters backed Proposition 227, which eliminated bilingual education in public schools. By the end of the 1990s, California seemed to have planted its flag on the unwelcoming end of the immigration reception spectrum.

The ensuing decades witnessed a sea change in California politics and the state's approach to immigration policy. The extreme anti-immigrant policies and politics of the 1990s galvanized grassroots organizations into action. Civil society groups and community organizations fought for immigrants' rights and rallied Latinos to become more politically involved.[52] Latino immigrants who were eligible became citizens, and eventually voters. Latinos who were already citizens, either by birth or through naturalization, began running for local and state office and voting in large numbers.[53] The result was a shift in California state politics over the subsequent decades such that today California is one of the most reliably and heavily Democratic states in the country. It has become the most welcoming state in the union, having instituted a host of policies that are welcoming to immigrants.[54] Emblematic of just how much California has changed in its approach to immigration is the 2016 ballot initiative Proposition 58, which reinstated state-sponsored bilingual education. The measure, approved by nearly three-quarters of California voters, does nothing short of doing away with Proposition 227, the ballot initiative that eliminated bilingual education eighteen years earlier. In 2020, Proposition 16, which would have reinstated affirmative action in state hiring, did not pass. Still, the state is a dramatically different policy context for immigrants today compared to a generation ago.

Arizona and New Mexico have also seen some changes in their approaches to immigration policy. For a time, New Mexico appeared to move in an unwelcoming direction. The state's former governor, Susanna Martinez, championed a rollback of the state's provision allowing unauthorized immigrants to apply for and hold driver's licenses. The state prison system also once had a 287(g) agreement with the federal government, allowing state prisons to carry out immigration enforcement. Both of these measures appear to be more of a blip than a trend: not only was Martinez only partially successful in her effort to revise the state's driver's license laws, but New Mexico only sparsely used its 287(g) agreement, which it ended in 2013.[55] The state recently elected a Democratic governor, Michelle Lujan Grisham, whose pro-immigrant politics seem to have returned New Mexico to its previous trajectory.

For its part, Arizona may be undergoing a change reminiscent of California's metamorphosis. Since the fever pitch of unwelcoming policymaking in the early 2000s, Arizona has witnessed notable changes in the state's unwelcoming bent. The most pronounced change is the state casting its electoral votes for the Democratic presidential candidate, Joe Biden, in the 2020 election. Biden ran on a platform that included welcoming immigration policies, including a pathway to citizenship for undocumented immigrants and reestablishing the White House Task Force on New Americans, which was first established by George W. Bush's administration and later reestablished within the White House under President Obama. Also, after the state elected Mark Kelly to the U.S. Senate in 2020, both of Arizona's senatorial seats were occupied by Democrats.

Arizona's turn to blue in the 2020 election is part of a series of changes going back a decade, when Arizona passed SB 1070. Much like California's Proposition 187, SB 1070 roused a coalition of Latino, LGBTQ, and labor activists and organizations that galvanized voters to elect more progressive candidates.[56] In 2016, Maricopa County voters ousted Sheriff Joe Arpaio and elected Democrat Paul Penzone. The Maricopa County Sheriff's Department still cooperates with ICE under Penzone, but the immigration raids and the anti-immigration politics trumpeted by Arpaio are largely things of the past. Phoenix, Arizona's largest city and the fifth-largest in the nation, recently elected Democratic mayor Kate Gallego, a champion of immigrant rights. In 2018, the state elected its first Democratic senator since 1995, Kyrsten Sinema. Sinema and fellow Democratic senator Mark Kelly are hardly vocal proponents of immigrants' rights, but both generally follow the Democratic Party's accommodating position on immigration. The state's current Republican governor, Doug Doucey, has a more mixed record on immigration, although he vocally opposed some of the harshest moves on immigration policy by the Trump White House. Arizona's electorate is also shifting in much the same way that California's electorate changed in the 1990s and early 2000s: it is increasingly Latino, Democratic, and pro-immigrant. We are not arguing that Arizona is destined to follow California's path, but the seeds that grew into the political change that made California a welcoming state appear to be planted and sprouting in Arizona.

The Promises and Limits of Immigration Federalism

State policies and politics do not operate in a vacuum. They intersect with federal and local policies and politics such that action at one level of government can enhance or restrict the measures at other levels. If immigration across the country is a patchwork, the various patches are still sewn to a federal fabric.

States have taken cues from local governments. The recent flurry of state immigration policies got its start in municipalities, with cities and counties instituting measures that were at first mostly unwelcoming, but later turned welcoming.[57] Also, local government officials have taken cues from the federal government, which sets the legal parameters within which they can set local versions of immigration policies.[58] But those policies often bump up against very different approaches taken by the state and federal governments. In recent years, states, cities, and counties have proclaimed themselves sanctuary jurisdictions, indicating that they will not cooperate with federal immigration enforcement. In response, as Texas did in 2016, some states have moved to ban sanctuary jurisdictions. Other states, such as California, chose to align themselves with the sanctuary movement being embraced in their counties and cities by declaring the entire state a sanctuary for immigrants.[59] The federal government met those state policies with lawsuits, but courts ultimately sided with California.

When Arizona passed SB 1070, the federal government sued the state, claiming that Arizona violated the supremacy clause, which gives the federal government authority over states, including when it comes to immigration. The federal government won only a partial victory in that case. It is not just that the federal government's policies take precedent; federal policies determine the terms of legal belonging and structure the grounds for immigrants' experiences at the state and local levels. Subfederal jurisdictions can institute measures that limit or compound the negative effects of the federally defined legal exclusion of immigrants, as New Mexico and Arizona have done.[60]

But welcoming policies in states should not relieve the federal government of its responsibility to institute policies that create a greater sense of belonging for all. The federal government ultimately has the responsibility to institute measures that create a greater sense of belonging for the greatest number of people. As we have shown with our investigation of two states, welcoming policies are a significant step in that direction. Unfortunately, the Trump administration made a hard, swift, and unrelenting move in the opposite direction, enacting policies that excluded immigrants, limited their rights, punished them disproportionately relative to their violation of immigration laws, and scapegoated them for all that ails the United States.

With Trump out of office and a more immigrant-friendly Biden administration now in place, one quick action could do more for strengthening immigrants' sense of belonging than any policy in recent memory: legalize a large share of the estimated 10.5 million individuals who are currently unauthorized. We agree with our respondents from across the political spectrum who told us that a pathway to citizenship for those immigrants is a smart policy. It would have the greatest positive impact on a sense of belonging not just for the immigrants who would benefit but also for their future generations and even the United States as a whole.

We base that conclusion on the evidence that we have presented throughout the book and on research by social scientists who have offered clear evidence that legalization is a boon to the integration of immigrants. When the federal government has offered unauthorized immigrants a pathway to legalize through, for example, the amnesty provision of the 1986 Immigration Reform and Control Act, immigrants experienced dramatic improvements in their socioeconomic fortunes and so did their children and grandchildren.[61] Even limited legal protection for unauthorized immigrants, like DACA, yields improvements to the mental health of U.S.-born children of immigrants and the social and economic outcomes of those who receive protection.[62] If, as the evidence shows, legalization facilitates integration across the generations, then it also facilitates a greater sense of belonging. That outcome is beneficial for both the beneficiaries of legalization and for the United States as a whole. If federal lawmakers care about creating a greater sense of belonging—and we think they should—then they should follow the lead of welcoming states in crafting a set of immigration policies that foster a sense of belonging among immigrants in particular and in the American population in general. No measure would do more to achieve that end than mass legalization.

NOTES

Chapter 1: The State of Immigration Policy

1. All interview respondent names are pseudonyms. We use the term "Latino" to refer to people who are from Latin American countries or from Spain. There has been quite a bit of debate in recent years about how to describe this group of individuals. While the gender-neutral term "Latinx" has gained some popularity, the best evidence suggests that only about 2 percent of people with Latin American ancestry in the United States use it, making it one of the least prevalent self-identifiers (Carrasco 2019). We choose instead to use the terms most preferred by this population: "Hispanic" and "Latino."

2. See Sam and Berry 2016.

3. Walton and Brady 2017, 272.

4. Ramón and Cardinal Brown 2018.

5. Bloemraad and de Graauw 2012; Colbern and Ramakrishnan 2020; Jiménez 2011. The exception is refugee policy. The Office of Refugee Resettlement works with non-governmental organizations to resettle and integrate refugees and asylees through English language acquisition, access to health care, job training, and mental health services.

6. Colbern and Ramakrishnan 2020; de Graauw 2015; Provine and Varsanyi 2020.

7. On the varied state immigration laws, see Reich 2017, 2019.

8. Pham and Van 2019.

9. Alabama's HB56 takes a similarly aggressive approach. Enacted in 2011, that bill allows police officers to request proof of legal presence in the United States from an individual they stop if they have "reasonable suspicion" that the individual might be an unauthorized immigrant. The bill also bans unauthorized immigrants from attending public colleges and universities, requires public schools to ascertain whether their students are undocumented (though it does not prohibit undocumented students from attending school), prohibits transporting or harboring unauthorized immigrants, and prohibits landlords from renting to unauthorized immigrants and employers from knowingly hiring unauthorized immigrants for any job in Alabama. Several provisions of the law were blocked by the courts.

10. Colbern and Ramakrishnan 2020. On Alabama, see Jones and Brown 2017.
11. Colbern and Ramakrishnan 2020; Pham and Van 2019; Ybarra, Juárez Pérez, and Sanchez 2019.
12. Colbern and Ramakrishnan 2020.
13. Gulasekaram and Ramakrishnan 2015; Pham and Van 2019; Ybarra, Juárez Pérez, and Sanchez 2019.
14. Chávez and Provine 2009; Gulasekaram and Ramakrishnan 2015; Hopkins 2010; Ramakrishnan and Wong 2010; Varsanyi et al. 2012; Walker and Leitner 2011; Williamson 2018; Zingher 2014.
15. Filindra and Pearson-Merkowitz 2013a; Ybarra, Sanchez, and Sanchez 2015.
16. Abrajano and Hajnal 2015; Avery, Fine, and Márquez 2017; Filindra and Pearson-Merkowitz 2013b.
17. Pastor 2018; see also Colbern and Ramakrishnan 2020.
18. De Graauw 2015; de Graauw and Vermeulen 2016; see also Majka and Longazel 2017.
19. See McCann and Jones-Correa 2020.
20. Sumner 1906, 77.
21. Hainmueller and Hopkins 2014; Hochschild 2016.
22. Zolberg 2006.
23. FitzGerald and Cook-Martín 2014; Higham 1955; Zolberg 2006.
24. Asia is the largest source region for newly arrived immigrants (Pew Research Center 2020a).
25. Chávez 2008.
26. Portes and Rumbaut 2001.
27. Armenta 2017; Patler and Golash-Boza 2017; Ryo and Peacock 2018.
28. Menjívar and Abrego 2012; Ryo and Peacock 2018; Santos et al. 2018.
29. García 2019.
30. Pedraza and Ariana Osorio 2017; Pedraza, Nichols, and LeBrón 2017.
31. Jones 2019.
32. Kaushal 2008.
33. Sunstein 1996.
34. Jost, Gaucher, and Stern 2015.
35. As Anne Schneider and Helen Ingram (1993, 340) put it, "the agenda, tools, and rationales of policy impart messages to target populations that inform them of their status as citizens and how they and people like themselves are likely to be treated by government."
36. Asad 2020; Ybarra et al. 2019. For the negative effects on mental health and children's school performance, see Capps et al. 2020; Santos et al. 2018.
37. Torche and Sirois 2019.
38. Portes and Rumbaut 2001.
39. Félix, González, and Ramírez 2008; Pantoja, Ramirez, and Segura 2001; Pantoja and Segura 2003; Sanchez, Masuoka, and Abrams 2019; Schildkraut 2011.
40. Bourhis et al. 2009; Pfafferott and Brown 2006.
41. Huo et al. 2010; Huo and Molina 2006; Vroome, Verkuyten, and Martinovic 2014.
42. Abrego 2008.

43. Okamoto et al. 2020.
44. Schneider and Ingram 1993, 334.
45. Chávez 2008.
46. Jiménez 2010.
47. Portes and Rumbaut 2001; Waters 1999.
48. Bloemraad and Trost 2008. Throughout the book, we use "white" as shorthand for "non-Hispanic white."
49. Torpey 2000.
50. Molina 2014.
51. Molina 2014; Molina, HoSang, and Gutiérrez 2019.
52. Zolberg 2006.
53. Roediger 2005.
54. Blumer 1958; Bobo and Smith 1998; Williamson 2018.
55. Craig, Rucker, and Richeson 2018; Domke, McCoy, and Torres 1999; Hopkins 2010; Hutchings et al. 2011; Jardina 2019; Outten et al. 2012; Stephan 2014.
56. DellaPosta, Shi, and Macy 2015; Iyengar, Sood, and Lelkes 2012.
57. Cadava 2020.
58. Barreto and Segura 2014; Telles and Ortiz 2008.
59. Hartigan 1999; McDermott 2006.
60. Kaufmann 2018.
61. Kaufmann 2018, 2019.
62. Cadava 2020.
63. Schildkraut 2011.
64. For an account of African Americans' attitudes about immigration, we refer the reader to Niambi Carter's (2019) research. While outside of the scope of our current research, understanding how other ethno-racial groups are affected by welcoming or unwelcoming immigration policies is also an important enterprise. Theoretically, this may be an even more complex issue than studying how Latinos and whites respond. On the one hand, support for strict immigration policies is generally correlated with policies that are punitive or restrictive of members of other ethno-racial minority groups, in part because these various policies have some common causes, such as threats to status or economic standing, and function to maintain a social status quo that benefits particular powerful groups more than others. On the other hand, how different ethno-racial minority groups respond to restrictive immigration policies specifically depends on how the group perceives the policy, their position with respect to it, and their relationship with the group directly targeted by the policy (for example, as sharing an identity as a minority group, or as having a different identity, or as being in competition; see Abascal 2015, Jones 2019). See Wong (2018) for an analysis of evangelical Asian Americans' and Latinos' views about immigration.
65. Colbern and Ramakrishnan 2020.
66. Andrews 2018; García 2019.
67. Colbern and Ramakrishnan 2020.
68. Michener 2018.
69. Colbern and Ramakrishnan 2020.

Chapter 2: A Tale of Two States

1. Murphy 1985.
2. Noel 2011.
3. Jacobson, Tichenor, and Durden 2018.
4. Gonzales 2015.
5. Jacobson, Tichenor, and Durden 2018.
6. Berman 1992, cited in Jacobson, Tichenor, and Durden 2018; Noel 2014, 27.
7. Tichenor and Jacobson 2019, 5.
8. Noel 2014.
9. Ibid.
10. Ibid.
11. Tichenor and Jacobson 2019.
12. Jacobson, Tichenor, and Durden 2018.
13. Fox 2012.
14. Tichenor and Jacobson 2019.
15. Pham and Van 2019; Ybarra et al. 2019.
16. Menjívar and Abrego 2012.
17. Provine and Varsanyi 2020.
18. Magaña and Lee 2013.
19. Greene Sterling and Joffe-Block 2021.
20. Colbern and Ramakrishnan 2020; Pham and Van 2019. The Immigrant Climate Index puts Arizona's unwelcoming bent in numeric terms.
21. See Lasch et al. 2018.
22. See ibid., 1707. According to Christopher Lasch and his colleagues, "The five policy types that have been adopted by jurisdictions to resist entanglement of state and local law enforcement in federal immigration enforcement include: (1) barring investigation of civil and criminal immigration violations by local law enforcement, (2) limiting compliance with immigration detainers and immigration warrants, (3) refusing U.S. Immigration and Customs Enforcement ('ICE') access to local jails, (4) limiting local law enforcement's disclosure of sensitive information, and (5) precluding local participation in joint operations with federal immigration enforcement" (Lasch et al. 2018, 1707).
23. U.S. Immigration and Customs Enforcement 2017.
24. Pedroza 2019.
25. Ibid.
26. Vasil Yasenov and his colleagues define immigration service providers "as organizations that provide low- or no-cost assistance with social immigration-related documents or forms and/or legal representation in immigration proceedings. We used three criteria. The provider must (1) be an organization; (2) qualify by the broad U.S. Federal Title 8 standards as a representative for immigration legal services; and (3) advertise online as providing free or low-cost legal services to immigrants and/or refugees" (Yasenov et al. 2020, 4).
27. See the Cities for Action website at https://www.citiesforaction.us/.

28. Pham and Van 2019.
29. Pham and Van 2019.
30. Quoted in Tichenor and Jacobson 2019, 12.
31. Provine and Varsanyi 2020. In 2016, Governor Susanna Martinez signed into law a bill that allows unauthorized immigrants to obtain a "driver's authorization card" instead of a driver's license.
32. Named for the portion of federal law from which they derive, 287(g) agreements are partnerships between immigration and customs enforcement and local law enforcement agencies wherein the federal government trains local law enforcement to enforce immigration policy. Historically, there have been three models of 287(g) participation. In the first—and the one in which the state of New Mexico has participated—the state and local jurisdictions could opt to use a *jail enforcement model* in which ICE deputizes law enforcement to question suspected noncitizens who have been arrested and to place immigration detainers on those who are verified to be noncitizens. A second model, the *warrant service officer model*, allows ICE to train and deputize local and state law enforcement officials to conduct immigration enforcement activities. Finally, the *task force model* allows deputized law enforcement to question and arrest individuals who have violated federal immigration laws. There is also a hybrid model that combines components of the three others.
33. Tichenor and Jacobson 2019, 12.
34. Lasch et al. 2018.
35. U.S. Immigration and Customs Enforcement 2017.
36. According to Welcoming America, whose member cities and counties, like Albuquerque, must commit to the organization's welcoming standard. For details, see the Welcoming America website at https://www.welcomingamerica.org/welcoming-standard.
37. Yasenov et al. 2020.
38. Gulasekaram and Ramakrishnan 2015.
39. The online appendix is available at https://www.russellsage.org/publications /states-belonging.

Chapter 3: The Immigration Policy Climate and Latinos' Sense of Belonging

1. Walton and Brady 2017, 272.
2. Citrin and Sears 2014; Masuoka and Junn 2013; Schildkraut 2011; Telles and Ortiz 2008.
3. New Mexico has a greater percentage of U.S.-born and English-dominant Latinos than Arizona (see table 2.1), as does our sample: 78 percent of Latinos in our New Mexico sample were U.S.-born versus 54 percent of Latinos in our Arizona sample; 82 percent of New Mexico respondents used the English version of the survey versus 60 percent of Arizona respondents.
4. Because the models include an interaction between state and nativity, the coefficient on Arizona can be interpreted as the impact of living in Arizona for the foreign-born. The coefficient on the interaction shows whether the effect of living in

Arizona is different for the U.S.-born than it is for the foreign-born (Brambor, Clark, and Golder 2006).

5. Because 155 respondents declined to give their income, income is included as a series of dummy variables, with "less than $25,000" as the omitted category.

6. Democratic and Republican "leaners" are coded as partisans. The omitted category in our models is whether the respondent declined to answer the question on partisan affiliation.

7. Barreto and Pedraza 2009; Hajnal and Lee 2011; Wong et al. 2011.

8. Abrajano and Hajnal 2015; Sides, Tesler, and Vavreck 2018.

9. This dichotomous variable equals 1 if respondents live in Arizona and 0 if they live in New Mexico.

10. When the dependent variable is a continuous scale (individual discrimination), we use ordinary least squares regression; for all other dependent variables, which are ordinal, we use ordered probit models. Predicted probabilities are calculated using "margins" in STATA. All independent variables besides nativity and state of residence are set to their mean or modal values. One variable we do not include in our models is racial identification. Although it is possible that racial identification is related to perceptions of belonging, this question is beyond the scope of the current project. The survey respondents do not differ by state in their racial identification; in both states, for example, over 75 percent of Latino respondents identified racially as Latino ($p = 0.44$). This lack of variation means that any differences we find across the two states with respect to belonging would not be due to differing patterns of racial identification. The online appendix contains the full regression results.

11. We find that Republicans were less likely than Democrats, independents, and nonpartisans to say that their state was unwelcoming to immigrants.

12. We use pseudonyms for all respondents to protect their anonymity.

13. Okamoto et al. 2020.

14. Response options were "none at all," "a little," "some," or "a lot."

15. Partisanship did not affect Latino responses to this question.

16. We also asked two questions about individual-level discrimination: how often people felt that they were treated with less courtesy than other people, and how often they felt that they were treated with less respect than other people owing to their race and ethnicity. See David R. Williams's (2016) Everyday Discrimination Scale. The correlation for these two items is 0.71. Responses were combined into a single scale that runs from 1 to 6, with 1 being the lowest level of perceived discrimination ($\alpha = 0.83$, median = 2.26, standard deviation = 1.35; median = 2.23 in Arizona and 2.29 in New Mexico). Income was our only significant predictor of individual-level discrimination; respondents with higher incomes and those who refused to give their income were less likely to perceive this type of discrimination than other respondents.

17. Our results also show an important effect of partisanship: Republicans were less likely to perceive group-level discrimination and Democrats were more likely than nonpartisans to perceive group-level discrimination (see online appendix).

18. Tajfel and Turner 1979; see also Hogg, Abrams, and Brewer 2017.
19. Tajfel 1974, 69.
20. Leach et al. 2008.
21. Tajfel 1982.
22. Tajfel and Turner 1979.
23. Salice and Sánchez 2016.
24. Zhou 1992.
25. Gonzales 2016; Salgado 2018.
26. Du Bois 1903.
27. Ogbu 1991.
28. Feliciano 2005; Kasinitz, Mollenkopf, and Waters 2010; Lajevardi et al. 2020.
29. Lajevardi et al. 2020.
30. Menjívar and Abrego 2012; see also Armenta 2017.
31. Greene Sterling and Joffe-Block 2021.
32. The Trump administration rescinded DACA in September 2017. In June 2020, the Supreme Court ruled that DACA was to remain in place, the administration's rescindment having been arbitrary and lacking in a policy justification.
33. Gonzales 2016.
34. Salgado 2018.
35. We started our search in 2005, the year in which Congress first failed at comprehensive immigration reform and when state-level activity on immigrant policy began to ramp up. We ended our search at the end of 2016, just before the Trump presidency began. Our search of the *Arizona Republic* used Global Newsstand; our search of the *Albuquerque Journal* used Access World News. Note that we only analyzed the number of articles that came from our search terms; we do not have a database of the articles themselves.
36. Pratto and John 1991; see also Barlow et al. 2012.
37. Okamoto et al. 2020.
38. Cornell and Hartmann 2006.
39. Jones-Correa et al. 2018; Schildkraut 2011.
40. In a random assignment, some respondents were asked first about the United States and some were asked first about their state.
41. See online appendix for regression results with additional controls.
42. See Cohen (2018) for a theoretical exploration of the role of time in considerations of citizenship.
43. Schildkraut 2011.
44. Pérez 2016.
45. On "legal passing," see García 2019.
46. See the online appendix for statistical results.
47. Hopkins and Washington 2020).
48. McCann and Jones-Correa 2020.
49. Sunstein 1996.
50. Gaertner and Dovidio 2000; Huo 2003; Putnam 2007; Schildkraut 2011; Theiss-Morse 2009.

Chapter 4: The Immigration Policy Climate and Whites' Sense of Belonging

1. Glasford, Pratto, and Dovidio 2008.
2. The wording of the survey question upon which we base this analysis is: "In general, do you think that the state of [Arizona/New Mexico] tries to make immigrants feel: very welcome, somewhat welcome, somewhat unwelcome, very unwelcome?"
3. Kaufmann 2019.
4. Democratic and Republican "leaners" are coded as partisans. The omitted category in our models is those respondents who declined to answer the question on partisan affiliation.
5. With the inclusion of the interaction terms, the coefficient on state of residence can be interpreted as the impact of living in Arizona among Democrats and the coefficient on being Republican can be interpreted as the impact of being Republican (relative to Democrat) in New Mexico. The coefficient on the interaction term can tell us whether the effect of partisanship varies with state of residence and whether the effect of state of residence varies with partisanship. As in chapter 2, when the dependent variable is a continuous scale (individual discrimination), we use ordinary least squares regression; for all other dependent variables, which are ordinal, we use ordered probit models. Predicted probabilities are calculated using "margins" in STATA. All independent variables besides party and state of residence are set to their mean or modal values.
6. Jacobson, Tichenor, and Durden 2018; Noel 2011.
7. See Salgado 2018.
8. Pratto and John 1991; see also Barlow et al. 2012.
9. We accessed state demographics for 2010 at CensusViewer, "Population of Arizona," http://censusviewer.com/state/AZ.
10. Abrajano and Hajnal 2015.
11. Pew Research Center 2018; see also Kaufmann 2018.
12. Albertson and Gadarian 2015; Merolla et al. 2013.
13. Leach et al. 2008.
14. As the full model results in the online appendix show, the coefficient on being Republican is not significant.
15. Jiménez 2017.
16. Diaz and Ore 2020.
17. Alba and Nee 2003; Domínguez and Maya-Jariego 2008; Jiménez 2017; Lay 2012.
18. Kleen 2018.
19. Alesina and La Ferrara 2000, 2002; Putnam 2007.
20. We also measured perceptions of individual-level discrimination by asking how often people felt that they were treated with less courtesy than other people and how often they felt that they were treated with less respect than other people, owing to their race and ethnicity. We combined responses into a single scale that runs from 1 to 6, with 1 being the lowest level of perceived discrimination and 6 the highest ($\alpha = 0.85$, median = 2.10 [2.04 in Arizona and 2.17 in New Mexico],

standard deviation = 1.28). As the full model results in the online appendix show, partisanship was a strong predictor, with Republicans, independents, and non-partisans more likely than Democrats to perceive individual-level discrimination. State residence was not statistically significant, nor were any of the interactions between state residence and partisanship.

21. Gómez-Quiñones 1994; Jacobson, Tichenor, and Durden 2018; Varsanyi and Provine 2016.
22. DellaPosta, Shi, and Macy 2015; Iyengar, Sood, and Lelkes 2012.
23. Abrajano and Hajnal 2015.
24. Daniller 2019; Kaufmann 2019.
25. Bonilla-Silva 2006; McDermott and Samson 2005.
26. As with many Americans, several interview respondents did not identify with a particular party. Yet it became clear through our discussions that they aligned more with one party than the other. If they called themselves independent, libertarian, or something else, we describe them as such, though we may include their views when we are characterizing the views of people on the left (typically Democrats) and on the right (typically Republican).
27. Hartigan 1999; McDermott 2006.
28. Kaufmann 2019.
29. Gest 2016; Jardina 2019.
30. Gaertner et al. 2016.
31. For interested readers, our appendix includes correlations among all of our belonging measures by state and party. They show that most correlations are low. In some instances, the correlations between state-level measures and their national-level equivalents are just over 0.5. They include feeling like an outsider in one's state and in the United States (Arizona Republicans), perceptions of discrimination against whites (all four groups), and thinking that others felt like the respondent belonged (all four groups).
32. Smith 1993.
33. Schildkraut 2011.
34. Smith 1997.
35. Zolberg 2006.
36. Fox and Miller-Idriss 2008; Jiménez 2017.
37. Craig, Rucker, and Richeson 2018.
38. Kaufmann 2018.
39. Flores and Schachter 2018.
40. Jardina 2019; Schildkraut 2019b.
41. Kaufmann 2018, 2019.
42. Abrajano and Hajnal 2015.
43. See Jardina 2019.
44. Abrajano and Hajnal 2015; Hochschild 2016.
45. Kinder and Sanders 1996.
46. McDermott 2006.
47. Jardina 2019; Sides, Tesler, and Vavreck 2018; Tesler and Sears 2010.

48. The full model results in the online appendix show that whites with higher incomes tend to be less alienated and to express greater feelings of belonging than those with lower incomes; we found a similar pattern with Latinos in chapter 2. Education was sometimes significant, with higher levels of education associated with greater levels of belonging.

49. Lay 2012; Williamson 2018.

Chapter 5: What If the Immigration Climate Were Changed?

1. Walton and Brady 2017.
2. Huo et al. 2018a.
3. Huo et al. 2018b.
4. FitzGerald and Cook-Martín 2014; Higham 1955; Zolberg 2006.
5. Haslam, Reicher, and Platow 2011; Turner 1991.
6. We asked respondents to report the extent to which they experienced three emotions—"happy," "angry," or "sad"—after they read the proposal. Responses to "angry" and "sad" were recoded and combined with responses to "happy" to form one indicator of how positive respondents felt about the proposal.
7. We assessed sense of belonging in the state by asking respondents two questions: (1) To what extent would the proposal make you feel more at home? (2) Would it make you more likely to move out of state? Responses to the second question were recoded and combined with responses to the first question to form one indicator of belonging in the state.
8. Analysis of Variance (ANOVA) conducted on the positive feelings respondents felt after reading one of the two proposals (welcoming or unwelcoming) produced a significant three-way interaction: policy proposal by ethno-nativity by party identification, $F_{(4,1427)} = 3.72$, $p = 0.005$. Analysis conducted on sense of belonging produced the same significant three-way interaction, $F_{(4,1403)} = 3.43$, $p = 0.008$. The significant interactions suggest that foreign-born Latinos, U.S.-born Latinos, and U.S.-born whites responded differently to the two proposals depending on their party identification. To understand these relationships, we present findings for the ethno-nativity groups separately. For each group, we describe how responses to welcoming versus unwelcoming proposals were similar or different for Democrats, Republicans, and independents.
9. Jiménez 2010; Telles and Ortiz 2008.
10. Abrajano and Hajnal 2015; Sides, Tesler, and Vavreck 2018.
11. Abrajano and Hajnal 2015.
12. The same cannot be said of foreign-born Latinos, who, regardless of their political orientation, respond positively to welcoming immigration policies.
13. IRCA included an amnesty program for unauthorized immigrants who had been living and working in the United States since January 1, 1982. Under the amnesty provision, these individuals could apply for a temporary legal status and, later, legal permanent residency and ultimately citizenship (see Jiménez 2011).

14. Torpey 2000.
15. Menjívar and Abrego 2012; Provine and Varsanyi 2020.
16. Provine and Varsanyi 2020.
17. Andrews 2018.
18. Smith 1997.
19. Ibid.
20. Craig and Richeson 2014; Danbold and Huo 2015; Hainmueller and Hopkins 2014.
21. Cheryan and Monin 2005; Portes and Rumbaut 2001; Schildkraut 2011.
22. Jiménez 2010.
23. Abrajano and Hajnal 2015.
24. In the 2016 American National Election Study (ANES), only 39 percent of whites identified themselves as a Republican or a Republican-leaning independent. See ANES, "Time Series Study 2016," https://www.electionstudies.org/studypages/anes_timeseries _2016/anes_timeseries_2016htm.
25. Prior research has shown that more local contextual factors, like the pace of immigration-driven demographic change, partisanship, and politicized messages, can shape attitudes about immigration and immigration policy (Kopan and Agiesta 2017). Our data do not permit such analyses, but it is an important direction for future research.
26. One potential barrier to the adoption of welcoming policies, despite evidence of their positive effects on a broad segment of immigrant-receiving communities, is that elected officials in Arizona may find it advantageous to cater to constituents who are more likely to be politically engaged (for example, conservative and Republican whites). To explore this possibility, we examined data from the 2016 Cooperative Congressional Election Study, which has large numbers of respondents from Arizona and New Mexico. Those data indicate that white respondents of all partisan orientations in Arizona were extremely likely to report that they voted in the 2016 presidential election, and that self-identified Republicans were only slightly more common than self-identified Democrats (32 percent versus 29 percent). We also looked at ideology and found that the divide among whites was larger for ideology than it was for party: white conservatives outnumbered white liberals (41 percent to 27 percent). By contrast, whites in New Mexico were far more likely to identify as Democrats than as Republicans (36 percent versus 21 percent) and were more evenly distributed across the ideological categories (Ansolabehere and Schaffner 2017).

Chapter 6: Immigration Policy Preferences in a Divided United States

1. Haynes, Merolla, and Ramakrishnan 2016.
2. Abrajano and Hajnal 2015; Jardina 2019; Sides, Tesler, and Vavreck 2018.
3. Kaufmann 2018; Pew Research Center 2018; Schildkraut 2019a; Sides, Tesler, and Vavreck 2018.
4. Gulasekaram and Ramakrishnan 2015; Pew Research Center 2019; Pham and Van 2019.
5. The wording for this question was developed by consulting the 2016 American National Election Study.

6. In our appendix, we present statistical models that examine these preferences more fully. Those results show that for both white and Latino respondents, Republicans were less likely than Democrats to support this option. For both groups, perceiving one's state as unwelcoming made support more likely. For Latinos, being born in the United States made support less likely. State residence was not significant for Latinos, but whites in Arizona were less likely to express support for this option.

7. Smith 1997.

8. Cohen 2018.

9. Under federal law, unauthorized immigrants are not permitted to receive federal benefits.

10. According to the 1986 Immigration Reform and Control Act, employers are in compliance so long as they do not "knowingly" hire employees who are unauthorized immigrants. The law also requires prospective employees to show their prospective employer proof of legal U.S. residency, and for employers to retain a copy of that proof.

11. Calavita 1992.

12. Schildkraut 2019a.

13. Jiménez 2010.

14. Schildkraut 2011.

15. Garip 2017.

16. Ngai 2004.

17. Kurtzleben 2018.

18. In the online appendix, we present statistical models that examine these preferences more fully. Those results show that for both white and Latino respondents, perceiving the state as unwelcoming and identifying as a Democrat were associated with more support for the act. For Latinos, speaking English in the home was associated with opposition. As in chapter 3, we find that U.S.-born Latinos in Arizona were more likely to support the act than U.S.-born Latinos in New Mexico, and white respondents in New Mexico were more likely to support it than white respondents in Arizona.

19. Smith 1997.

20. Salgado 2018.

21. Pettigrew et al. 2011. On the contact hypothesis and immigrants, see Kotzur, Tropp, and Wagner 2018.

22. Hainmueller et al. 2017; Wong et al. 2017.

23. Gramlich 2019.

24. Kurtzleben 2018.

25. Research shows that individuals overestimate the partisan divide (Westfall et al. 2015) and the degree to which Democrats and Republicans dislike each other (Moore-Berg et al. 2020).

26. Zamora 2017.

27. It was Trump's grandfather who came to the United States from Germany.

28. Andrews 2018.

29. Massey, Durand, and Pren 2016.

30. Schildkraut 2019a.
31. Barreto and Segura 2014.
32. Voss and Bloemraad 2011.
33. Barreto and Segura 2014.
34. Page and Gilens 2017.

Chapter 7: Conclusion

1. Schneider and Ingram 1993; Zolberg 2006.
2. Walton and Brady 2017.
3. See Sam and Berry 2016.
4. Huo, Binning, and Begeny 2015.
5. Walton and Brady 2017, 272.
6. Hainmueller and Hopkins 2014; Hochschild 2016.
7. Haslam, Reicher, and Platow 2011; Williamson 2018.
8. Portes and Rumbaut 2001.
9. Schildkraut 2011.
10. Gonzales 2016; Hainmueller et al. 2017; Menjívar and Abrego 2012; Santos et al. 2018; Torche and Sirois 2019.
11. Chávez 2008; Jiménez 2010; Pérez 2016.
12. Norton and Sommers 2011.
13. DellaPosta, Shi, and Macy 2015; Iyengar, Sood, and Lelkes 2012.
14. Abrajano and Hajnal 2015.
15. Kaufmann 2018, 2019; Pew Research Center 2018.
16. Andrews 2018; García 2019; Lay 2012; Williamson 2018.
17. Pratto and John 1991; see also Barlow et al. 2012.
18. Daniller 2019; Pew Research Center 2020a.
19. Pew Research Center 2016.
20. DellaPosta, Shi, and Macy 2015; Iyengar et al. 2019.
21. *The Atlantic* 2019.
22. Baldassarri and Park 2020.
23. Younis 2020.
24. Ibid.; Pew Research Center 2018.
25. Daniller 2019.
26. Pew Research Center 2020a.
27. Hopkins and Washington 2020.
28. Abrajano and Hajnal 2015.
29. Kaufmann 2018.
30. Pew Research Center 2020b.
31. Iyengar et al. 2019.
32. Although there are exceptions; see the American Legislatures project at Measuring American Legislatures, https://americanlegislatures.com/.
33. Gulasekaram and Ramakrishnan 2015; Pham and Van 2019.

34. Williamson 2018.
35. Lay 2012, 144.
36. Ibid., 151.
37. Tuan 1998.
38. Center for Study of Hate Crimes and Extremism 2021.
39. Jones 2019; see also Jiménez 2016.
40. Carter 2019.
41. Kaufmann 2019.
42. Jones 2019; Richeson and Craig 2011.
43. Abascal 2015; Carter and Pérez 2016.
44. Waters and Kasinitz 2016.
45. Waters and Pineau 2015.
46. Alba and Nee 2003.
47. Alba 2009; Rothstein 2017; Sharkey 2013.
48. Alba 2020.
49. Ibid.; Darity and Mullen 2020.
50. HoSang 2010.
51. Ibid.
52. Colbern and Ramakrishnan 2020; HoSang 2010; Pastor 2018.
53. Pantoja, Ramirez, and Segura 2001; Pantoja and Segura 2003.
54. Colbern and Ramakrishnan 2020; Pham and Van 2019.
55. Provine and Varsanyi 2020.
56. Mayo-Adam 2020.
57. Gulasekaram and Ramakrishnan 2015; Pham and Van 2019.
58. Williamson 2018.
59. Ramakrishnan and Colbern 2015.
60. Patler and Golash-Boza 2017; Ryo and Peacock 2018.
61. Bean, Brown, and Bachmeier 2015.
62. Hainmueller et al. 2017; Wong et al. 2017.

REFERENCES

Abascal, Maria. 2015. "Us and Them: Black-White Relations in the Wake of Hispanic Population Growth." *American Sociological Review* 80(4): 789–813.

Abrajano, Marisa, and Zoltan Hajnal. 2015. *White Backlash: Immigration, Race, and American Politics*. Princeton, N.J.: Princeton University Press.

Abrego, Leisy. 2008. "Legitimacy, Social Identity, and the Mobilization of Law: The Effects of Assembly Bill 540 on Undocumented Students in California." *Law and Social Inquiry* 33(3): 709–1071.

Alba, Richard. 2009. *Blurring the Color Line: The New Chance for a More Integrated America*. Cambridge, Mass.: Harvard University Press.

———. 2020. *The Great Demographic Illusion: Majority, Minority, and the Expanding American Mainstream*. Princeton, N.J.: Princeton University Press.

Alba, Richard D., and Victor Nee. 2003. *Remaking the American Mainstream: Assimilation and Contemporary Immigration*. Cambridge, Mass.: Harvard University Press.

Albertson, Bethany, and Shana Kushner Gadarian. 2015. *Anxious Politics: Democratic Citizenship in a Threatening World*. New York: Cambridge University Press.

Alesina, Alberto, and Eliana La Ferrara. 2000. "Participation in Heterogeneous Communities." *Quarterly Journal of Economics* 115(3): 847–904.

———. 2002. "Who Trusts Others?" *Journal of Public Economics* 85(2): 207–34.

Andrews, Abigail. 2018. *Undocumented Politics: Place, Gender, and the Pathways of Mexican Migrants*. Oakland: University of California Press.

Ansolabehere, Stephen, and Brian F. Schaffner. 2017. "Cooperative Congressional Election Study Common Content 2016." DOI: 10.7910/DVN/GDF6Z0, Harvard Dataverse, V4, UNF:6:WhtR8dNtMzReHC295hA4cg== [fileUNF].

Armenta, Amada. 2017. *Protect, Serve, and Deport: The Rise of Policing as Immigration Enforcement*. Oakland: University of California Press.

Asad, Asad L. 2020. "Latinos' Deportation Fears by Citizenship and Legal Status, 2007 to 2018." *Proceedings of the National Academy of Sciences* 117(16): 8836–44.

Atlantic, The. 2019. "*The Atlantic* Devotes Its December Issue to a Special Report: 'How to Stop a Civil War.'" *The Atlantic*, November 12. https://www.theatlantic.com/press-releases/archive/2019/11/atlantics-december-2019-issue/601795/.

Avery, James M., Jeffrey A. Fine, and Timothy Márquez. 2017. "Racial Threat and the Influence of Latino Turnout on State Immigration Policy." *Social Science Quarterly* 98(2): 750–65.

Baldassarri, Delia, and Barum Park. 2020. "Was There a Culture War? Partisan Polarization and Secular Trends in U.S. Public Opinion." *Journal of Politics* 82(3): 809–27.

Barlow, Fiona K., Stephania Paolini, Anne Pedersen, Matthew J. Hornsey, Helena R. M. Radke, Jake Harwood, Mark Rubin, and Chris G. Sibley. 2012. "The Contact Caveat: Negative Contact Predicts Increased Prejudice More than Positive Contact Predicts Reduced Prejudice." *Personality and Social Psychology Bulletin* 38(12): 1629–43.

Barreto, Matt, and Francisco Pedraza. 2009. "The Renewal and Persistence of Group Identification in American Politics." *Electoral Studies* 28(4): 595–605.

Barreto, Matt, and Gary Segura. 2014. *Latino America: How America's Most Dynamic Population Is Poised to Transform the Politics of the Nation.* New York: Public Affairs.

Bean, Frank D., Susan K. Brown, and James Bachmeier. 2015. *Parents without Papers: The Progress and Pitfalls of Mexican American Integration.* New York: Russell Sage Foundation.

Berman, David R. 1992. *Reformers, Corporations, and the Electorate: An Analysis of Arizona's Age of Reform.* Niwot: University Press of Colorado.

Bloemraad, Irene, and Els de Graauw. 2012. "Diversity and Laissez-Faire Integration in the United States." In *Diverse Nations, Diverse Responses: Approaches to Social Cohesion in Immigrant Societies,* edited by Paul Spoonley and Erin Tolley. Queen's Studies Series. Montreal: McGill-Queen's University Press.

Bloemraad, Irene, and Christine Trost. 2008. "It's a Family Affair: Intergenerational Mobilization in the Spring 2006 Protests." *American Behavioral Scientist* 52(4): 507–32.

Blumer, Herbert. 1958. "Race Prejudice as a Sense of Group Position." *Pacific Sociological Review* 1(1): 3–7.

Bobo, Lawrence, and Ryan A. Smith. 1998. "From Jim Crow Racism to Laissez-Faire Racism: The Transformation of Racial Attitudes." In *Beyond Pluralism: The Conception of Groups and Group Identities in America,* edited by Wendy Freedman Katkin, Ned C. Landsman, and Andrea Tyree. Urbana: University of Illinois Press.

Bonilla-Silva, Eduardo. 2006. *Racism without Racists: Color-Blind Racism and the Persistence of Racial Inequality in the United States.* Lanham, Md.: Rowman & Littlefield Publishers.

Bourhis, Richard Y., Annie Montreuil, Geneviève Barrette, and Elisa Montaruli. 2009. "Acculturation and Immigrant/Host Community Relations in Multicultural Settings." *Intergroup Misunderstanding: Impact of Divergent Social Realities* (June): 39–61.

Brambor, Thomas, William Roberts Clark, and Matt Golder. 2006. "Understanding Interaction Models: Improving Empirical Analyses." *Political Analysis* 14: 63–82.

Cadava, Geraldo. 2020. *The Hispanic Republican: The Shaping of an American Political Identity, from Nixon to Trump.* New York: HarperCollins.

Calavita, Kitty. 1992. *Inside the State: The Bracero Program, Immigration, and the INS.* New York: Routledge.

Capps, Randy, Jodi Berger Cardoso, Kalina Brabeck, Michael Fix, and Ariel G. Ruiz Soto. 2020. "Immigration Enforcement and the Mental Health of Latino High School Students." Washington, D.C.: Migration Policy Institute (September). https://www.migrationpolicy.org/research/immigration-enforcement-mental-health-latino-students.

Carrasco, Mario. 2019. "Progressive Latino Pollster: 98% of Latinos Do Not Identify with 'Latinx' Label." ThinkNow Research, November 1. https://medium.com/@ThinkNowTweets/progressive-latino-pollster-trust-me-latinos-do-not-identify-with-latinx-63229adebcea.

Carter, Niambi M. 2019. *American While Black: African Americans, Immigration, and the Limits of Citizenship.* New York: Oxford University Press.

Carter, Niambi M., and Efrén O. Pérez. 2016. "Race and Nation: How Racial Hierarchy Shapes National Attachments." *Political Psychology* 37(4): 497–513.

Center for the Study of Hate and Extremism. 2021. "FACT SHEET: Anti-Asian Prejudice March 2021." San Bernadino: California State University at San Bernadino (CSUSB). https://www.csusb.edu/sites/default/files/FACT%20SHEET-%20Anti-Asian%20Hate%202020%20rev%203.21.21.pdf.

Chávez, Jorge M., and Doris Marie Provine. 2009. "Race and the Response of State Legislatures to Unauthorized Immigrants." *Annals of the American Academy of Political and Social Science* 623(1): 78–92.

Chávez, Leo R. 2008. *The Latino Threat: Constructing Immigrants, Citizens, and the Nation.* Stanford, Calif.: Stanford University Press.

Cheryan, Sapna, and Benoit Monin. 2005. "'Where Are You Really From?': Asian Americans and Identity Denial." *Journal of Personality and Social Psychology* 89(5): 717–30.

Citrin, Jack, and David O. Sears. 2014. *American Identity and the Politics of Multiculturalism.* New York: Cambridge University Press.

Cohen, Elizabeth F. 2018. *The Political Value of Time.* New York: Cambridge University Press.

Colbern, Allan, and S. Karthick Ramakrishnan. 2020. *Citizenship Reimagined: A New Framework for State Rights in the United States.* Cambridge: Cambridge University Press.

Cornell, Stephen E., and Douglas Hartmann. 2006. *Ethnicity and Race: Making Identities in a Changing World,* 2nd ed. Sociology for a New Century Series. Thousand Oaks, Calif.: Pine Forge Press.

Craig, Maureen A., and Jennifer Richeson. 2014. "More Diverse Yet Less Tolerant? How the Increasingly Diverse Racial Landscape Affects White Americans' Racial Attitudes." *Personality and Social Psychology Bulletin* 40(6): 750–61.

Craig, Maureen A., Julian M. Rucker, and Jennifer A. Richeson. 2018. "Racial and Political Dynamics of an Approaching 'Majority-Minority' United States." *Annals of the American Academy of Political and Social Science* 677(1): 204–14.

Danbold, Felix, and Yuen J. Huo. 2015. "No Longer 'All-American'? Whites' Defensive Reactions to Their Numerical Decline." *Social, Psychological, and Personality Science* 6(2): 210–18.

Daniller, Andrew. 2019. "Americans' Immigration Policy Priorities." Washington, D.C.: Pew Research Center (November 12). https://www.pewresearch.org /fact-tank/2019/11/12/americans-immigration-policy-priorities-divisions -between-and-within-the-two-parties/.

Darity, William A., and A. Kirsten Mullen. 2020. *From Here to Equality: Reparations for Black Americans in the Twenty-First Century*. Chapel Hill: University of North Carolina Press.

De Graauw, Els. 2015. "Polyglot Bureaucracies: Nonprofit Advocacy to Create Inclusive City Governments." *Journal of Immigrant and Refugee Studies* 13(2): 156–78.

De Graauw, Els, and Floris Vermeulen. 2016. "Cities and the Politics of Immigrant Integration: A Comparison of Berlin, Amsterdam, New York City, and San Francisco." *Journal of Ethnic and Migration Studies* 42(6): 989–1012.

DellaPosta, Daniel, Yongren Shi, and Michael Macy. 2015. "Why Do Liberals Drink Lattes?" *American Journal of Sociology* 120(5): 1473–1511.

Diaz, Christina J., and Peter D. Ore. 2020. "Landscapes of Appropriation and Assimilation: The Impact of Immigrant-Origin Populations on U.S. Cuisine." *Journal of Ethnic and Migration Studies* (September 9): 1–25.

Domínguez, Silvia, and Isidro Maya-Jariego. 2008. "Acculturation of Host Individuals: Immigrants and Personal Networks." *American Journal of Community Psychology* 42(3): 309–27.

Domke, David, Kelley McCoy, and Marcos Torres. 1999. "News Media, Racial Perceptions, and Political Cognition." *Communication Research* 26(5): 570–607.

Dovidio, John F., Deborah Schildkraut, Yuen Huo, and Tomás R. Jiménez. 2016. Survey of Immigration and Belonging. New Haven, Conn.: Yale University.

Du Bois, W.E.B. 1903. *Souls of Black Folk*. Chicago: A. C. McClurg & Co.

Feliciano, Cynthia. 2005. *Unequal Origins: Immigrant Selection and the Education of the Second Generation*. El Paso, Tex.: LFB Scholarly Publishing.

Félix, Adrián, Carmen González, and Ricardo Ramírez. 2008. "Political Protest, Ethnic Media, and Latino Naturalization." *American Behavioral Scientist* 52(4): 618–34.

Filindra, Alexandra, and Shanna Pearson-Merkowitz. 2013a. "Together in Good Times and Bad? How Economic Triggers Condition the Effects of Intergroup Threat." *Social Science Quarterly* 94(5): 1328–45.

———. 2013b. "Research Note: Stopping the Enforcement 'Tide': Descriptive Representation, Latino Institutional Empowerment, and State-Level Immigration Policy." *Politics and Policy* 41: 814–32.

FitzGerald, David Scott, and David Cook-Martín. 2014. *Culling the Masses: The Democratic Origins of Racist Immigration Policy in the Americas*. Cambridge, Mass.: Harvard University Press.

Flores, René D., and Ariela Schachter. 2018. "Who Are the 'Illegals'? The Social Construction of Illegality in the United States." *American Sociological Review* 83(5): 839–68.

Fox, Cybelle. 2012. *Three Worlds of Relief: Race, Immigration, and the American Welfare State from the Progressive Era to the New Deal.* Princeton, N.J.: Princeton University Press.

Fox, Jon E., and Cynthia Miller-Idriss. 2008. "Everyday Nationhood." *Ethnicities* 8(4): 536–76.

Gaertner, Samuel, and John F. Dovidio. 2000. *Reducing Intergroup Bias: The Common Ingroup Identity Model.* Philadelphia: Psychology Press.

Gaertner, Samuel L., John F. Dovidio, Rita Guerra, Eric Hehman, and Tamar Saguy. 2016. "A Common In-group Identity: A Categorization-Based Approach for Reducing Intergroup Bias." In *Handbook of Prejudice, Discrimination, and Stereotyping,* 2nd ed., edited by Todd Nelson. New York: Psychology Press.

García, Angela S. 2019. *Legal Passing: Navigating Undocumented Life and Local Immigration Law.* Oakland: University of California Press.

Garip, Filiz. 2017. *On the Move: Changing Mechanisms of Mexico-U.S. Migration.* Princeton, N.J.: Princeton University Press.

Gest, Justin. 2016. *The New Minority: White Working Class Politics in an Age of Immigration and Inequality.* New York: Oxford University Press.

Glasford, Demis E., Felicia Pratto, and John F. Dovidio. 2008. "Intragroup Dissonance: Responses to Ingroup Violation of Personal Values." *Journal of Experimental Social Psychology* 44(4): 1057–64.

Gómez-Quiñones, Juan. 1994. *Roots of Chicano Politics, 1600–1940.* Albuquerque: University of New Mexico Press.

Gonzales, Felipe B. 2016. *Política: Nuevomexicanos and American Political Incorporation, 1821–1910.* Lincoln: University of Nebraska Press.

Gonzales, Phillip B. 2015. "New Mexico Statehood and Political Inequality: The Case of Nuevomexicanos." *New Mexico Historical Review* 90(1): 31–52.

Gramlich, John. 2019. "How Americans See Illegal Immigration, the Border Wall and Political Compromise." Washington, D.C.: Pew Research Center (January 16). https://www.pewresearch.org/fact-tank/2019/01/16/how-americans-see -illegal-immigration-the-border-wall-and-political-compromise/.

Greene Sterling, Terry, and Jude Joffe-Block. 2021. *Driving While Brown: Sheriff Joe Arpaio versus the Latino Resistance.* Oakland: University of California Press.

Gulasekaram, Pratheepan, and S. Karthick Ramakrishnan. 2015. *The New Immigration Federalism.* New York: Cambridge University Press.

Hainmueller, Jens, and Daniel J. Hopkins. 2014. "Public Attitudes toward Immigration." *Annual Review of Political Science* 17: 225–49.

Hainmueller, Jens, Duncan Lawrence, L. Martén, Bernard Black, Lucila Figueroa, Michael Hotard, Tomás R. Jiménez, Fernando Mendoza, Maria I. Rodrigues, Jonas J. Swartz, and David Laitin. 2017. "Protecting Unauthorized Immigrant Mothers Improves Their Children's Mental Health." *Science* 357(6355): 1041–44.

Hajnal, Zoltan L., and Taeku Lee. 2011. *Why Americans Don't Join the Party: Race, Immigration, and the Failure (of Political Parties) to Engage the Electorate.* Princeton, N.J.: Princeton University Press.

Hartigan John, Jr. 1999. *Racial Situations: Class Predicaments of Whiteness in Detroit.* Princeton, N.J.: Princeton University Press.

Haslam, S. Alexander, Stephen D. Reicher, and Michael J. Platow. 2011. *The New Psychology of Leadership: Identity, Influence, and Power.* New York: Psychology Press.

Haynes, Chris, Jennifer Merolla, and S. Karthick Ramakrishnan. 2016. *Framing Immigrants: News Coverage, Public Opinion, and Policy.* New York: Russell Sage Foundation.

Higham, John. 1955. *Strangers in the Land: Patterns of American Nativism, 1860–1925.* New Brunswick, N.J.: Rutgers University Press.

Hochschild, Arlie Russell. 2016. *Strangers in Their Own Land: Anger and Mourning on the American Right.* New York: New Press.

Hogg, Michael A., Dominic Abrams, and Marilynn B. Brewer. 2017. "Social Identity: The Role of Self in Group Processes and Intergroup Relations." *Group Processes and Intergroup Relations* 20(5): 570–81.

Hopkins, Daniel J. 2010. "Politicized Places: Explaining Where and When Immigrants Provoke Local Opposition." *American Political Science Review* 104(1): 40–60.

Hopkins, Daniel J., and Samantha Washington. 2020. "The Rise of Trump, the Fall of Prejudice? Tracking White Americans' Racial Attitudes via a Panel Survey, 2008–2018." *Public Opinion Quarterly* 84(1): 119–40.

HoSang, Daniel Martinez. 2010. *Racial Propositions: Ballot Initiatives and the Making of Postwar California.* Berkeley: University of California Press.

Huo, Yuen J. 2003. "Procedural Justice and Social Regulation across Group Boundaries: Does Subgroup Identity Undermine Relationship-Based Governance?" *Personality and Social Psychology Bulletin* 29(3): 336–48.

Huo, Yuen J., Kevin R. Binning, and Christopher T. Begeny. 2015. "Respect and the Viability of Ethnically Diverse Institutions." In *Towards Inclusive Organizations: Determinants of Successful Diversity Management at Work,* edited by Sabine Otten, Karen van der Zee, and Marilynn B. Brewer. New York: Psychology Press.

Huo, Yuen J., John F. Dovidio, Tomás R. Jiménez, and Deborah J. Schildkraut. 2018a. "Not Just a National Issue: Effect of State-Level Reception of Immigrants and Population Changes on Intergroup Attitudes of Whites, Latinos, and Asians in the United States." *Journal of Social Issues* 74(4): 716–36.

———. 2018b. "Local Policy Proposals Can Bridge Latino and (Most) White Americans' Response to Immigration." *Proceedings of the National Academy of Sciences of the United States of America* 115(5): 945–50.

Huo, Yuen J., and Ludwin E. Molina. 2006. "Is Pluralism a Viable Model of Diversity? The Benefits and Limits of Subgroup Respect." *Group Processes and Intergroup Relations* 9(3): 359–76.

Huo, Yuen J., Ludwin E. Molina, Kevin R. Binning, and Simon P. Funge. 2010. "Subgroup Respect, Social Engagement, and Well-being: A Field Study of an Ethnically Diverse High School." *Cultural Diversity and Ethnic Minority Psychology* 16(3): 427–36.

Hutchings, Vincent, Ashley Jardina, Robert Mickey, and Haynes Walton. 2011. "The Politics of Race: How Threat Cues and Group Position Can Activate White

Identity." Paper presented at the annual meeting of the American Political Science Association, Seattle, February 17–19.

Iyengar, Shanto, Yphtach Lelkes, Matthew Levendusky, Neil Malhotra, and Sean J. Westwood. 2019. "The Origins and Consequences of Affective Polarization in the United States." *Annual Review of Political Science* 22(1): 129–46.

Iyengar, Shanto, Gaurav Sood, and Yphtach Lelkes. 2012. "Affect, Not Ideology: A Social Identity Perspective on Polarization." *Public Opinion Quarterly* 76(3): 405–31.

Jacobson, Robin Dale, Daniel Tichenor, and T. Elizabeth Durden. 2018. "The Southwest's Uneven Welcome: Immigrant Inclusion and Exclusion in Arizona and New Mexico." *Journal of American Ethnic History* 37(3): 5–36.

Jardina, Ashley. 2019. *White Identity Politics.* New York: Cambridge University Press.

Jiménez, Tomás. 2010. *Replenished Ethnicity: Mexican Americans, Immigration, and Identity.* Berkeley: University of California Press.

———. 2011. "Immigrants in the United States: How Well Are They Integrating into Society?" Washington, D.C.: Migration Policy Institute (May).

———. 2016. "Fade to Black: Multiple Symbolic Boundaries in 'Black/Brown' Contact." *Du Bois Review: Social Science Research on Race* 13(1): 159–80.

———. 2017. *The Other Side of Assimilation: How Immigrants Are Changing American Life.* Oakland: University of California Press.

Jones, Jennifer A. 2019. *The Browning of the New South.* Chicago: University of Chicago Press.

Jones, Jennifer A., and Hana E. Brown. 2017. "American Federalism and Racial Formation in Contemporary Immigration Policy: A Processual Analysis of Alabama's HB56." *Ethnic and Racial Studies* 42(4): 531–51.

Jones-Correa, Michael, Helen B. Marrow, Dina G. Okamoto, and Linda R. Tropp. 2018. "Immigrant Perceptions of U.S.-Born Receptivity and the Shaping of American Identity." *RSF: The Russell Sage Foundation Journal of the Social Sciences* 4(5): 47–80.

Jost, John T., Danielle Gaucher, and Chadley Stern. 2015. "The World Isn't Fair: A System Justification Perspective on Social Stratification and Inequality." In *APA Handbook of Personality and Social Psychology*, vol. 2, *Group Processes*, edited by Mario Mikulincer, Phillip R. Shaver, John F. Dovidio, and Jeffry A. Simpson. Washington, D.C.: American Psychological Association.

Kasinitz, Philip, John Mollenkopf, and Mary C. Waters. 2010. *Inheriting the City: The Children of Immigrants Come of Age.* New York: Russell Sage Foundation.

Kaufmann, Eric. 2018. *Whiteshift: Populism, Immigration, and the Future of White Majorities.* New York: Harry N. Abrams.

———. 2019. "Americans Are Divided by Their Views on Race, Not Race Itself." *New York Times*, March 18.

Kaushal, Neeraj. 2008. "In-State Tuition for the Undocumented: Education Effects on Mexican Young Adults." *Journal of Policy Analysis and Management* 27(4): 771–92.

Kinder, Donald R., and Lynn M. Sanders. 1996. *Divided by Color: Racial Politics and Democratic Ideals.* Chicago: University of Chicago Press.

Kleen, Brendon. 2018. "More People Moving to Maricopa County than Anywhere in the U.S." *Phoenix Business Journal*, October 15. https://www.bizjournals.com /phoenix/news/2018/10/15/more-people-moving-to-maricopa-county-than.html.

Kopan, Tal, and Jennifer Agiesta. 2017. "CNN/ORC Poll: Americans Break with Trump on Immigration Policy." CNN, March 17. https://www.cnn.com/2017 /03/17/politics/poll-oppose-trump-deportation-immigration-policy/index.html.

Kotzur, Patrick F., Linda R. Tropp, and Ulrich Wagner. 2018. "Welcoming the Unwelcome: How Contact Shapes Contexts of Reception for New Immigrants in Germany and the United States." *Journal of Social Issues* 74(4): 812–32.

Kurtzleben, Danielle. 2018. "What the Latest Immigration Polls Do (and Don't) Say." NPR, January 23. https://www.npr.org/2018/01/23/580037717/what-the-latest -immigration-polls-do-and-dont-say.

Lajevardi, Nazita, Kassra A. R. Oskooii, Hannah L. Walker, and Aubrey L. Westfall. 2020. "The Paradox between Integration and Perceived Discrimination among American Muslims." *Political Psychology* 41(3): 587–606.

Lasch, Christopher N., R. Linus Chan, Ingrid V. Eagly, Dina F. Haynes, Annie Lai, Elizabeth M. McCormick, and Juliet P. Stumpf. 2018. "Understanding 'Sanctuary Cities.'" *Boston College Law Review* 59(5): 1704–74.

Lay, J. Celeste. 2012. *A Midwestern Mosaic: Immigration and Political Socialization in Rural America: The Social Logic of Politics.* Philadelphia: Temple University Press.

Leach, Colin Wayne, Martijn van Zomeren, Sven Zebel, Michael L. W. Vliek, Sjoerd F. Pennekamp, Bertjan Doosje, Jaap W. Ouwerkerk, and Russell Spears. 2008. "Group-Level Self-definition and Self-investment: A Hierarchical (Multicomponent) Model of In-group Identification." *Journal of Personality and Social Psychology* 95(1): 144–65.

Magaña, Lisa, and Erik Lee. 2013. "Arizona's Immigration Policies and SB 1070." In *Latino Politics and Arizona's Immigration Law SB 1070*, edited by Lisa Magaña and Erik Lee. New York: Springer.

Majka, Theo, and Jamie Longazel. 2017. "Becoming Welcoming: Organizational Collaboration and Immigrant Integration in Dayton, Ohio." *Public Integrity* 19(2):151–63.

Massey, Douglas S., Jorge Durand, and Karen A. Pren. 2016. "Why Border Enforcement Backfired." *American Journal of Sociology* 121(5): 1557–1600.

Masuoka, Natalie, and Jane Junn. 2013. *The Politics of Belonging: Race, Public Opinion, and Immigration.* Chicago: University of Chicago Press.

Mayo-Adam, Erin. 2020. *Queer Alliances: How Power Shapes Political Movement Formation.* Palo Alto, Calif.: Stanford University Press.

McCann, James, and Michael Jones-Correa. 2020. *Holding Fast: Resilience and Civic Engagement among Latino Immigrants.* New York: Russell Sage Foundation.

McDermott, Monica. 2006. *Working-Class White: The Making and Unmaking of Race Relations.* Berkeley: University of California Press.

McDermott, Monica, and Frank L. Samson. 2005. "White Racial and Ethnic Identity in the United States." *Annual Review of Sociology* 31: 245–61.

Menjívar, Cecilia, and Leisy Abrego. 2012. "Legal Violence: Immigration Law and the Lives of Central American Immigrants." *American Journal of Sociology* 117(5): 1380–1421.

Merolla, Jennifer L., Adrian Pantoja, Ivy Cargile, and Juana Mora. 2013. "From Coverage to Action: The Immigration Debate and Its Effects on Participation." *Political Research Quarterly* 66(2): 332–35.

Michener, Jamila. 2018. *Fragmented Democracy: Medicaid, Federalism, and Unequal Politics.* New York: Cambridge University Press.

Molina, Natalia. 2014. *How Race Is Made in America: Immigration, Citizenship, and the Historical Power of Racial Scripts.* Oakland: University of California Press.

Molina, Natalia, Daniel Martinez HoSang, and Ramón A. Gutiérrez. 2019. *Relational Formations of Race Theory, Method, and Practice.* Oakland: University of California Press.

Moore-Berg, Samantha L., Lee-Or Ankori-Karlinsky, Boaz Hameiri, and Emile Bruneau. 2020. "Exaggerated Meta-Perceptions Predict Intergroup Hostility between American Political Partisans." *Proceedings of the National Academy of Sciences* 117(26): 14864–72.

Murphy, Dan. 1985. *New Mexico, the Distant Land: An Illustrated History.* Sun Valley, Calif.: Windsor Publications.

Ngai, Mae M. 2004. *Impossible Subjects: Illegal Aliens and the Making of Modern America.* Princeton, N.J.: Princeton University Press.

Noel, Linda C. 2011. "'I Am an American': Anglos, Mexicans, Nativos, and the National Debate over Arizona and New Mexico Statehood." *Pacific Historical Review* 80(3): 430–67.

———. 2014. *Debating American Identity: Southwestern Statehood and Mexican Immigration.* Tucson: University of Arizona Press.

Norton, Michael I., and Samuel R. Sommers. 2011. "Whites See Racism as a Zero-Sum Game That They Are Now Losing." *Perspectives on Psychological Science* 6(3): 215–18.

Ogbu, John U. 1991. "Immigrant and Involuntary Minorities in Comparative Perspective." In *Minority Status and School: A Comparative Study of Immigrant and Involuntary Minorities,* edited by Margaret A. Gibson and John U. Ogbu. New York: Garland Publishing.

Okamoto, Dina G., Linda R. Tropp, Helen B. Marrow, and Michael Jones-Correa. 2020. "Welcoming, Trust, and Civic Engagement: Immigrant Integration in Metropolitan America." *Annals of the American Academy of Political and Social Science* 690(1): 61–81.

Outten, H. Robert, Michael T. Schmitt, Daniel A. Miller, and Amber L. Garcia. 2012. "Feeling Threatened about the Future: Whites' Emotional Reactions to Anticipated Ethnic Demographic Changes." *Personality and Social Psychology Bulletin* 38(1): 14–25.

Page, Benjamin I., and Martin Gilens. 2017. *Democracy in America? What Has Gone Wrong and What We Can Do about It.* Chicago: University of Chicago Press.

Pantoja, Adrian D., Ricardo Ramirez, and Gary M. Segura. 2001. "Citizens by Choice, Voters by Necessity: Patterns in Political Mobilization by Naturalized Latinos." *Political Research Quarterly* 54(4): 729–50.

Pantoja, Adrian D., and Gary M. Segura. 2003. "Fear and Loathing in California: Contextual Threat and Political Sophistication among Latino Voters." *Political Behavior* 25(3): 265–86.

Pastor, Manuel. 2018. *State of Resistance: What California's Dizzying Descent and Remarkable Resurgence Mean for America's Future.* New York: New Press.

Patler, Caitlin, and Tanya Maria Golash-Boza. 2017. "The Fiscal and Human Costs of Immigrant Detention and Deportation in the United States." *Sociology Compass* 11(11, November): e12536.

Pedraza, Francisco I., Vanessa Cruz Nichols, and Alana M. W. LeBrón. 2017. "Cautious Citizenship: The Deterring Effect of Immigration Issue Salience on Health Care Use and Bureaucratic Interactions among Latino U.S. Citizens." *Journal of Health Politics, Policy, and Law* 42(5): 925–60.

Pedraza, Francisco I., and Maricruz Ariana Osorio. 2017. "Courted and Deported: The Salience of Immigration Issues and Avoidance of Police, Health Care, and Education Services among Latinos." *Aztlán* 42(2): 247–64.

Pedroza, Juan Manuel. 2019. "Deportation Discretion: Tiered Influence, Minority Threat, and 'Secure Communities' Deportations." *Policy Studies Journal* 47(3): 624–46.

Pérez, Efrén O. 2016. *Unspoken Politics: Implicit Attitudes and Political Thinking.* New York: Cambridge University Press.

Pettigrew, Thomas F., Linda R. Tropp, Ulrich Wagner, and Oliver Christ. 2011. "Recent Advances in Intergroup Contact Theory." *International Journal of Intercultural Relations* 35(3): 271–80.

Pew Research Center. 2014. "Demographic and Economic Profiles of Hispanics by State and County, 2014." Washington, D.C.: Pew Research Center. https://www.pewresearch.org/hispanic/states/.

———. 2015. "2015, Hispanic Population in the United States Statistical Portrait." Washington, D.C.: Pew Research Center. https://www.pewresearch.org/hispanic/2017/09/18/2015-statistical-information-on-hispanics-in-united-states-current-data/.

———. 2016. "A Wider Ideological Gap between More and Less Educated Adults." Washington, D.C.: Pew Research Center (April 26). https://www.pewresearch.org/politics/2016/04/26/a-wider-ideological-gap-between-more-and-less-educated-adults/.

———. 2018. "Shifting Public Views on Legal Immigration into the U.S.: Many Unaware That Most Immigrants in the U.S. Are Here Legally." Washington, D.C.: Pew Research Center (June 28). https://www.pewresearch.org/politics/2018/06/28/shifting-public-views-on-legal-immigration-into-the-u-s/.

———. 2019. "Unauthorized Immigrant Population Trends for States, Birth Countries and Regions." Washington, D.C.: Pew Research Center (June 12). https://www.pewresearch.org/hispanic/interactives/unauthorized-trends/.

———. 2020a. "74% Favor Legal Status for Those Brought to U.S. Illegally as Children as Supreme Court Weighs DACA." Washington, D.C.: Pew Research Center.

———. 2020b. "Majorities across Racial, Ethnic Groups Express Support for the Black Lives Matter Movement." Washington, D.C.: Pew Research Center.

Pfafferott, Inga, and Rupert Brown. 2006. "Acculturation Preferences of Majority and Minority Adolescents in Germany in the Context of Society and Family." *International Journal of Intercultural Relations* 30(6): 703–17.

Pham, Huyen, and Pham Hoang Van. 2019. "Subfederal Immigration Regulation and the Trump Effect." *New York University Law Review* 94(1): 125–70.

Portes, Alejandro, and Rubén G. Rumbaut. 2001. *Legacies: The Story of the Immigrant Second Generation.* Berkeley: University of California Press.

Pratto, Felicia, and Oliver P. John. 1991. "Automatic Vigilance: The Attention-Grabbing Power of Negative Social Information." *Journal of Personality and Social Psychology* 61(3): 380–91.

Provine, Marie, and Monica W. Varsanyi. 2020. "The Politics behind the Documents: Comparing Immigrant Driver's License Policy Development in New Mexico and Arizona." In *Paper Trails: Migrants and Documents in an Era of Legal Insecurity,* edited by Sarah Horton and Josiah Heyman. Durham, N.C.: Duke University Press.

Putnam, Robert D. 2007. "E Pluribus Unum: Diversity and Community in the Twenty-First Century." 2006 Johan Skytte Prize Lecture. *Scandinavian Political Studies* 30(2): 137–74.

Ramakrishnan, S. Karthick, and Allan Colbern. 2015. "The California Package: Immigrant Integration and the Evolving Nature of State Citizenship." *Policy Matters* 6(3): 1–19.

Ramakrishnan, S. Karthick, and Tom Wong. 2010. "Partisanship, Not Spanish: Explaining Municipal Ordinances Affecting Undocumented Immigrants." In *Taking Local Control: Immigration Policy Activism in U.S. Cities and States,* edited by Monica Varsanyi. Stanford, Calif.: Stanford University Press.

Ramón, Cristobal, and Theresa Cardinal Brown. 2018. "An Immigration Patchwork in the States: How Partisanship, Regionalism, and Shifting Priorities Impact State Immigration Laws." Washington, D.C.: Bipartisan Policy Center (November).

Reich, Gary. 2017. "Immigrant Legislation, across and within the United States." *Research and Politics* 4(4): 1–7.

———. 2019. "One Model Does Not Fit All: The Varied Politics of State Immigrant Policies, 2005–16." *Policy Studies Journal* 47(3): 544–71.

Richeson, Jennifer A., and Maureen A. Craig. 2011. "Intra-Minority Intergroup Relations in the Twenty-First Century." *Daedalus* 140(2): 166–75.

Roediger, David R. 2005. *Working toward Whiteness: How America's Immigrants Became White.* New York: Basic Books.

Rothstein, Richard. 2017. *The Color of Law: A Forgotten History of How Our Government Segregated America.* New York: Liveright.

Ryo, Emily, and Ian Peacock. 2018. "A National Study of Immigration Detention in the United States." Los Angeles: Center for Law and Social Science Research Papers Series.

Salgado, Casandra D. 2018. "Mexican American Identity: Regional Differentiation in New Mexico." *Sociology of Race and Ethnicity* 6(2): 179–94.

Salice, Alessandro, and Alba Montes Sánchez. 2016. "Pride, Shame, and Group Identification." *Frontiers in Psychology* 4(403). DOI: 10.3389/fpsyg.2016.00557.

Sam, David L., and John W. Berry. 2016. *The Cambridge Handbook of Acculturation Psychology.* New York: Cambridge University Press.

Sanchez, Gabriel, Natalie Masuoka, and Brooke Abrams. 2019. "Revisiting the Brown-Utility Heuristic: A Comparison of Latino Linked Fate in 2006 and 2016." *Politics, Groups, and Identities* 7(3): 673–83.

Santos, Carlos E., Cecilia Menjívar, Rachel A. VanDaalen, Olga Kornienko, Kimberly A. Updegraff, and Samantha Cruz. 2018. "Awareness of Arizona's Immigration Law SB 1070 Predicts Classroom Behavioral Problems among Latino Youths during Early Adolescence." *Ethnic and Racial Studies* 41(9): 1672–90.

Schildkraut, Deborah J. 2011. *Americanism in the Twenty-First Century: Public Opinion in the Age of Immigration.* New York: Cambridge University Press.

———. 2019a. "Ambivalence in American Public Opinion about Immigration." In *New Directions in Public Opinion,* edited by Adam J. Berinsky, 3rd ed. New York: Routledge Press.

———. 2019b. "The Political Meaning of Whiteness for Liberals and Conservatives." *The Forum* 17 (3): 421–46.

Schneider, Anne, and Helen Ingram. 1993. "Social Construction of Target Populations: Implications for Politics and Policy." *American Political Science Review* 87(2): 334–47.

Sharkey, Patrick. 2013. *Stuck in Place: Urban Neighborhoods and the End of Progress toward Racial Equality.* Chicago: University of Chicago Press.

Sides, John, Michael Tesler, and Lynn Vavreck. 2018. *Identity Crisis: The 2016 Presidential Campaign and the Battle for the Meaning of America.* Princeton, N.J.: Princeton University Press.

Small, Mario Luis. 2009. "'How Many Cases Do I Need?' On Science and the Logic of Case Selection in Field-Based Research." *Ethnography* 10(1): 5–38.

Smith, Rogers M. 1993. "Beyond Tocqueville, Myrdal, and Hartz: The Multiple Traditions in America." *American Political Science Review* 87(3): 549–66.

———. 1997. *Civic Ideals: Conflicting Visions of Citizenship in U.S. History.* New Haven, Conn.: Yale University Press.

Stephan, Walter G. 2014. "Intergroup Anxiety: Theory, Research, and Practice." *Personality and Social Psychology Review* 18(3): 239–55.

Sumner, William Graham. 1906. *Folkways: A Study of the Sociological Importance of Usages, Manners, Customs, Mores, and Morals.* Boston: Ginn & Company.

Sunstein, Cass R. 1996. "On the Expressive Function of Law." *University of Pennsylvania Law Review* 144(5): 2021–53.

Tajfel, Henri. 1974. "Social Identity and Intergroup Behavior." *Social Science Information* 13(2): 65–93.

———. 1982. "Social Psychology of Intergroup Relations." *Annual Review of Psychology* 33: 1–39.

Tajfel, Henri, and John C. Turner. 1979. "An Integrative Theory of Intergroup Conflict." In *The Social Psychology of Intergroup Relations,* edited by William G. Austin and Stephen Worchel. Monterey, Calif.: Brooks/Cole.

Telles, Edward E., and Vilma Ortiz. 2008. Generations of Exclusion: Mexican Americans, Assimilation, and Race. New York: Russell Sage Foundation.

Tesler, Michael, and David Sears. 2010. *Obama's Race: The 2008 Election and the Dream of a Post-Racial America.* Chicago: University of Chicago Press.

Theiss-Morse, Elizabeth. 2009. *Who Counts as an American? The Boundaries of National Identity*. New York: Cambridge University Press.

Tichenor, Daniel J., and Robin Jacobson. 2019. "Tenuous Belonging: Diversity, Power, and Identity in the U.S. Southwest." *Journal of Ethnic and Migration Studies* 46(12): 2480–96.

Torche, Florencia, and Catherine Sirois. 2019. "Restrictive Immigration Law and Birth Outcomes of Immigrant Women." *American Journal of Epidemiology* 188(1): 24–33.

Torpey, John C. 2000. *The Invention of the Passport: Surveillance, Citizenship, and the State*. New York: Cambridge University Press.

Tuan, Mia. 1998. *Forever Foreigners or Honorary Whites? The Asian Ethnic Experience Today*. New Brunswick, N.J.: Rutgers University Press.

Turner, John C. 1991. *Social Influence*. Milton Keynes, U.K.: Open University Press.

U.S. Immigration and Customs Enforcement (ICE). 2017. "Enforcement and Removal Operations: Weekly Declined Detainer Outcome Report for Recorded Declined Detainers Feb 11–Feb 17, 2017." Washington, D.C.: ICE.

Varsanyi, Monica W., Paul G. Lewis, Doris Provine, and Scott Decker. 2012. "A Multilayered Jurisdictional Patchwork: Immigration Federalism in the United States." *Law and Policy* 34(2): 138–58.

Varsanyi, Monica, and Doris Marie Provine. 2016. "Divergent States: Explaining Immigration Policy Trajectories in New Mexico and Arizona." Presentation at the Center for the Study of Law and Society, University of California at Berkeley, March 23.

Voss, Kim, and Irene Bloemraad. 2011. *Rallying for Immigrant Rights: The Fight for Inclusion in 21st Century America*. Berkeley: University of California Press.

Vroome, Thomas, Maykel Verkuyten, and Borja Martinovic. 2014. "Host National Identification of Immigrants in the Netherlands." *International Migration Review* 48(1): 76–102.

Walker, Kyle E., and Helga Leitner. 2011. "The Variegated Landscape of Local Immigration Policies in the United States." *Urban Geography* 32(2): 156–78.

Walton, Gregory M., and Shannon T. Brady. 2017. "The Many Questions of Belonging." In *Handbook of Competence and Motivation: Theory and Application*, 2nd ed., edited by Andrew J. Elliot, Carol S. Dweck, and David S. Yeager. New York: Guilford Press.

Waters, Mary C. 1999. *Black Identities: West Indian Immigrant Dreams and American Realities*. Cambridge, Mass.: Harvard University Press.

Waters, Mary C., and Philip Kasinitz. 2016. "The War on Crime and the War on Immigrants: Racial and Legal Exclusion in the Twenty-First Century United States." In *Anxiety and National Identity: Immigration and Belonging in North America and Europe*, edited by Nancy Foner and Patrick Simon. New York: Russell Sage Foundation.

Waters, Mary C., and Marisa Gerstein Pineau, eds. 2015. *The Integration of Immigrants into American Society*. Washington, D.C.: National Academies of Science, Engineering, and Medicine.

Westfall, Jacob, Leaf Van Boven, John R. Chambers, and Charles M. Judd. 2015. "Perceiving Political Polarization in the United States: Party Identity Strength and Attitude Extremity Exacerbate the Perceived Partisan Divide." *Perspectives on Psychological Science* 10(2): 145–58.

Williams, David R. 2016. "Measuring Discrimination Resource." Cambridge, Mass.: Harvard University (June). https://scholar.harvard.edu/files/davidrwilliams/files/measuring_discrimination_resource_june_2016.pdf.

Williamson, Abigail Fisher. 2018. *Welcoming New Americans? Local Governments and Immigrant Incorporation.* Chicago: University of Chicago Press.

Wong, Janelle S. 2018. *Immigrants, Evangelicals, and Politics in an Era of Demographic Change.* New York: Russell Sage Foundation.

Wong, Janelle, S. Karthick Ramakrishnan, Taeku Lee, and Jane Junn. 2011. *Asian American Political Participation: Emerging Constituents and Their Political Identities.* New York: Russell Sage Foundation.

Wong, Tom K., Greisa Rosas Martinez, Adam Luna, Henry Manning, Adrian Reyna, Patrick O'Shea, Tom Jawetz, and Philip E. Wolgin. 2017. "DACA Recipients' Economic and Educational Gains Continue to Grow." Washington, D.C.: Center for American Progress (August 28). https://www.americanprogress.org/issues/immigration/news/2017/08/28/437956/daca-recipients-economic-educational-gains-continue-grow/.

Yasenov, Vasil, David Hausman, Michael Hotard, Duncan Lawrence, Alexandra Siegel, Jessica Sadye Wolff, David Laitin, and Jens Hainmueller. 2020. "Identifying Opportunities to Improve the Network of Immigration Legal Services Providers." Working paper. Stanford, Calif.: Stanford University, Immigration Policy Lab (August 6). https://arxiv.org/pdf/2008.02230.pdf.

Ybarra, Vickie D., Melina Juárez Pérez, and Gabriel R. Sanchez. 2019. "Do Perceptions Match Reality? Comparing Latinos' Perceived Views of State Immigration Policy Environments with Enacted Policies." *Policy Studies Journal* 47(3): 774–92.

Ybarra, Vickie D., Lisa M. Sanchez, and Gabriel R. Sanchez. 2015. "Anti-Immigrant Anxieties in State Policy: The Great Recession and Punitive Immigration Policy in the American States, 2005–2012." *State Politics and Policy Quarterly* 16(3): 313–39.

Younis, Mohamed. 2020. "Americans Want More, Not Less, Immigration for First Time." Washington, D.C.: Gallup (July 1). https://news.gallup.com/poll/313106/americans-not-less-immigration-first-time.aspx.

Zamora, Lazaro. 2017. "Comparing Trump and Obama's Deportation Priorities." Washington, D.C.: Bipartisan Policy Center (February 27). https://bipartisanpolicy.org/blog/comparing-trump-and-obamas-deportation-priorities/.

Zhou, Min. 1992. *Chinatown: The Socioeconomic Potential of an Urban Enclave.* Philadelphia: Temple University Press.

Zingher, Joshua N. 2014. "The Ideological and Electoral Determinants of Laws Targeting Undocumented Migrants in the U.S. States." *State Politics and Policy Quarterly* 14(1): 90–117.

Zolberg, Aristide R. 2006. *A Nation by Design: Immigration Policy in the Fashioning of America.* New York: Russell Sage Foundation.

INDEX

Boldface numbers refer to figures and tables.